A Natural Right *to* Die

Recent Titles in
Contributions in Legal Studies

The Appearance of Equality: Racial Gerrymandering, Redistricting, and the Supreme Court
Christopher M. Burke

Religion, Law, and the Land
Brian Edward Brown

The Supreme Court's Retreat from Reconstruction: A Distortion of Constitutional Jurisprudence
Frank J. Scaturro

Respecting State Courts: The Inevitability of Judicial Federalism
Michael E. Solimine and James L. Walker

Basic Principles of Property Law: A Comparative Legal and Economic Introduction
Ugo Mattei

Inherent Rights, the Written Constitution, and Popular Sovereignty: The Founders' Understanding
Thomas B. McAffee

Constitutional Structure and Purposes: Critical Commentary
Michael Conant

Constitutional Interpretation: Illusion and Reality
Jeffrey M. Shaman

Prisoners' Rights: The Supreme Court and Evolving Standards of Decency
John A. Fliter

The Four Faces of Affirmative Action: Fundamental Answers and Actions
W. Robert Gray

Choice of Law for American Courts: A Multilateralist Method
Edwin Scott Fruehwald

Whittaker: Struggles of a Supreme Court Justice
Richard Lawrence Miller

A Natural Right *to* Die

Twenty-Three Centuries of Debate

Raymond Whiting

Contributions in Legal Studies, Number 101

GREENWOOD PRESS
Westport Connecticut • London

Library of Congress Cataloging-in-Publication Data

Whiting, Raymond, 1959-
A natural right to die : twenty-three centuries of debate / Raymond Whiting.
p. cm.—(Contributions in legal studies, ISSN 0147–1074 ; no. 101)
Includes bibliographical references and index.
ISBN 0–313–31474–8 (alk. paper)
1. Right to die—Law and legislation—United States—History. 2. Right to die—Law and legislation—History. 3. Natural law—History. I. Title. II. Series.
KF3827.E87W48 2002
344.73'04197—dc21 00–069129

British Library Cataloguing in Publication Data is available.

Library of Congress Catalog Card Number: 00–069129
ISBN: 0–313–31474–8
ISSN: 0147–1074

First published in 2002

Greenwood Press, 88 Post Road West, Westport, CT 06881
An imprint of Greenwood Publishing Group, Inc.
www.greenwood.com

Printed in the United States of America

The paper used in this book complies with the Permanent Paper Standard issued by the National Information Standards Organization (Z39.48–1984).

10 9 8 7 6 5 4 3 2 1

To my Grandparents:

Raymond (Dick) Smith Whiting
Dorothy Lucille (Pettengill) Whiting
Claude Arthur Wood
Mary Louise (Tuttle) Wood

and to all of you reading this book who have watched,
are currently watching, or will ever have to watch a loved one slowly die

Contents

Preface

To a great extent, this book began during the Fall of 1979 when, as a college sophomore, I watched my Grandfather's long struggle with cancer come to an end. My Grandfather died much as he lived, on his own terms. When he determined that the good fight was over, he reached down and plucked the intravenous needle from his arm and, when the medical staff tried to return it, he staunchly refused permission. Finally, he and the staff reached what struck me, then, as a bizarre compromise. They would tape the needle to his arm without inserting it into his vein, in a medical charade. With this last act of control, my Grandfather hastened the end of his life and simultaneously opened a point of inquiry in mine. "Why the charade?" "Did my Grandfather act properly?" "What did the law have to say?"

For the next thirteen years I quietly clipped articles and collected references, amassing several file boxes of stories, articles and court cases. Then, in the Fall of 1992, a strange thing happened. My former wife, and still great friend, Robin Whiting got a job caring for a quadriplegic. He was a large powerful man who, despite his physical condition, still asserted great control over his own life. In his conversation with Robin, he mentioned that he had once gone to the Georgia Supreme Court and won the right to turn off his respirator and, thus, terminate his life at will. This idea struck a chord and sent me digging through my boxes, only to retrieve a file with numerous clippings about his case. I had been tracking his very man's life for many years. With these clippings in hand, I was granted a rare personal interview and the real work on this book began.

The truth be told, however, this book would never have come to be, if it were not for the help and assistance of many of my friends and colleagues. I am deeply grateful to Robin Whiting for her help in getting me started on this book and for the many hours of tender care she provided our children while I was closeted away writing. I must also extend my endless gratitude to my colleague

Professor Debra R. Van Tuyll and my dear friend Father Robert Bader, who both spent countless hours editing my manuscripts without any thought of personal gain. Such friends and colleagues are hard to come by.

I must also extend great thanks to my student assistants Sara Silverman and Craig Albert who, in performing their jobs, demonstrated not just a willingness to work but an excitement at the idea of participating in the publication of this work.

Finally, I must thank two people for providing me with the encouragement I needed to complete the final, and tedious, work that must be done if one is going to actually present one's work to the world. I thank Janice Williams for her hours of counsel and encouragement on the many occasions when I felt that I could never be satisfied with my own work. And I thank my department chair, Dr. Jeanne Jensen, who continuously reminded me that the elusive goal of reaching full professor was likely to stay that way unless I finally put my dreams into a physical form.

Introduction: The "Right to Die" Debate

This book was written to develop a new approach to the "right to die" debate. It is hoped that if readers can be provided with the foundation needed to understand the historical basis upon which the claim of such a right can be based, as well as the main points that support and oppose the legalization of the "right to die," the debate might shift away from an argument over whether the "right to die" is "right or wrong" to one that emphasizes the degree to which we, as a society, wish to control the inevitable acts that will be performed in support of those who believe that there is a "right to die."

In attempting to reach this goal, this work also examines current public policy issues from a new direction, taking as its basic approach the idea that society has become so distracted by the arguments for or against euthanasia that we have failed to recognize the fact that euthanasia is now a common practice in the United States. In political reality, the United States has few options when it comes to the legal status of the "right to die," since euthanasia has been both secretly and openly practiced in the United States for at least twenty years, and there is no reason to believe that this state of affairs will change. The reality of this debate is that the frequency of acts of euthanasia will only continue to increase, whether government recognizes such a right or not.

The underlying structure and development of the theory of rights, as it evolved from the pre-Socratic age to the present, are also documented in this book. In this way, the reader learns that the "right to die" question is not simply a question of law, majority or moral will, but rather a cultural question that involves some of the fundamental theories of the Western world. This work reveals that the "right to die" controversy is related to basic questions about the proper role of society, as well as the proper position of the individual within society. This author has combined historical overview of the argument with a discussion of contemporary attitudes and opinions, so that the reader can come to understand the shifts in political thought that have made the current contest over the "right to die" so divisive. By linking these issues to the current public policy disputes, the book lays the basis for a more analytical approach to understanding the arguments made by both sides of the conflict, as well as the current options open to U.S. policy makers. This book also provides new insight into the ways in which our current public policies are influenced, and in some ways predetermined, by the political theories of the past.

While many books have delved into the subject of the "right to die," no attempt has been made to substantially demonstrate the historic nature of this question beyond the borders of the United States. Most works in the area of the "right to die" examine ethical questions concerning medical treatment or the legal status of assisted-suicide cases. While such contributions have been important, this work seeks to examine the political reality of the asserted right. By demonstrating that the "right to die" is not simply a modern fad or a new idea, it can be shown that we are not dealing with a momentary item on the political agenda but rather with an idea that has taken over 2000 years to reach maturity. With such a rich history, it is myopic to think that one can come to fully understand the nature of this debate by concentrating solely on the positive law of the modern age. The long history of this debate provides a deeper understanding for both sides of the controversy. It also provides support for those who would maintain that no government can give its citizens the right to take their own lives, while simultaneously demonstrating the historical foundation of the arguments that the right to self-ownership and autonomy mandates the existence of a "right to die." By examining the whole spectrum of the historical debate, readers can come to understand not only the origins of the controversy, but also the different perspectives each age has contributed to this contemporary issue.

The answer to the "right to die" controversy contains within it important consequences for life in the United States and the whole of the Western world. The "right to die" controversy is not an issue that will soon slip from the political agenda of our day. Quite to the contrary, there is compelling evidence to suggest that many countries, particularly the United States, have trapped themselves into a position that will lead either to the unchecked use of euthanasia against potentially innocent and unwilling victims or to the legalization of the "right to die" under the control of state regulators. It is important to our future that decisions in this area are made with a thorough understanding of the rights and societal obligations involved.

In an environment of public debate that features such emotional events as the exploits of Jack Kevorkian, the publication of how-to suicide manuals such as *Final Exit*, and the counterattacks of "right to life" groups, the historical and political reality of the question can frequently be lost. This work demonstrates that "right to die" practices and policies have evolved in the United States to such an extent that we are left with only two options: We can both legalize and regulate euthanasia in order to guarantee the safety of all, or we can continue to allow a secret and dangerous black market in death to exist in our country.

While this book begins by attempting to familiarize the reader with the terminology of the field, together with world attitudes and opposing viewpoints that relate to the "right to die" controversy, this author strongly recommends that the reader first read the two personal interviews that are included as appendices to this book. For many readers, these interviews will provide valuable personal perspectives that can serve as a backdrop against which more technical discussions of the "right to die" can stand. The purpose of these sections of the book is to lay the foundations the reader needs to understand the various rights claimed by both sides of the debate.

Having established a modern foundation for the "right to die," the book then introduces the reader to the historical basis of the debate, stretching back over twenty-three centuries. The reader comes to understand that the "right to die" debate is inextricably tied to the evolution of natural law theory and the creation of the autonomous individual. Finally, the reader is shown how the theory of natural rights was embedded in the American Constitution, thus opening the door for many to claim that there is a "right to die" in the United States.

This author begins the first chapter by identifying the foundation of American attitudes toward the process of death, since the seventeenth century, and the factors that influenced these shifting attitudes. The chapter discusses the role of a world that was booming with new ideas and in which industry was increasingly influencing societal affairs. It identifies the role of religion, which was showing signs of fading out as a major force, and the development of the new paradigm of science. It discusses the idea that, as religion was replaced by the modern paradigm of science, the individual gradually began to recognize increased control over his or her own destiny as well as nature itself.

At the same time that mysticism was being replaced by experimentation, the legal theory of logical positivism began to replace the more ethereal concepts of morality, love, and dignity; many would argue that our concept of death was impoverished as a result. Death was transformed from a social process to a merely biological one. Science took a hold over the role of the family, as medical treatment became the backbone for a terminally ill patient, and the role of the family decreased from loving and sincere care to an almost obligatory support. Death was stripped of its spiritual and social quality, turned into a terminating event that was to be feared, and thus hidden away in sterile institutions, rather than accepted and experienced within the home and in the company of one's friends and family.

Chapter 2 outlines the history of organized efforts to advocate for the "right to die." This survey covers such organizations as the Hemlock Society, Concern for Dying, and the World Federation of Societies for the Right to Die. This chapter also covers the positions of such leading institutions as the Roman Catholic Church, which has organized a formidable political wing to oppose the "right to die" and euthanasia; the American Medical Association, which has formally opposed the legalization of such a right; and the American Bar Association, which has played important roles on both sides of the controversy.

The chapter attempts to separate the myriad of terms frequently used while talking about the "right to die" and attempts to outline briefly some of the major events that have influenced the evolution of this field of thought, ranging from appeal cases in the early 1900s to the major precedent-setting antics and five criminal trials of Dr. Jack Kevorkian (Doctor Death) in the last years of the century.

Chapter 3 discusses the legality surrounding euthanasia and assisted suicide, as it pertains to most of the Western world's developed nations, beginning with an outline of the stance of the United States and the fact that most states have their own laws surrounding the much-heated topic, the "right to die."

This chapter identifies the development of the "right to die" debate in Great Britain, Australia, and several other developed nations. The chapter also looks at the advent of this debate in several emerging nation. As a result of these investigations, the chapter suggests that the Western world appears to have a growing support for some form of legalized euthanasia.

Chapters 4 and 5 discuss the questions that can be raised concerning what an individual is actually claiming when he or she asserts the existence of a "right." Chapter 4 investigates the different definitions of a "right." Through this inquiry, the reader can better assess whether or not anyone can logically assert the existence of a "right to die." The discussion of rights covers such topics as the potential existence of natural rights as embodied in the Declaration of Independence, and perhaps in the Constitution, and how the evolution of the American conception of individual liberties and civil rights has been influenced by the natural law theories of the past.

Chapter 5 outlines the major positions of groups that oppose the acceptance of any "right to die" legislation, demonstrating that most nonreligious opposition can be placed in roughly three categories: the wedge or slippery-slope argument, the need to protect innocent life, and the incompatibility of the "right to die" with the medical profession. In addition, this chapter covers a more generalized argument that any recognition of the "right to die" would place the desires of a single individual above the community's interest in the general preservation of life.

Chapter 5 also confirms that these secular arguments against the "right to die" are often intermingled with, or supported by, religious opposition. In this area, the Roman Catholic Church has played a major role in organizing opposition to the legalization of any "right to die." The National Right to Life Committee has been an effective lobbying arm for the church. Their principal argument against legalization is that life is a gift from God, which does not belong to the individual, and that suffering is not an absolute evil but rather an opportunity for spiritual growth and atonement of sins. Finally, this chapter attempts to map out a possible middle way by attempting to develop a theory of euthanasia that can be viewed as compatible with many of these objections.

Chapter 6 begins to introduce the historical context in which the "right to die" debate must be set, if it is to be properly understood. This chapter argues that while, for more than twenty-three centuries, political philosophers have proposed various answers to the human dilemma, for the entire period only one theory has continually played a significant role in the evolution of Western political thought: the theory of natural law. Natural law theories, in various incarnations, served as the catalyst for the transformation of a collection of legal principles and philosophical schools of thought into the legal system of the Roman Empire, the authority of the Catholic Church in the medieval state, and the battle cry of the Protestant Reformation. This chapter argues that natural law theory has served as one of the cornerstones for the development of social contract theory and the evolution of the theory of individual rights that played such an important role in both the American and the French revolutions.

Because of the relationship between the "right to die" claims of our current society and the slow evolution of individual rights within natural law theory, it is important for readers to understand how the development of natural law made such a claim possible. The origins of natural law theory can be traced back to the works of Heraclitus, Sophocles, and Aristotle; however, it was the Stoics, in approximately 300 B.C., who from these rudimentary beginnings developed a theory that could serve as the foundation for both legal and political institutions of the Roman Empire. The Roman doctrine of natural law borrowed heavily from Greek philosophy and particularly from the Stoics. This chapter identifies how the Romans used natural law theory to create the ideas of a universal law.

In the hands of the Roman jurist Cicero, the Roman Empire developed the idea that some laws are fundamental and thus cannot be changed by human action or desire. The chapter outlines how this idea of a fundamental law becomes the foundation of the later claim for the existence of such rights as the "right to free speech," the "right to religious freedom," and the "right to die."

Chapter 7 attempts to explain how natural law theory experienced several transformations that enabled it to serve as the foundation of authority for the medieval Catholic Church. It explains how St. Thomas Aquinas took on the task of redefining natural law and bringing it into line with the teachings of Aristotle. This necessitated, once again, a recognition of the importance of the State to the full development of mankind, elevating its role to the top of the authoritative hierarchy. Under such a design, natural law was once again viewed as the source of rules that are necessary for the state to attain justice. Just as it had served the Roman Empire, natural law theory served to provide Christianity the ethical justification it needed for its legal and social structures. In essence, the ideas of Cicero and other Roman jurists, such as Seneca, were Christianized by St. Ambrose, St. Jerome, and most important St. Augustine and incorporated into church doctrine, resulting in the use of natural law as one of the foundations of canon law.

This chapter points out that, although the Christian Church of the Middle Ages had no intention of doing so, its interpretations of natural law laid the foundation for the development of the theory of human rights. It makes it clear that it was from this foundation that the philosophers of the Renaissance and the Reformation first developed a full theory of individual rights. Through this process, Western legal theory was slowly being transformed by the Roman Church clerics who introduced natural law theory into an important part of the law of "equity," and, in doing so, allowed the individual to claim to have entitlement that the secular government could not justly remove without violating some form of fundamental right.

Chapter 8 details how the theory of natural rights, 1,500 years in the making, became the foundation of the "right to die." It argues that it was not until the complete development of natural rights theory that the individual emerged from the protective shell of society as an autonomous political being. Natural law theory from the time of Cicero had inherently implied the existence of "rights," but not until the late sixteenth century was such an idea accepted as authoritative.

Chapter 8 also points to the work of Hugo Grotius and other natural law theorists, whose arguments that natural law guaranteed the existence of natural rights fueled revolutionary ideologies and threatened the dominance of both the church and the state in the lives of individuals. It argues that it is from this foundation that Protestant philosophers began to systematically challenge the Roman Catholic view of the state and the papacy and that writers such as Locke and Hobbes challenge even the divine right of kings.

Chapter 9 more explicitly sets forth the way in which the historical debate over the "right to die" coincided with the evolution of natural law theory. It argues that natural law theory represented the human desire to discover some immutable yardstick against which to measure the right actions of the state and of the citizens within it. It points out that the controversy over the "right to die" has a history equally as long as, and intermingled with that of natural law theory and that the concept of "suicide," with all its negative connotations, was not a part of the human language until approximately 1662. This chapter also points out that this fact should not be taken to mean that self-killing was not common or that it was not an issue of historical debate. There is no lack of references to the act of self-killing among the ancient Greeks, but it may be surprising to many modern readers to learn that there was a lack of any sense of condemnation toward such acts. Quite to the contrary, acts of self-killing were often elevated to the level of heroic acts. In fact, such acts were often characterized as portraits of bravery, sacrifice, and virtue.

While Chapter 9 points out that no evidence of condemnation can be found to support a contention that Athenian civil law considered such acts to be an offence against the state, it also points out that this should not be taken to mean that self-killing was universally accepted. The literature does indicate some quasi-religious grounds for opposing self-killing; and Socrates himself argued, while drinking hemlock as part of his death sentence, that it was wrong for a man to willingly take his own life, because it belonged not to him but to the gods. Similarly, Plato and Aristotle condemned self-killing as an act not against the gods, but against the state.

This chapter points out that while self-killing was clearly common in the ancient world, it was the Stoics who first raised the issue of a "right" to die. It argues that, in doing so, they developed a positive philosophy of self-killing based on natural law theory that maintained that the decision to live or die was entirely in the hands of the individual; it also argues that these ideas were translated into Roman law. Thus, the chapter indicates that, contrary to popular belief, no legal consequences were attached to an act of self-killing, outside of the military, and that the morality of such an act was not an issue of concern to the state so long as the act was attributed to any number of permissible factors including, but not limited to, tedium, sickness, extreme grief, insolvency, or madness.

Chapter 9 also points out that, interestingly enough, the Christians of the first century seemed to follow the Roman traditions concerning self-killing and reacted pastorally rather than condemning such acts. It was not until the fourth century that Christianity began to systematically disapprove of such acts.

The chapter argues that, with the advent of the Renaissance and the waning authority of the Catholic Church, secular philosophy once again began addressing the issue of the "right to die" in a positive light. It points out that Renaissance philosophy began to create a vision of mankind as a collection of autonomous individuals who possessed not only liberty over their own bodies but also an inalienable right to self-determination. Thus, by the late 1500s, John Donne had constructed a sympathetic view of rational acts of self-killing; later, in the eighteenth century, the right of an individual to take his own life would be defended by such theorists as Montesquieu and Hume.

Chapter 10 explains how natural law theory provided the spark needed to create both a viable theory of rights and the American Revolution. In addition, it explains how important these ideas were to the foundation of our nation and its legal systems. It argues that, to a great extent, the creation of the modern state and the development of an understanding of individual liberties was the product of the ideas unleashed by the Protestant Reformation. The authority of natural law was so strong among the early American Puritans that even John Winthrop, a civil rather than a religious official, maintained the view that society should be ordered in accordance with the dictates of natural law.

In addition to this religious influence, the chapter argues that thinkers such as Locke, Pufendorf, Milton, Montesquieu, and Blackstone, all of whom were advocates of natural law and natural rights theory, began to influence early American political thought. Under such conditions the early American jurists lost or simply disregarded any distinction between the theories of natural law and natural rights.

Chapter 10 further points out that, despite initial opposition by some, the popularity of natural law theories among early American political activists provided a common basis of agreement upon which America could claim moral authority. As a result, such leading American statesmen as Hamilton, Allen, Otis, Adams, and Dickinson all proudly waved the banner of natural law as providing justification for an American Revolution. Finally, the chapter demonstrates that Thomas Jefferson used natural law and natural rights theory as the binding principle upon which to base the Declaration of Independence.

Chapter 11 attempts to demonstrate how natural law principles were embedded into the early American legal system. The period of history following the American Revolution was marked by legal and political disorder. Many ex-colonists came to view themselves as having slipped back into the state of nature; as a result, many failed to recognize the authority of any surviving governmental entities.

This chapter argues that such political confusion and the clear break with the English common law system left American judges with a need to make judicial determinations without the availability of statutory law. To resolve this difficulty, American jurists simply returned to the principles of natural law that had been so influential during the earliest periods of American colonial history.

This shift caused clear distinctions between American and English legal philosophy of the eighteenth century. These distinctions caused the American legal system to embrace natural law concepts while their English counterparts clung to common law traditions. Resulting American legal and political philosophy recognized that there were two distinct realms of law. The first was positive law, which may consist of legislative enactments or recognition of tradition and the second was the realm of natural law.

In this way, the first ten amendments to the Constitution sought to express the American understanding of natural law and to embed them in the Constitution as an expression of the natural rights that flow from that theory. Thus, with the stabilization of the various states and the creation of a national government, the ardent appeal to natural law was transformed into an appeal to the fundamental laws now embodied in the Constitution.

Chapter 12 explains that, while the theory of natural law and natural rights is inextricably bound up with the Constitution, many of today's legal positivists strongly contest the idea that natural law has any relevance in today's society. They revolt against the idea that natural law theory creates within our legal philosophy a type of dualism in which we recognize the importance of positive law while holding some areas of human action as being beyond the authority of the state.

An examination of American legal history demonstrates that natural law principles have always played an important role in our judicial development. While this chapter makes it clear that, after the Revolution, many Americans saw the principle of natural law as far too unstable to serve as the foundation for an emerging nation, it makes it equally clear that many jurists believed that the incorporation of natural rights theory into the Constitution provided the theory of natural law with the stability needed not only to base decisions upon but also to override positive law.

Chapter 12 argues that, as a result of this strong belief in natural rights, judicial decisions throughout American history have reflected the belief that natural law was incorporated into the Constitution. Frequent references to natural law can be found in the decisions of American jurists up until the early 1800s, at which time a strong democratic movement made the overruling of positive legislative authority unpopular. However, even then, ongoing references to natural law can be found in the decisions of several justices.

The chapter points out that, when the debate over the morality of slavery began to gather steam during the mid to late 1830s, frequent references to natural law were used by both abolitionists and the advocates of slavery. This debate fermented until American jurists, from the 1850s to the 1950s, slowly evolved a principle of fundamental law and vested rights. In this sense, the Fourteenth Amendment to the U.S. Constitution was intended to give practical effect to the Declaration of Independence and its statement of inalienable rights. In 1874, the Supreme Court used a "higher law" or "natural law" interpretation of the Fourteenth Amendment as a basis for reinvigorating the principle of judicial review, which allowed courts to once again overturn the positive law enactments of legislatures. It was these ideas that were eventually embodied in the due process clause of the Fourteenth Amendment.

While the symmetry between the principles of due process and the theory of fundamental rights was widespread throughout the judiciary, it by no means was a universal belief. With the rise of the analytical theory of jurisprudence, under the tutelage of John Austin, the references to fundamental law became increasingly infrequent. The struggle between those who maintained a belief in the concept of fundamental law and the analytical school of jurisprudence continued for many years and, to a great extent, continues to this day.

Chapter 13 explains the importance of natural law theory, not only to the issue of the "right to die" but also to the whole of that entity we call the United States. It argues that this principle serves as a theoretical beacon, guiding our lumbering society through the process of history, leading us away from the dangers of excessive authoritarianism, majoritarianism, and mandated social conformity.

This chapter points out that, in this way, natural law has commonly been used in the United States as a principle upon which to base revolutionary shifts in political thought pertaining to the appropriate use of state authority and that this makes the theory particularly relevant to today's debate over the "right to die." While any attempt to pay homage to the theory of natural law will send shivers down the spines of those political theorists who have been taught to reject natural law out of hand, in the end such legal positivists must face their theories' own inconsistency with the principles that Americans hold most dear.

Roscoe Pound once noted that, despite the lack of support from the legal philosophers of his day, the average American clearly clung to an understanding of the Constitution that included the principles of natural law and natural rights as manifested in the concept of fundamental law. The philosophical school of jurisprudence maintains that positivists have failed to grasp the full understanding of those factors that make law binding on the minds, as well as the bodies, of humankind.

The relevance of such concepts to the debate over the "right to die" is that the theory helps to establish the boundaries of permissible action but does not determine which actions, in and of themselves, are good or bad. Under such a construction, once the parameters of government are set, the majority has no power to interfere with the actions that take place within these defined boundaries. It was precisely for the protection of individual rights that the founders placed limits on unrestrained majoritarianism.

The importance of these ideas is that they identify American government as a government of limited powers. Natural law principles in the Constitution lead to the recognition of fundamental personal rights. Jacques Maritain argues that the natural law demands the recognition that "every human person has the right to make his own decisions with regard to his personal destiny. . . . The state can forcibly requisition the services of each of us . . . but the state becomes tyrannical if it tries to 'become master of men's souls.'" Put concisely, the essence of natural law principles, as incorporated into the Constitution, is that each American enjoys the right of self-ownership, which may very well include the right to die as one sees fit.

Chapter 14 applies the conclusions drawn from the study of the American interpretation of natural law and natural rights theory to the current issue of the "right to die." In reaching the answer to this question, the chapter examines the proper role of the state in such events as passive euthanasia, active euthanasia, and the standards emerging within the U.S. courts.

The chapter outlines the need within American society to strike a balance between the impulses of the majority and the liberty interests of the individual. It outlines the state's interest in regulating the activities of our daily lives to produce social order and stability and the interest of American citizens to be free from government regulation. In outlining these powers and rights, the chapter recognizes that we all have undisputed rights to life, privacy, self-ownership, and autonomy in private decisions of conscience. In applying these concepts to the "right to die," the chapter outlines what role our government might legitimately play in the successively difficult questions of passive euthanasia, active euthanasia, and assisted suicide.

Finally, the chapter examines the alternatives open to the United States in its effort to regulate euthanasia. It examines the ability of the United States to effectively use three different systems of regulation that span a scale of severity from absolute prohibition to regulated permissibility. In the end, this author concludes that only one of these options is open to the United States and that, in pursuing it, our whole society would be better off concentrating on efforts to provide the dying individual with the attributes of care necessary to experience a meaningful personal state of comfort, peace, and love.

Chapter 1

Contemporary Attitudes about Death

Socrates:

> To fear death, gentlemen, is no other than to think oneself wise when one is not, to think one knows what one does not know. No one knows whether death may not be the greatest of all blessings for a man, yet men fear it as if they know that it is the greatest of evils. (Plato 1975, 29 A-b)

Death was once a part of life, an accepted part of the human condition. It was a communal occasion that brought friends and family together in an effort to bring comfort and dignity to the dying and the bereaved. Death was a social process rather than a medical event. In any context, it is a process that brings us all face to face with our own finite existence.

Social attitudes about death have undergone significant changes over the centuries (Aries 1981, 15). One need travel back only a few centuries to find a time when an individual who was dying would do so surrounded by his family, friends, and neighbors; the bedchamber of the dying was a place for adults and children alike. This was the case until at least the eighteenth century, when society's attitudes about death slowly began to change (Aries 1974).

Within the Western world, the roots of these shifting attitudes about death can be found in the emergence of science as the predominant paradigm and in the seventeenth-century development of the concept of individuality. As a result of these two concepts, the bonding power of religious beliefs and church authority were slowly supplanted by tenets of science, which emphasized dominion over one's own destiny as well as over nature itself (Toynbee et al. 1968). Religion was replaced with science, and mysticism with experimentation. While few can argue against the assertion that human knowledge about our physical world was considerably advanced by this shift, it is equally true that the elevation of logical positivism over the more ethereal concepts of morality, love, and dignity impoverished our understanding of human processes of death (Feifel 1964,

415-420). As a result, death was transformed from a social process to a merely biological one. It was stripped of its spiritual signature—as a process of transition—and re-envisioned as a terminating event to be feared rather than accepted.

This fear is manifested in nineteenth- and even twentieth-century Western medical tradition in which the doctor and family, acting in concert, frequently conspire to shield the dying individual from the realization that death is near (Feifel 1990, 538). In the twenty years between 1930 and 1950, advances in medical technology led society to cast off the idea of death as a natural process, as well as to shun the *person* who happened to be dying, and death became an institutionalized process rather than a private one. It evolved into an event that took place not at home, but in the hospital, with many individuals entering medical facilities only after the determination was made that death was imminent (Aries 1974, 27-29). As a result, modern medical facilities served dually as sites of healing and as places to hide the dying from society. In this context death became essentially a technical failure, occurring only when all available medical options had been exhausted. Doctors, once revered for their capacity to heal, have now become the midwives of death, deciding when and under what conditions death is to take place. The patient frequently dies alone or unconscious; it is a moment that has been robbed of its poignancy, a moment designed to serve the needs of the living rather than dying (Aries 1974, 26).

As a result of this change in social attitudes, the open discussion of death and dying became strictly taboo. To discuss such a topic was to invite disaster, to bring about bad luck. Consequently, to rhapsodize on the subject of death was no more acceptable in polite society than a blunt discussion of sex (Dickinson 1993, 4). By the 1950s, America's social attitudes concerning death began to show signs of change. The events of World War II, with its Nazi death camps and bloody battlefronts, forced the nation to come to grips with the existence of a host of social problems and issues, and the veneer surrounding America's detached attitude about death began to crack. Throughout the 1950s and 1960s, the growing awareness of the dire circumstances of many social issues began to weaken the grip of logical positivism on the intellectual sectors of American society. Logically enough, American scholars also began to examine the many issues surrounding the process of death and dying (Feifel 1990, 537-538).

By the 1960s, the American attitude with respect to death began to broaden, with most citizens reporting that it was important to discuss the possibility of death with their loved ones and to make plans against its eventuality (Riley 1970). This openness engendered a concomitant explosion of intellectual interest in the topic of death and its many facets. Universities and professional schools alike began teaching courses on varied topics concerned with death; and finally, in 1969, Elizabeth Kubler-Ross published her now famous book, formally consecrating the now familiar phrase "death and dying" (Feifel 1990, 539; Kubler-Ross 1969).

The 1970s saw the publication of numerous books and articles on the subject, and America began to come to grips with its fears. As a result of this new social freedom and the continuing advancement of medical technology, Americans began to discuss new ideas concerning the ever-changing role of the medical profession in the process of dying, the importance of a person's dying with dignity, and the possibility that the individual is possessed of an actual right to die. As new moral conundrums arose, medical professionals began to reevaluate their role in the dying process. Medical scholars began to suggest that prolonging life might not, in and of itself, always be an appropriate goal, particularly in those cases in which the prospect of healing was truly limited. Instead, it was reasoned that the simple provision of comfort care was a more desirable medical goal (Feifel 1977). Toward that end, the United States realized a rapid growth in the Hospice Care movement (Bass 1985).

Still, advances in medical technology and the possibility of a protracted death—in which one is artificially supported by mechanical respirators, heart pumps, and feeding tubes—pushed the issue of the "right to die" into the legislative and judicial arena. In response, numerous legislatures passed laws both protecting and regulating the rights of their citizens to control precisely what medical procedures may or may not be performed on them. In addition, the American judiciary affirmed a host of rights: the right of a dying person to refuse medical treatment, the right of a state to set standards of proof for the determination of an incompetent patient's wishes, and the rights of attending physicians, as well as the rights of society as a whole. However, all of this has served to raise more questions than it has answered, and Americans still search for a common understanding of what it means to die well.

Some openly advocate both active and passive euthanasia, an idea that until relatively recently was reserved for the more radical sectors of society. Others advocate that life is too precious and emphasize that the trivialization of death, with its social costs, can only lead to a disregard for a person's right to life.[1]

Ultimately, if American society is to reach agreement on these ponderous issues, we will have to take one of two alternative paths. We must develop a common understanding of what it means to die; we must agree on whether death is a beginning or an end, whether it is something to be fought against or accepted; or we can agree to allow each individual to decide his or her own course of action. As a society we must determine whether we will allow all those who wish to live the legal right and moral support necessary to pursue life, while allowing all those who wish to die the right to pass from this life with dignity.

Chapter 2

A Brief Modern History and Definition of Terms

Over the course of the last hundred years, a controversy has grown in the United States over the individual's right to terminate his or her own life once it has been decided that, because of illness or infirmity, life is no longer worth living. During the last several decades, this debate has spawned the creation of numerous organizations that advocate recognition of what has popularly become known as the "right to die." Primary among these organizations are the Hemlock Society, with 160,000 members; the Society for the Right to Die, with 147,000 members; Concern for Dying; and the World Federation of Societies for the Right to Die, founded in 1980 (Meucci 1988,17-20).[1] In addition some leading professional institutions, such as the American Medical Association (Hentoff 1987) and the American Bar Association (Meucci 1988), have developed positions intended to assist their members in evaluating the efficacy of any given course of action available to the modern terminal patient.

At least one writer concerned about this topic has suggested that our nation's current preoccupation with the "right to die" may arise concomitantly out of the strong traditions of free expression, personal choice, and individual liberties that are integral to the American identity (Jacoby 1980, 33-64). If this assertion is true, the current debate may be viewed as a logical extension of those values expressed by our early American ancestors: stoicism, determination, and self-reliance, juxtaposed against the values of caring and mutual support that might be nurtured more in a less individualistic society (McKay 1983, 41).

Individuals who accept this view of the debate find themselves nonetheless horrified by the increasing popularity and support for the concept of euthanasia. They see it as an idea that leads to a disregard for those individuals whom society has devalued, ultimately resulting in the involuntary termination of those whom society may simply label as not worthy of life (Cole 1989, 393-406).

Many doctors and nurses in the United States share this view of life and feel an acute need to preserve it. Naturally enough, many medical personnel feel an obligation to use all the medical technology available to them to prolong the ongoing existence of their patient's physical body, regardless of the effect that such treatment may have on the psychological or spiritual well-being of the recipient. As one observer put it, many of our current physicians seem to be caught up in the American practice of "winning" (Ogg 1980).

The difficulty with this view is that it fails to consider how extraordinarily medical technology has changed the practice of dying in American society. Eighty years ago, the national life expectancy was under 55 years of age and the majority of individuals died in their own homes. As a result of this everyday exposure to the process of dying, death was viewed as a normal experience (Ogg 1980). Today, however, most dying individuals are shuffled off to sterile institutions to undergo the ritual of death. As a result, the process of dying is hidden from social view, and those facing it are often subjected to impersonal care, loneliness, and dehumanization. The process of death is no longer part of the mainstream of our social consciousness, and many view their personal obligation to the dying as a matter better left in the hands of trained professionals when in fact it is one of the most necessary and unavoidable learning experiences in life.

The need to delay death is not, however, universally and automatically accepted by the medical establishment. A growing number of doctors recognize that there is a time to do all that is possible to save a life and a time to concede that further efforts would not only be futile, but perhaps inhumane. This involves the simple recognition that just any manifestation of human life is not necessarily valuable to the individual enduring it and that the opinion of that individual, while somewhat loaded, might also be one arrived at through introspection and careful consideration. Recognizing this problem, the American Medical Association's judicial council has ruled that a physician may ethically "cease or omit treatment to let a terminally ill patient die," and the Medical Society of the State of New York now allows the issuance of "Do Not Resuscitate" orders that instruct medical personnel not to use emergency measures to restore life to a dying patient (Newman 1983, 74-85).[2]

Given the polarization endemic to "right to die" issues, our judicial system and legislatures find themselves under mounting pressure when plaintiffs and/or constituents ask them, on an ever-increasing basis, to rule on or legislate about the individual's right to die. Thus, legal scholars are forced to reconsider old definitions about what constitutes suicide, how to treat issues of assisted suicide (Mojica and Murrell 1991, 471-504), and how to reconcile the ethical dilemmas posed by such questions (Harner 1991). They are being forced to make such decisions with little or no judicial and legislative history, all in an area in which no consistency has been brought to bear (Mullins 1991, 827-859).

THE EVOLUTION OF TERMINOLOGY

Before launching into a whirlwind tour of the modern history of the "right to die" movement, it is first prudent to note that the terminology that has arisen out of this debate has not always been consistent. While today most discussions occur under the general heading of "right to die," several other terms have commonly been used to discuss essentially the same concept throughout the last century, many of which are still found in the literature today. It is therefore not uncommon to find authors making reference to "the right to die with dignity," "death with dignity," "a natural death," or even the right to "abate treatment" (Glick 1992, 8). While each of these terms places its own unique spin on the concept, all are essentially just different ways of referring to euthanasia.

The term *euthanasia* comes from the Greek concept of a good or easy death, often involving some element of self-control. The difficulty with this term is that it has come to have politically negative connotations and is often associated with the harsh and deplorable acts of the Nazis, who killed so many in the name of "the social good." The word is sometimes taken to be synonymous with the act of killing those whom society deems socially undesirable, against their will. In fact, this meaning is still so strong in Germany today that the term euthanasia is rarely used within that country (*New York Times*, 6 December 1986, 6). While Americans have not shown the same level of reluctance to use the term itself, it is clear that many are still uncomfortable with any label attached to the concept.

Taken generally, the word euthanasia can refer to several distinct categories of action. While traditional use of the term has been restricted to those cases involving individuals who suffer from some terminal illness or debilitating condition, the connotations can vary widely. The most important dichotomy housed under this term is the one between voluntary and involuntary euthanasia. Voluntary euthanasia refers to those actions taken by request and with approval—to bring about the end of a competent person's life. Conversely, involuntary euthanasia implies the taking of a life either without the person's consent and knowledge or, taken in its most sinister sense, against his or her will.

In addition, it is common to find distinctions within the literature between "passive" and "active" euthanasia. Used in this way, the term serves to discriminate between methods used to bring about death. Theoretically, passive methods of euthanasia would involve only the non-initiation or the withdrawal of life-prolonging medical procedures, while active methods would include the introduction of some outside agent, be it chemical or physical, to hasten the onset of death. While some would argue that the distinction between active and passive methods is illusory (Kamisar 1958, 969-71), particularly when euthanasia involves the withdrawal of such necessary elements to ongoing life as nutrition and hydration, it is a distinction that has been generally accepted within the public and the courts.

In reaction to the broad connotations that have been ascribed to the word "euthanasia," many who support the right of terminally ill and disabled individuals to end their lives have attempted to generate phrases that connote only the voluntary aspects of euthanasia. This is, in fact, the intent of the phrase "a right to die." However, there is no consensus on whether that phrase should be taken to refer only to passive methods of bringing about death or whether it should include advocacy for active methods as well. Some argue that the traditional meaning of the "right to die" does not include the concept of active euthanasia; if so, the definition would exclude such acts as "mercy killing," in which the use of medication or a weapon prematurely ends the life of another, and "assisted suicide," in which the means are provided to the individual to occasion his or her own death (Glick 1992, 11). It is clear, however, that in some other countries at least (the Netherlands, for example), assisted suicide is indeed included under the moniker of "right to die" (*New York Times*, 31 October 1986, 6). Given the vague and ill-defined nature of the mere terminology linked to this issue, it is little wonder that many choose to create their own lexicon rather than use a term that may inadvertently endorse a view the author did not intend.

THE EVOLUTION OF THE "RIGHT TO DIE" IN AMERICA

It seems clear that until comparatively recently there was no debate about the "right to die"; the terms in which we have couched our contemporary debate would have seemed irrational a few generations ago. Mankind had not yet become sufficiently advanced to cheat death through the use of medical technology, and the occurrence of drawn-out and lingering illnesses was necessarily rare. However, in those cases that did occur, either through disease or injury, the law would have been clear. The common law considered suicide a crime against society, and anyone who assisted another in the commission of a suicide, regardless of the purity of their motives, would have been judged to have committed some form of homicide.[3]

By the mid 1800s, this attitude had begun to change, and society began to look at acts of self-killing less as crimes and more as indications of social and psychological illnesses. As a result of these changing views, the law and, to some extent, the church began to moderate their views of suicide, eventually resulting in its decriminalization in most of the American states (Mojica and Murrell 1991, notes 16-20).

By the 1870s, the idea that the terminally ill should have a "right to die" was fully articulated in Great Britain by a small but influential group of intellectuals who argued for the legalization of such a right (Kamisar 1958, 696-1042). Despite these efforts to foster recognition of a "right to die" in England, American legal scholars showed little to no interest in the subject. This is not to say, however, that American law was not changing, for indeed it was. Yet the changes in the American legal attitude toward the "right to die" took place not as a result of proposed legislative action but, much more quietly, as a result of judicial determination.

As early as 1902, the Texas Court of Criminal Appeals made a dramatic break with the common law and ruled that an individual who had committed suicide was not guilty of a crime against the state and, even more astonishing, that an individual who knowingly provided another with the means to commit suicide was not guilty of murder so long as no active role had been played in the employment of those means (*Grace v. State* 1902). The Texas court made its position even clearer in 1925, when it ruled that, in the absence of statutory authority, the provision of poison to another for the known purpose of aiding that person in the commission of suicide not only did not constitute murder but did not even rise to the level of manslaughter (*Aven v. State* 1925). However, it should be noted that these early Texas rulings were innovations in the law that many legislatures specifically defeated by passing statutes making any form of mercy killing or assisted suicide a criminal act; manslaughter convictions, usually with light or suspended sentences, were not uncommon (Humphry and Wickett 1986).

This new willingness to rethink the legal implications of self-killing manifested itself, in the 1930s, with the creation of an American society for the promotion of euthanasia. The Euthanasia Society of America was largely an outgrowth of its British counterpart, known as Britain's Voluntary Euthanasia Legalization Society, and followed its lead in attempting to convince lawmakers to pass legislation formally recognizing the right of the terminally ill to control the time and nature of their deaths. Despite the fact that the proposed bills took great pains to spell out detailed procedures and safeguards, thereby ensuring that the person requesting euthanasia was in fact terminally ill and had voluntarily made the request, no legislature in the United States or Great Britain was yet willing to consider legalizing euthanasia (Russell 1977, 64-86).

However, the Euthanasia Society of America did not allow this apparent legislative obstinence to impede their efforts. To the contrary, the society was buoyed by public opinion polls throughout the decade indicating that 46% of Americans were willing to consider the legalization of euthanasia (Humphry and Wickett 1986, 18). Supported by such data, the society, in 1938, attempted on several occasions to persuade New York State legislators to introduce euthanasia legislation for debate. Each attempt was thwarted by a coalition of social groups, which included the Roman Catholic Church and various medical associations. As a result of their opposition and strong lobbying efforts, not a single legislator was willing to attach his name to the bill (*New York Times,* 1 January 1938, 21; 27 January 1939, 21; 14 February 1939, 2).

In the face of these defeats, Dr. Foster Kennedy, the president of the Euthanasia Society of America, publicly adopted a substantially more radical position with respect to the proper employment of euthanasia in American society. Kennedy announced that he believed that euthanasia should be used to shorten the painful lives of those individuals who had been born defective. He argued that this was the most humane treatment of such individuals, one that would further serve to reduce the psychological and financial strain such cases placed on their families (*New York Times,* 14 February 1939, 2). Despite Kennedy's hopes that his expansive view of euthanasia might generate greater public support, New York State legislative initiatives addressing the legalization of voluntary euthanasia failed in both 1941 and 1946. The latter proposal failed in spite of the fact that it was accompanied by a petition signed by 50 Protestant ministers and 1,500 doctors. After this failure, the society was moved to redirect its efforts from New York to New Hampshire, where Dr. Hermann Sanders had injected air into the vein of a terminally ill patient in order to bring about his death. Amazingly, even though Dr. Sanders readily admitted the truth of all allegations made against him, state prosecutors were unable to obtain a conviction. Despite this apparent show of support among the inhabitants of New Hampshire, the Society's legislative initiative of 1950 once again failed (*New York Times,* 3 January 1950, sect. 7:1).

It is extremely likely that the advent of World War II and the horrors of the Holocaust were significantly detrimental to the society's efforts to pass legislation. Many drew parallels between the atrocities of the Nazis' euthanistic policies, particularly in light of Dr. Kennedy's open advocacy for the use of euthanasia in the case of the physically and mentally disabled (Humphry and Wickett 1986, 36). However, the shock of the Holocaust was not long lived. Prior to the 1950s, modern medicine was not sufficiently advanced to generate much debate on the subject of euthanasia. Generally speaking, patients in a persistent vegetative state died from secondary illnesses and/or dehydration without excessive passage of time. Pneumonia, tuberculosis, and influenza were common before the widespread use of antibiotics. Heretofore, most people died at home and thus did not have the aid—or burden—of modern medical machinery. Advances in surgery and in disease and infection control, along with the advent of new technology such as intravenous feeding tubes, cardiopulmonary bypass machines, and ventilators, served not only to improve the general health of society, but also to increase the frequency with which individuals were kept technically alive, but in conditions that may be seen as personally undesirable (Glick 1992, 12-14). As a result, there was renewed interest in the cause of voluntary euthanasia in America. This reawakening was given a significant boost, in 1956, by a series of lectures given by James Carpentier in which he strongly advocated the need and, in some instances, the duty to provide euthanasia for terminally ill individuals suffering from untreatable pain.[4] The lectures roused strong debate concerning the morality of euthanasia and brought the issue back into the forefront of American public controversies (Kamisar 1958, 696).

Recognizing the growing controversy caused by modern medical technology, the Roman Catholic Church, under the leadership of Pope Pius XII, issued directives intended to aid Catholics in their efforts to distinguish between types of medical care that they were obligated to receive (ordinary care) and medical treatments that they could morally refuse (extraordinary care). Included in the category of extraordinary care was the use of resuscitators and ventilators in those cases in which a clear medical determination of death had occurred, but the Pope went on to warn against the excessive use of pain medication that might interfere with consciousness and so with the individual's ability to prepare for death.[5]

This renewed interest in the issue of euthanasia notwithstanding, the next ten years produced no significant activities in the field. The lack of legislative and judicial activity was not representative of a lack of interest and, viewed in retrospect, simply appears to have been an example of the proverbial calm before the storm. As the events of the late 1960s erupted into a virtual firestorm of social controversy, the "right to die" issue was once again thrust into the mainstream of American politics.

In 1967, the first exemplar living will was introduced by the Euthanasia Society of America. One year later, a Florida physician-legislator put the nation's first "right to die" proposal before a state legislature. Despite the fact that the legislation was defeated, these activities helped bring about the creation of the Hasting Center, in 1969, and the Kennedy Institute of Ethics at Georgetown University, in 1970 (Glick 1992, 62).

By the mid 1970s, attempted suicide had been decriminalized in every state in the nation (Mojica and Murrell 1991, 487).[6] In fact, a large number of states went even further and passed legislation that specifically "declared that the withholding or withdrawal of life sustaining procedures [did] not constitute suicide" (Mojica and Murrell 1991, 487-488, note 138).[7] The entire landscape of the "right to die" movement was changed forever, in 1973, by the emergence of "right to die" claims based for the first time not on religious beliefs but on the concept of a right to privacy.

Prior to the mid 1970s, judicial activity in "right to die" cases was primarily limited to cases in which patients had chosen to refuse lifesaving medical treatment on religious grounds, as contained in the free exercise clause of the First Amendment. Nonetheless, such a claim was subject to the Court's determination of whether government intervention would unduly burden the challenger's freedom of religion and, if so, whether some compelling state interest existed that could justify the burden (*Sherbert v. Verner* and *Wisconsin v. Yoder*). Moreover, when the Supreme Court handed down its now historic 1973 decision in the case of *Roe v. Wade,* it not only opened the door for the legalization of abortion, it also acknowledged the idea that the individual's right to privacy was so strong that it extended to fundamental questions of life and death. From this point forward, the majority of "right to die" cases focused less on religious free exercise claims than on the individual's right to control what happens to his or her own body without the interference of government. It was precisely this type of argument that opened the way for the 1976 landmark case of *In re Quinlan.*

The Quinlan case involved a 22-year-old woman who, for reasons never fully determined, had lost consciousness and fallen into a persistent vegetative state. Ms. Quinlan was maintained in this state for several months by a respirator and feeding tube, without which she would have died. Eventually her father brought a petition before the New Jersey Supreme Court requesting permission to withdraw "all extraordinary medical procedures," which, in the opinion of the family, included the respirator but not the equipment necessary for artificial feeding (*In re Quinlan* 1976). In deciding the case, the New Jersey Supreme Court specifically chose not to base its decision on the free exercise clause of the First Amendment; it elected, rather, to set the standard for all "right to die" cases by basing its decision to allow the removal of the respirator on Ms. Quinlan's right to privacy, as exercised through her parent/guardian (*In re Quinlan* 1976). In the course of rendering this decision, the court relied upon the statements of the attending physician and the hospital's "ethics committee," attesting to the fact that "there was no reasonable possibility of [Karen's] ever emerging from her present comatose condition to a cognitive, sapient state," as a critical element in its determination to allow discontinuation (*In re Quinlan* 1976).[8]

In his comprehensive history of the "right to die," Henry Glick describes the Quinlan case as a galvanizing event. One result was that the total number of articles published concerning the "right to die" in the years "1975 and 1976 equaled or exceeded all articles published in the previous decade." He goes on to note that "from 1976 until the end of 1990, dozens of appellate court cases were decided in 17 states, affecting the use of life-support systems and other treatment of the terminally ill and those in a persistent vegetative state" (Glick 1992, 15). The impact of the Quinlan case immediately made itself felt in California by virtue of the enactment of the nation's first living will law. By 1977, seven states had passed similar living will statutes and nearly all states had corresponding legislation before their legislatures (Glick 1992, 15).

In keeping with the trend toward a more liberal interpretation of the "right to die," in 1983 the Michigan Court of Appeals laid down a new interpretation of assisted suicide in the common law. In the case of *People v. Campbell* the court reversed its previous rulings, stating "that it is 'extremely doubtful' that aiding or soliciting a suicide was a crime at common law, and that suicide, by definition, excludes homicide." The court held that the act of providing a gun and bullets to a person who had expressed the intent to commit suicide, while "morally reprehensible," was not a crime under the existing law of Michigan,[9] and it invited the legislature to adopt a provision regarding "inciting suicides" (Mojica and Murrell 1991, 495). While at the time of its decision, the court's new interpretation of the permissibility of assisted suicide under common law must have been little more than an interesting interpretation of the current status of the law, the true significance of the court's decision would not be felt until seven years later when, in 1990, Dr. Jack Kevorkian, relying on the *Campbell* decision and the lack of any Michigan statute making assisted suicide a crime, used his now infamous "suicide machine" to induce the death of three women (two from the State of Washington) in the State of Michigan. Dr. Kevorkian's actions were intended to draw public attention and to stimulate debate concerning the "right to die" and the proper role of the medical community in this process. As a result of his actions, Dr. Kevorkian was indicted on first-degree murder; however, all charges were eventually dismissed, the court finding that the doctor had not caused the deaths of the women but had merely provided them with the means by which they could take their own lives. The court further concluded that the state had no law against assisting in a suicide and that therefore the doctor's actions could not be said to constitute a crime (*New York Times*, 14 December 1990, 1; 25 October 1991, 1).

By 1983, state courts had begun to support the "right to die" more aggressively, in some instances even setting aside the limiting provisions of state living will legislation. In the case of *Barber v. Superior Court*, the court ruled that, the provisions of the California living will statute notwithstanding, its citizens had the right to refuse medical treatment and that this right could not be limited by any interpretation of the state's statute. In 1984, a Georgia court also recognized that the right to die existed, independent of state legislation, and accepted statements of a mature teenager who was legally a minor, but who had clearly expressed a desire not to be kept alive by artificial means prior to events that left him in a coma. By doing so, the court extended the right to die beyond statutory authority and allowed the removal of all life-supporting systems. Finally, in 1985, the New Jersey Supreme Court handed down the landmark decision of *In re Conroy,* in which it ruled that even artificial feeding and hydration could be removed from an otherwise dying patient in the same way that any other medical treatment could be withdrawn.[10]

In his book The *Right to Die: Policy Innovation and Its Consequences*, Henry Glick reports that, statistically, the *Conroy* decision stimulated similar legislation in several other areas. He notes that, at the very least, "following *Conroy*, the artificial administration of food and hydration became one of the most controversial right to die issues in years" (Glick 1992, 149-150).

It is clear that the decade of the 1980s was a time in American history when the public refocused its interest in the "right to die" issue. This increased interest was demonstrated by a dramatic upsurge in the publication of "right to die" articles in professional journals, as well as in the mass media. In addition, the 1980s saw more national organizations than ever articulating their support for the "right to die." Simultaneously, state courts and legislative bodies took up the issue of the "right to die," with a gusto not before seen in the United States (Glick 1992, 90).

If the 1980s can accurately be said to have produced a marked increase in "right to die" advocacy, then the 1990s can best be described as an explosion of the same. In June of 1990, the landscape of the "right to die" debate was changed forever as a result of the first U.S. Supreme Court decision addressing a variety of issues relating specifically to the "right to die." The case was that of *Cruzan v. Director, Missouri Department of Health*. In its five-to-four decision, articulated in the writings of Chief Justice Rehnquist, the Court upheld the right of the State of Missouri to require clear and convincing evidence of Ms. Cruzan's desire not to have her life artificially sustained once she fell into a persistent vegetative state. The Court went on to hold that the state had a further right to guard against any potential abuse of authority by her surrogate or guardian.

This case recognized the power of a state (Missouri) to regulate the withdrawal of medical treatment from citizens who are terminally ill or in a persistent vegetative state. In addition, the Court ruled that each state has broad leeway to develop its own standard of proof for determining a person's wishes to have treatment removed or uninitiated. In reaching this decision, the Court expressed a preference for written directives, noting that past oral statements were generally suspect in legal transactions.

Finally, the Court rejected the argument that a legal distinction can be made between the withdrawal of medical procedures providing food and hydration and those relating to other bodily functions. In the end, the Court concluded that once the patient's wish not to have his or her life artificially sustained has been established, the removal of all medical treatments, regardless of their nature, was allowed.

The *Cruzan* decision was handed down on June 15 of 1990. In July of the same year, the Hemlock Society of Oregon attempted unsuccessfully to pass an assisted suicide referendum in the State of Washington. This failure came as a surprise to many, given that polling data had indicated broad support for assisted-suicide. The effect that the Cruzan case had on the Washington referendum is uncertain (*New York Times*, 6 July 1990, A7).

In November 1990, Ms. Cruzan's case was back in the news when her court-appointed guardian filed a new petition to remove life support from Ms. Cruzan. Supported by new testimony from three of her friends, the Missouri trial court now ordered the removal of Nancy Cruzan's feeding tube.

Despite the fact that this new ruling was never contested by the State of Missouri, several "right to life" organizations filed petitions in both state and federal courts seeking to stay or overturn the trial court decision. When those efforts were unsuccessful, a crowd of some 25 protesters were arrested while attempting to force their way into Nancy Cruzan's hospital room, supposedly to force the reinitiation of tube feeding. Their efforts were unsuccessful, and Cruzan died twelve days after the removal of her feeding tube on December 26, 1990 (Glick 1992, 4).

By the end of 1990, Dr. Kevorkian had initiated a series of assisted suicides in the State of Michigan and had propelled the issue onto the front pages of newspapers and TV news reports across the nation. Commenting on Dr. Kevorkian's actions, the editor of the *New England Journal of Medicine* stated that the whole bizarre episode "underscored a very real problem . . . [but] whatever you thought of what Dr. Kevorkian does, it certainly wasn't murder. And we in medicine have got to come to better grips with the fact that increasing numbers of our patients will be seeking our assistance in ending their lives" (*New York Times*, 14 December 1990, B10).

Dr. Kevorkian's actions most certainly seemed to have encouraged Dr. Timothy E. Quill of Rochester, New York, to write an article for the *New England Journal of Medicine* in which he described his decision to prescribe barbiturates for one of his patients suffering from leukemia, knowing that she would use the medication not for treatment, but to end her life (*New York Times*, 6 and 7 June 1990, 1; 3 July 1991, 1; 25 October 1991, 1). Indeed, Dr.

Quill went farther than to simply prescribe the medication; he actively referred his patient to the Hemlock Society for any further assistance or information she might need (*New York Times*, 12 March 1991, B6). Because of these actions, prosecutors attempted to charge Dr. Quill with violation of New York State's law against assisting in a suicide attempt. In the end, however, the grand jury refused to indict Dr. Quill, despite his open admissions (*New York Times*, 27 July 1991, 1).

Almost immediately following the disposition of the Quill case, Derek Humphry, of the Hemlock Society, published his book entitled *Final Exit.* The book was on the best-seller list for almost the entire summer of 1991 (*New York Times*, 9 August 1991, A1). Although the book was assailed by many as a suicide handbook that might be used by the young or by those suffering from depression or other conditions that impair judgment, others hailed the book as a liberating publication that, for the first time, allowed those who wished to follow its dictates the right to control the time and nature of their deaths.

By the end of 1991, the United States Congress had taken steps to create a national policy in this area by passing the Patient Self-determination Act, which required all medical facilities receiving federal funds, including Medicare and Medicaid reimbursements, to inform all patients of their rights as a patient under applicable state laws and institutional regulations. The legislation further directed that the notification must include the right to refuse medical treatment, as well as the use of medical available treatment directives. The legislation was accompanied by an appropriation of 30 million dollars, to be spent between 1991 and 1994 on educational programs and implementing legislation (Glick 1992, 208-211).

By the end of 1994, popular support for the "right to die" within the State of Oregon had grown to such a level that a group known as Oregon Right to Die proposed the nation's third state referendum to allow terminally ill individuals to end their lives with the assistance of their doctors. Although similar legislation had failed both in Washington and California, public opinion polls showed that 60% of Oregon's citizens supported the proposal for allowing physician-assisted suicide. The legislation, known as Measure 16 or the Oregon Death with Dignity Act, proposed allowing doctors to provide terminally ill patients with a prescription for lethal doses of medication, provided two doctors agree that the patient has less than six months to live, that the patient has clearly rejected every alternative, and that three requests for such assistance have been made, the last of which is in writing (*New York Times*, 16 October 1994, A18). With the support of the state Democratic Party, the American Civil Liberties Union, and the National Organization for Women, in 1994 Oregon became the first state in the United States to pass a physician-assisted-suicide law (*New York Times*, 27 November 1994, A27).

In response to the passage of the Oregon measure, the National Conference of Catholic Bishops revised directives to assure that physician-assisted suicide would not be practiced in its 1,200 Catholic hospitals, which collectively make up the United States' largest private health care system. At the same time, however, the conference made it clear that its doctors would be allowed to administer painkilling medication, even to the point that such medication might hasten the death of a suffering patient (*New York Times*, 18 November 1994, A12; *Augusta Chronicle*, 18 November 1994, A2).

Finally, assuring that 1994 ended with a bang rather than a whimper, Dr. Jack Kevorkian reemerged after almost a year of inactivity to assist in the death of Margaret Garrish, a 72-year-old Michigan woman suffering from severe rheumatoid arthritis, who ended her life by the inhalation of carbon monoxide gas. Dr. Kevorkian's twenty-first assisted suicide was made even more controversial by the fact that the death occurred only hours after a Michigan law banning assisted suicide expired. In reference to his actions and the Oregon Death with Dignity Act, Dr. Kevorkian stated his belief that such a law was not necessary and that the Oregon act was too limited because it would not have allowed a physician to assist Ms. Garrish with her desire to end her life, as her condition was not terminal. Dr. Kevorkian further stated that the only law that was necessary was one that specified medical personnel as the proper individuals to assist patients in ending their lives (*New York Times*, 27 November 1994, A12).

In August of 1995, the Michigan Supreme Court adopted a new standard for determining when life-sustaining medical treatment could be withdrawn from a permanently unconscious adult. The court announced that it would apply a strict version of the "clear and convincing evidence" standard. In applying the test, the court refused to allow the withdrawal of life support from a severely brain-damaged man because he had only made clear statements about not wishing to be kept alive if he were in a permanently unconscious condition. The court ruled that these two conditions were sufficiently different to require a more specific statement. In essence the court ruled that only statements about specific conditions could be honored (*In re Martin* 1995).

The issue of unwanted medical treatment was taken up in 1996 by the Ohio Supreme Court, whose decision recognized that nonconsensual medical treatment was a form of battery that could entitle the recipient to some form of financial judgment. The case involved the performance of heroic measures to resuscitate the plaintiff despite the known existence of a do-not-resuscitate order. Several days after the treatment, the patient suffered a disabling stroke, which he asserted was caused by St. Frances-St. George Hospital's actions in resuscitating him. Despite this finding, the court ruled that the plaintiff could not establish by sufficient evidence that the hospital's actions had caused the stroke (*Anderson v. St. Frances-St. George Hospital* 1996). Similarly, the North Carolina Supreme Court ruled that the spouse of a nursing home resident was liable for all medical bills, even though the hospital provided the treatment against the spouse's wishes and in violation of a valid living will (*First HealthCare Corporation v. Rettinger* 1996). These cases represented a trend in many states' courts to place clear restrictions on the ability of private citizens to enforce living wills and medical directives unless they contained a high level of specificity and were acceptable to the treating medical institution. However, this trend was by no means universal. In the case of *In re Fiori* (1996), the Pennsylvania Supreme Court ruled that, in the absence of sufficient evidence as to a patient's wishes, a close family relative of an individual in a persistent vegetative state should be allowed to substitute his or her own judgment for that of the patient, as long as two qualified physicians agree and order the withdrawal of life-sustaining treatment.

In 1997 a Michigan Circuit Court for the County of Genesee put into practice the principle that a violation of a patient's wishes concerning life-sustaining treatment, even when given by a third party under a durable power of attorney for health care, is a battery. In the case of *Osgood v. Genesee Regional Medical Center,* the jury awarded a substantial monetary verdict based on the premise that unwanted medical treatment was a battery that caused mental anguish, as well as past and future expenses for medical care and treatment.

While the 1997 Michigan decision represented an important victory for euthanasia advocates, the importance of this event was by far outweighed by two U.S. Supreme Court decisions handed down in June of that year. In these decisions, the Court upheld the right of states to pass laws banning physician-assisted suicide within their borders. In the cases of *Vacco v. Quill* and *Washington v. Glucksberg,* the Court found that the New York and Washington state statutes making "assisting," "causing," or "aiding" in a suicide a crime did not violate either a physician's or a patient's right to equal protection or due process under the Fourteenth Amendment of the U.S. Constitution. In reviewing these cases, the U.S. Supreme Court unanimously reversed the ruling of the Second and Ninth Circuit Courts of Appeals, which had ruled that mentally competent, terminally ill patients had a constitutionally protected right to receive medication for the purpose of ending their lives. However, in making this decision, the Court also made it clear that its ruling did not represent a constitutional hostility towards assisted suicide but rather expressed the opinion that decisions as to the legal status of physician-assisted suicide should be left up to the individual states (*Kansas v. Naramore*).

As if to herald this latter portion of these Supreme Court rulings, in February of 1997 the Ninth Circuit Court of Appeals ruled, in the case of *Lee v. Oregon,* that Oregon's Death with Dignity Act (Measure 16), which legalized physician-assisted suicide, did not violate the Fourteenth Amendment Equal Protection rights of the people trying to use it, any more than the laws of state that prohibited assisted suicide. Challengers to the law had asserted that the measure lacked sufficient safeguards to protect the rights of the terminally ill patients seeking to use it. In making its unanimous decision, the Ninth Circuit Court ruled that the challengers had failed to show any threat of immediate harm to Oregon citizens and that their claim seemed to rest on a "chain of speculative contingencies." As a result, the Ninth Circuit helped establish the principle that states had the power to determine the legal status of assisted suicide within their boundaries. The decision of the Ninth Circuit was later appealed to the U.S. Supreme Court, but the Court declined even to hear the appeal.

While the U.S. Supreme Court had made it clear that each state had the right to decide for itself whether or not to permit assisted suicide, those states that criminalized the act continued to have the problem of getting the public to enforce their laws. The Supreme Court handed down its decision in the New York case of *Vacco v. Quill* in June of 1997, giving New York full authority to enforce its criminal ban on assisted suicide; but, just two months later, Dr. Marco Zancope, a veterinarian, openly admitted injecting a 33-year-old terminally ill women with a fatal dose of phenobarbital on August 28, 1997. This case became the first significant test of New York's ability to enforce its own law against assisted suicide. In theory it should have been an easy case. Dr. Zancope was not even a physician, he was a veterinarian, and he had openly admitted his acts. However, as is so often the case in assisted-suicide trials, the criminal justice system floundered in its efforts to move the case forward; in July of 1999, a Manhattan grand jury refused even to indict Dr. Zancope for his act. In short, despite the existence of a clear statute that had received Supreme Court approval, private citizens simply refused to consider Dr. Zancope's acts a crime (*New York Times*, 17 July 1999, B1).

Just as 1997 began with important decisions concerning a person's right to assisted suicide, it also ended with such decisions. During its 1997 session, the Oregon State Legislature bowed to the conservative anti-euthanasia pressures that had been brought to bear within its state just long enough to put up a state referendum aimed at repealing the state's physician-assisted suicide statute. The battle over this referendum was spirited, with the political wing of the Roman Catholic Church, the American Medical Association, and anti-abortion groups such as the National Right to Life Committee all pressing for the repeal of the original law. However, in the end, the citizens of the state declined to change their earlier decisions. In November of 1997, Oregon voters declined to rescind the nation's only physician-assisted-suicide law, by voting 60% to 40% against the referendum measure that sought to destroy the law. For the first time since its creation in 1994, doctors and patients were free to put their state-created right to assisted suicide into effect without a legal cloud hanging over their heads (Claiborne and Edsall 1997).

As a result of the defeat of the 1997 initiative to repeal its assisted-suicide statute, in 1998 the Oregon Health Services Commission recommended that physician-assisted suicide become a part of the "comfort care services" offered under the state's insurance system. Acting on this recommendation, the State of Oregon amended the Oregon Health Plan so that it began covering physician-assisted suicide for low-income Oregonians. Strangely enough, the same legislature passed a bill that would have prohibited the state's health care insurance system from making payments for any procedure that did not receive federal funding. This bill would have effectively prohibited Oregon from using state funds to cover either abortions or physician-assisted suicide. This later bill was, however, vetoed by Governor Kitzhaber and never went into effect. Finally, the State of Oregon sought to balance the state's health care systems by establishing a task force on pain and symptom management. The function of the task force is to encourage the state's medical professionals to find ways to better manage the type of chronic pain that can lead patients to seek assistance in ending their lives.

While the State of Oregon was quickly moving along with the full integration of its assisted-suicide statute into its state's health care system, the State of Washington was debating whether or not it would follow suit and pass an assisted-suicide statute of its own. This initiative soon become the central battle ground over the spread of death services. The Washington "Proposal B" was much stricter than the Oregon law and would have allowed only individuals who were mentally competent, terminally ill, and within the last few months of their lives to apply for assistance. Then their case would have to be reviewed by three physicians before a prescription for a lethal dose of medication could be prescribed. Even then, the patient would have to hold onto the prescription until a statutory waiting period had expired, during which time the patient could reconsider his or her decision to die. The statute would also have set up a state oversight committee that would have been charged with reviewing up to 25% of the cases in which the patient decided to use the lethal prescription.

Not surprisingly, the measure was strongly opposed by a wide variety of advocates from both sides of the euthanasia debate. The political wing of the Roman Catholic Church and other right-to-life groups are said to have spent up to five million dollars to advocate the defeat of the proposal (Hemlock Society 2000). Dr. Kevorkian, the most well known advocate of physician-assisted suicide at that time, openly spoke out against the proposal, saying that it was too restrictive and would limit rather than broaden a person's right to assisted suicide. Indeed, according to "Marian's Friends," a group named after one of Dr. Jack Kevorkian's early patients, the bill was specifically designed to limit access to assisted suicide to only those people who were terminally ill. As a result of this broad-base opposition, "Proposal B" was overwhelmingly defeated 29% to 71% (DeathNet, Assisted Suicide Proposal, 2000).

The last significant event of 1998 occurred when the Kansas Court of Appeals overturned a jury verdict convicting one Dr. Naramore of both second-degree murder of one of his patients and the attempted murder of another. The issues in the criminal case evolved around Dr. Naramore's medical treatment of two patients. In the first instance, the jury had been asked to determine whether Dr. Naramore's decision to discontinue the use of machines providing life support to a patient constituted second-degree murder. In the second instance, the case involved Dr. Naramore's treatment of a patient suffering from intractable pain, to whom he prescribed such high levels of medication that they could have hastened death. In this latter case, the jury was asked to determine whether the act of prescribing such levels of medication constituted attempted murder. In both cases, the jury returned a verdict of guilty, determining that the doctor had acted criminally. However, when the Kansas Court of Appeals reviewed the medical testimony given in the case, they determined that any jury who rationally reviewed the facts of the case would, "as a matter of law," have to find reasonable doubt concerning the criminal charges logged against him (*Kansas v. Naramore*).

While the ruling of the Kansas Court of Appeals was clearly a victory for Dr. Naramore, in reality it represented a loss for both sides of the euthanasia debate. While the Kansas Court of Appeals demonstrated its desire to give doctors a broad degree of discretion in determining how to best treat their patients, it did little to clarify the potential criminal liability that doctors could face for similar acts. As a result, those who favor physician-assisted suicide saw the *Naramore* case as one that would likely discourage many doctors from aggressively treating patients suffering from a terminal illness or a condition causing chronic pain. Conversely, opponents to the euthanasia movement in the United States saw the decision in the case as one more step in the legalization of a secret market in death, in which people may be unknowingly euthanized against their will.

As a result of cases like *Kansas v. Naramore,* the issue of a doctor's liability in the treatment of pain grew to become one of the principal issues of the euthanasia debate for 1999. Several legal cases and state laws concerning this issue were decided, helping to clarify the treatment policies open for doctors in many states. In fact, 1999 turned out to be a watershed year, during which a number of states took steps to clarify their positions on a variety of issues surrounding euthanasia.

In March of 1999, the Nebraska State Legislature took steps to provide its doctors, nurses, and pharmacists with immunity from prosecution for aggressively treating pain with controlled substances. The legislation provided immunity even when medical personnel prescribed medications in excess of their recommended dosages. The statute went further and required the state's medical board to develop a set of standards and procedures to guide doctors in this area (Choice in Dying 2000). While this action clearly benefitted health care providers who wished to use controlled substances to treat pain aggressively, even when the treatment might hasten death, it did little to clarify the status of euthanasia in the state. Instead, the statute attempted to make a distinction between aggressive pain treatment and assisting in a death, a distinction that many on both sides of the debate find difficult, if not impossible, to maintain.

Despite this difficulty, 1999 seemed to represent a year during which a large number of medical boards, state legislatures, and even law enforcement officials tried to strike a middle ground in the euthanasia debate by attempting to shield doctors from prosecution when their actions were taken to treat severe pain (*New York Times*, 9 August 1999, A-13). This shift seems to have been the result of not only half a century of debate about euthanasia but also the growing realization that patients' desires to turn to a physician for aid in dying is often directly related to the medical establishment's willingness and ability to effectively treat their pain (*New York Times*, 4 September 1999, A-8).

This realization not only affected the actions of states in which assisted suicide was technically illegal, but also caused the State of Oregon, the only state to fully legalize physician-assisted suicide, to pass several pieces of legislation encouraging, and in some instances mandating, its doctors to effectively treat the pain of their patients. Oregon began this drive by first encouraging its medical community to widely distribute information about pain management and relief. It then passed legislation that created a class of acknowledged specialists, who would be free to administer high doses of controlled medication for the treatment of "intractable pain" without the need for consultations with other physicians as required under its Death with Dignity Act. Oregon even went so far as to create a Pain Management Demonstration Project, which would use "non-state funds" to treat Oregon Health Plan patients who suffer from chronic pain (Choice in Dying, 2000). Finally, the issue of a doctor's liability for pain treatment came full circle, when the Oregon State Medical Board became the first state regulatory body in the nation to sanction one of its doctors for his failure to effectively treat the chronic pain of his patients (*New York Times*, 4 September 1999, A-14).

Following this trend, other states legislatively required or actively encouraged their medical communities to include pain management and end-of-life care procedures in their medical school curriculums and daily practices (Choice in Dying 2000). As a result of these actions, a new field of debate and controversy began to emerge over the issue of euthanasia. While effective pain management had become recognized as one of the key way to prevent people from desiring a physician's aid in dying, a growing number of anti-euthanasia activists began to fear that physician-assisted suicide was, in effect, being slipped in the back door. By allowing doctors to so aggressively treat some medical conditions, opponents feared that some doctors were in actuality being allowed to euthanize their patients. Even more troubling was the fact that, under the laws of many states, such actions could go on without any significant level of state supervision, thus raising the specter of patients being euthanized without their knowledge or against their will.

Responding to these fears, federal representatives Don Nickles (Senate) and Henry Hyde (House of Representatives) introduced the most significant piece of federal legislation in this area to date. Their bill was called the Pain Relief Promotion Act of 1999 (HR 2260/SB 1272) and it sought to amend the federal Controlled Substances Act so as to allow the use of controlled substances for the treatment of pain, while prohibiting any physician from prescribing medications for the purpose of causing or hastening the death of a patient. In reaching this goal, the act also specifically required the Attorney General of the United States to "give no force and effect to State law authorizing or permitting assisted suicide or euthanasia." Thus, one of the intentions of the act was to effectively nullify the Oregon Death with Dignity Act.

Support for this act within the House of Representatives was strongly fractured along party lines, with Republicans favoring the bill and Democrats opposing it (Vollmar 1999). Further complicating the debate was the fact that such a party alignment placed the Democratic Party in the position of supporting the "states' rights" claims of the Oregon delegation while placing the Republican Party in the position of advocating for national supremacy.

Opponents of the bill, such as Oregon Representative Blumenauer, strongly advocated that the House proposition would "trample on States' rights" (*Congressional Record*, Rep. Blumenauer, 27 October 1999) and place doctors in the position of having their medical judgments second-guessed by "prosecutors, police and nonmedical drug enforcement bureaucrats on a case-by-case basis" (*Congressional Record*, Rep. Blumenauer, 27 October 1999).

Many members of the medical community agreed with Representative Blumenauer's arguments, stating that they believed that the Pain Relief Promotion Act was flawed in the same way as its 1998 version (Lethal Drug Abuse Prevention Act) in that, despite the language of the act, it would place many doctors in a position where they would be afraid to aggressively treat a patient's pain for fear of being accused by family members, or even fellow doctors, of intentionally trying to hasten a patient's death (*New York Times*, 14 August 1999, A12). However, in the end one of the reasons the 1999 bill was able to win House support where the 1998 version was not was the fact that the American Medical Association (which had opposed both the Oregon law and the 1998 Lethal Drug Abuse Prevention Act) reversed itself and supported passage of the new House bill (Channel 6000 2000).

In commenting on the House of Representatives 271-156 vote in support for this resolution, Supreme Court Justice Sandra Day O'Connor bluntly stated that, in her opinion, the bill represented a significant example of Congress's "underdeveloped capacity for self-restraint" (*New York Times*, 29 October 1999, A35). Comments such as these, taken along with the Court's statements concerning the rights of states to make such decisions, virtually guaranteed that the passage of the act would spur another round of cases before the U.S. Supreme Court (*New York Times*, 28 October 1998, A29). This is particularly true, given that the Supreme Court made such clear statements about the rights of states to act in this area even though, at the time it made such statements, it knew Congress was working on the Lethal Drug Abuse Prevention Act, which was substantially designed to nullify Oregon's assisted-suicide law.

As the federal government debates the passage of legislation that would, in effect, nullify any state legislation allowing for physician-assisted suicide, state governments continue to define their own laws on the subject individually. In Oregon the state reports that, in its first year of operation, 15 people (seven women and eight men) have taken advantage of the Death with Dignity Act (*New York Times*, 18 February 1999, A1). Further, a review of the demographics of those who used the act to end their lives demonstrated that neither low levels of education, lack of health insurance, nor poor access to hospice care had a significant impact on who would choose to end his or her life under the act. Instead, Oregon's 1998 report indicated that the most common reason given for patients' desire to receive assistance in dying was their fear of losing autonomy and control over their bodily functions (Oregon Health Division 2000).

In the State of California, despite the failure of a 1992 ballot proposition, field polls showed strong support for assisted-suicide legislation and, as a result, the state legislature began serious debate on a legislative proposal to legalize physician-assisted suicide in California (Gunnison 2000). In the State of Florida, the state legislature passed legislation expanding when life-support measures can be withdrawn, or even withheld, to include terminal conditions, the end-stage of life, and when patients are in a persistent vegetative state (Choice in Dying 2000). In an even more dramatic fashion, a Florida county circuit court expands the boundaries of Florida's protection of a state right to die, by granting a court order allowing Georgette Smith, a 42-year-old quadriplegic, the right to have her ventilator removed, thus bringing about her subsequent death (Candiottii 1999).

Conversely, other states, such as Arkansas, sought to strengthen their laws by passing legislation making their criminal bans on assisted suicide more explicit, thereby increasing the likelihood of successfully prosecuting violators. Similarly, the State of North Dakota strengthened its ban on assisted suicide by passing legislation that would allow for compensatory and punitive damages, as well as the suspension or revocation of licenses of any health care provider who participates in such an act. Additionally, the State of Maryland, for the first time passed legislation prohibiting anyone from assisting in the suicide of another, and the State of Maine limited the ability of guardians or surrogates to withdraw or withhold life support from a ward who was terminally ill or in a persistent vegetative state.

Of course, no summary of major events in the area of the "right to die" would be complete without at least mentioning the exploits of Dr. Jack Kevorkian. By 1997, Dr. Kevorkian had participated in an estimated 130 deaths and had become increasingly brazen in his attempts to openly defy state laws against assisted suicide. He had already been tried four times and, each time, the prosecution had failed to get a conviction. As elected officials, state prosecutors had become reluctant even to bring charges against Dr. Kevorkian for fear of enraging a public who clearly had little desire to convict people for participating in a voluntary act of euthanasia. As a result, Dr. Kevorkian's actions poignantly pointed out the difficulty states could have in convincing a jury to enforce laws against assisted suicide. However, in 1999, Dr. Kevorkian's luck began to change. His actions became so brazen that a new prosecutor felt he had no choice but to bring charges against him; suddenly, Dr. Kevorkian was facing a fifth trial (*New York Times*, 20 March 1999, A1).

From the very beginning, Dr. Kevorkian's fifth murder trial was characteristically different from the previous four. Most notable is the fact that Dr. Kevorkian insisted on acting as his own attorney and, in doing so, demonstrated to the jury his lack of knowledge of the law. Within the courtroom, Dr. Kevorkian gave the impression of being inept and confused, frequently asking legally impermissible questions and raising ill-timed and inappropriate legal arguments for venue (*New York Times,* 24 March 1999, A-20). In the end, Dr. Kevorkian seemed almost to demonstrate a desire to be convicted. In his own defense, Dr. Kevorkian chose to call no witnesses and presented no evidence to contradict or challenge the prosecution's case. After only half a day of testimony from prosecutorial witnesses, the jury heard closing arguments and adjourned to deliberate. Not surprisingly, Dr. Kevorkian was convicted of second-degree murder (*New York Times*, 26 March 1999, A14).

At Dr. Kevorkian's sentencing hearing, the widow and the brother of the terminally ill man he was convicted of killing made passionate appeals to the judge for leniency, but to no avail. He was sentenced to 10 to 25 years in prison, making him eligible for parole in May of 2007 (*New York Times,* 14 April 1999, A1). Motions were made on behalf of Dr. Kevorkian to obtain a new trial based on the ineffective assistance of the attorney appointed by the court to assist him, but again to no avail (Vollmar 1999).

Dr. Kevorkian's saga clearly demonstrates the difficulty of enforcing laws against assisted suicide in many parts of the United States. Even after his conviction, a national poll demonstrated that most Americans believed that the jury that convicted Dr. Kevorkian of second-degree murder acted incorrectly. Nationally, only 39% of those polled agreed with the jury's verdict. Statistics such as these are closely aligned with a national sentiment that seems to approve of some form of limited physician-assisted suicide (Langer 2000).

As the 1999 Congress drew to a close, the most significant issue to be resolved was the status of the Pain Relief Promotion Act of 1999 (HR 2260/SB 1272). While the bill had received an affirmative vote in the House of Representatives and passed through one Senate committee, a vote by the whole Senate had been delayed. By its very nature the Senate is a more deliberative body, and many bills that receive House approval die in the Senate. To further complicate matters, the Pain Relief Promotion Act had reached the Senate very close to the end of its term, raising the strong possibility that opponents of the bill (particularly Senator Wyden from Oregon) would filibuster any attempt to pass it, thus delaying other significant pieces of legislation. As a result of these factors the bill's sponsors realize that, for all practical purposes, the Pain Relief Promotion Act of 1999 could not be passed until Congress come back into session the following year (DeathNet, Suicide Bill Delayed, 2000).

By April of 2000 the Senate had moved the Pain Relief Promotion Act through its Judiciary Committee by a vote of 10-8. This vote cleared the way for a vote in the Senate as a whole, but the Senate clearly seemed to desire ongoing discussion of the bill before it was brought up for a vote (DeathNe, Senate Judiciary Committee, 2000). While the backing of the American Medical Association had significantly strengthened support for the bill, articles appearing in such prestigious publications as the *Journal of the American Medical Association* demonstrated that many American doctors believed the act would hurt, rather than encourage, pain relief or palliative care in the United States (Orentlicher and Caplan 2000). In support of such assertions, Senator Feinstein of California argued that any doctors who prescribes large dosages of pain medication would be subjecting themselves to investigation by the Drug Enforcement Administration and, if they couldn't prove that they were free of any intent to hasten death, they would face up to 20 years in prison (DeathNet, Suicide Bill Delayed, 2000). As the debate continued, the likelihood of the bill passing before the close of the congressional session diminished. While a filibuster would be less effective so early in the Senate's calendar, Senator Wyden and his allies promised to introduce and debate numerous amendments to the bill if it was brought to the Senate floor for a vote. In doing so, he was prepared to consume a great deal of "election year time" debating a bill that then President Clinton was likely to veto without the possibility of Senate override (DeathNet, Suicide Bill Delayed, 2000). The Republican leadership determined that a far better strategy was to delay any action on the bill until after the 2000 presidential election. After all with the election of George W. Bush Jr. as President, the passage of a Pain Relief Promotion Act might not even be necessary.

As a part of his presidential campaign, Governor Bush made it clear that he opposed physician-assisted suicide and that he would sign any bill that passes through the Congress restricting its use. Further, President Bush made it clear that, even in the absence of such a bill, his administration would likely take the position that federal law already prohibits the use of federally regulated controlled substances for assisted suicide and that the Drug Enforcement Administration should be free to prosecute any doctor who uses federally controlled drugs for such purposes (DeathNet, Suicide Bill Delayed, 2000).

As debate over what actions Congress will take raged on, Oregon released its figures for its third year of operation under its Death with Dignity Act. In its review of activities under the act, Oregon found that, in 1999, 26 people had used assistance provided under the law to end their lives, as compared to 16 people in 1998. Once again, the majority of those who requested assistance in dying cited loss of autonomy as a major concern. A significant number also expressed the simple desire to control how and when they would die (Sullivan, Hedberg and Fleming 2000, 598-604).

In an effort to follow Oregon's example and become the second state to legalize assisted suicide, the State of Maine introduced its own Death with Dignity Act as a referendum item appearing on its 2000 ballot. Maine's version of the law would allow mentally competent, terminally ill patients with less than six months to live, to receive a prescription for a lethal dosage of medication which they could self administer. The law requires that all patients receive both a second opinion concerning their prognoses and consultation with a palliative care specialist to ensure that every effort has been made to relieve any pain that they may be feeling. The law also makes it clear that no medical personnel can be forced to participate in these practices and that mercy killings by lethal injection are not permitted under the act. Finally, the act requires patients to personally communicate their request for assistance on two occasions, as well as one written request with a 15 and 48 hour waiting period between them. Although this statute has been criticized as being unduly burdensome, it enjoyed strong support from "right to die" advocates and seemed to benefit from the fact that it was coming up for a vote in a presidential election year when so many other issues seemed to distract potential adversaries (Maine Legislature 2000).

In the end the hopes of "right to die" advocates were crushed once again.

The Main Death with Dignity act or "Question 1" was defeated by a 52% majority. The defeat was attributed by many to significant advertising expenditures made by "right to life" organizations officiated with the Catholic Church in the last month before the vote (Hemlock Society 2000).

Adding to the excitement of 2000, the World Federation of Right to Die Societies and the Hemlock Society sponsored a three day world conference on "Assisted Dying in the New Millennium—An International Perspective." The conference, scheduled for September 1-3 in Boston, Massachusetts, will unquestionably add momentum to the "pro-right to die" movements of many states, thus ensuring an ongoing debate on this subject for years to come (Vollmar 1999). However, as of March 1, 2000, the American states line up as follows: One state (the state of Oregon) has passed legislation to legalize physician-assisted suicide within its borders, thirty-nine states have passed statutes specifically prohibiting assisted suicide, six states (Alabama, Idaho, Massachusetts, Nevada, Vermont and West Virginia) prohibit assisted suicide through application of state common law, and four states (North Carolina, Ohio, Utah and Wyoming) have not passed laws either prohibiting or allowing assisted suicide (Longwood College 2000). Despite the fact that the vast majority of U.S. states have taken actions to specifically prohibit physician-assisted suicide within their borders, it is clear from many sources that assisted suicide goes on in the United States every day and in almost every state.

A review of the history of debate surrounding this subject in the United States makes it clear that, from the 1800s to the present, the American attitude with respect to the "right to die" has undergone a slow but steady transformation. Equally clear is the fact that controversy over the existence and advocacy of a "right to die" is not a novel issue, nor is it apt to fade from the public eye in the near future. To the contrary, the history of the movement in the United States demonstrates a growing momentum that, for all practical purposes, would appear to be inexorable. As the Oregon Death with Dignity Act continues to be put into practice, and as other states continue to try to enact similar legislation, these actions will undoubtedly serve as models for advocates of the "right to die" in other states. In addition, we can anticipate that future court activities, on both the state and national levels, will serve to further refine what is a growing issue of public concern.

Chapter 3

Attitudes around the World

In truth, the question of euthanasia is not a matter of great concern or controversy throughout the world. The reason for this is not, as one might suspect, the overarching influence of a culturally preeminent religion; neither is it the secularization of the political state. To the contrary, the issue of euthanasia and the controversies surrounding it are inextricably linked with the development of technology. Without both the sufficient development of a nation's technological base and a high economic standard for its citizenry, the issue of euthanasia simply never arises. Within technologically underdeveloped countries, opportunity for artificially prolonging life rarely presents itself.

Without the prerequisite technology, the controversy over artificially prolonging the existence of a dying patient is eliminated. Additionally, in countries with a poor economic base, the option of extensive medical care is beyond the means of the vast majority of its citizens. Consequently, the issue of artificially prolonged life never becomes a rallying point for public support, and the cause is subordinated to more immediate matters of survival. Thus, the struggle over the legal status of euthanasia is restricted mainly to economically developed nations (*The Economist*, 17 September 1994, 21).

In the West, passive euthanasia, a more or less accepted means of following the expressed wishes of a patient, occurs when opposition exists to the use of medical technology in the face of imminent death. The use of passive euthanasia has also increasingly come to place a higher premium on the control of pain, as opposed to the mere prolongation of life. This applies particularly in the case of a terminally ill patient. Despite the relative clarity of the trends within Western culture, the legal statutes remain unclear. While most Western countries, and 44 of the 50 American states, have laws that make assisted suicide illegal, several countries and one American state have nonetheless passed laws legalizing the act. The six remaining U.S. states have no laws on the subject. Furthermore, it is clear from medical journals and popular reports that, even where it is technically illegal, assisted suicide is not an uncommon occurrence. In both the United States and Europe, such acts are often supported by the populace, the majority of whom express support for the theoretical ideas of assisted suicide and euthanasia in national opinion polls (*The Economist,* 17 September 1994, 14).

What follows certainly should not be taken as an exhaustive inventory of worldwide attitudes with respect to euthanasia, but rather as an introduction to the developing attitudes and trends prevalent within technologically developed nations. An effort has been made to include all of the major developed nations that have a clearly identifiable, or at least developing, policy on euthanasia.

THE UNITED STATES

As stated earlier, it has become customary in the United States to accept passive euthanasia as a matter of private concern between patients and their doctors. The American Medical Association has recognized this practice and has incorporated it into its codes, stating that a doctor "has an ethical obligation to honor the resuscitation preferences expressed by the patient." As a result of this level of acceptance, the *American Medical News* reports that 70% of all those who die in American hospitals do so only after life-sustaining treatment has been withdrawn (Helme 1992, 9).

While the trend is toward the acceptance of euthanasia, the United States has not equally embraced all forms of the act, and it is clear that only expressly voluntary euthanasia has any significant level of public support. Involuntary euthanasia is unquestionably considered homicide, regardless of its active or passive nature (White 1994, 142). Despite occasional advocacy for involuntary euthanasia, Americans have always maintained a strong moral and legal prohibition against such acts and have held them in violation of a person's right to life, self-determination, and privacy (Lacampagne 1983, 533, 538-539, 547). Furthermore, in most U.S. states, active euthanasia—even if voluntary—is considered murder, regardless of the willingness or medical condition of the patient or of the motives of the actor (Hirsch 1990, 799). However, it is clear that social attitudes toward active, voluntary euthanasia are in flux and that support for assisted suicide is growing.

AUSTRALIA

As part of a federation, each of Australia's six states and two territories has the right to institute its own unique laws regarding euthanasia, similar to the way U.S. states have independent lawmaking authority, although this power can be superseded by the national legislature. Therefore, while active euthanasia is currently illegal throughout the nation, this is only because the national government has blocked the efforts of states and territories to enact laws legalizing euthanasia, despite the fact that support is growing for the recognition and legalization of such legislation (Helme 1992, 7; Robinson 1999).

In May of 1995, the Northern Territories of Australia passed the nation's first law allowing voluntary euthanasia or doctor–assisted suicide. The law addressed the need for increased palliative care, or end–of–life and pain management, and included a provision allowing patients to request and receive assistance from their doctors in terminating their life (Docker 2000). The law, called the *Rights of Terminally Ill Act,* was strongly opposed by the Australian Medical Association, as well a number of "right to life" groups. It took over a year to work out the details necessary to make the bill operational, and it did not go into effect until July 1, 1996. By that time, similar bills had been introduced into several other Australian states. Polls taken at the time indicated that 81% of all Australian adults, 60% of doctors, and 78% of nurses favored some form of voluntary euthanasia (Robinson 1999).

The "right to die" movement seemed to be picking up speed in Australia until 1997, when the movement was dealt a significant blow. On 25 March, 1997, the Australian national Senate followed the previous vote of the House in disallowing the Northern Territories' *Rights of Terminally Ill* law in a 38-33 vote (Robinson 1999).

Despite this action, the debate over euthanasia is still an issue of significance in Australia. The *Medical Journal of Australia* polled 354 doctors and found that 107 had patients who had requested aid in hastening the time of their deaths; furthermore, these physicians reported that they had, in fact, assisted their patients to die. Better than twice that 107 expressed support for the legalization of such a right (*The Economist*, 17 September 1994, 21). In addition to the burgeoning support from the medical community, the State of Victoria has gone so far as to pass legislation that makes it a criminal act to provide medical treatment to an individual against his or her expressed will. The same legislation authorized designated medical proxies to make treatment decisions for the patient, should he or she become unable to do so. South Australia and the Northern Territories have also enacted Natural Death Acts, which grant their citizens the power to execute medical directives similar to what Americans know as living wills (Helme 1992, 8).

These measures have not been sufficient to quell the debate over euthanasia in Australia. In response to the actions of the national legislature, one Dr. Philip Nitschke began conducting informal informational clinics on euthanasia throughout Australia. The most recent area to invite Dr. Nitschke was Tasmania, where a 2000 poll indicated that 64.8% approved of providing information about euthanasia in this manner (Haley 2000). As of August 1999, Dr. Nitschke had reported that 13 people who had attended his informational clinics had committed suicide (Vollmar 1999).

BELGIUM

In December of 1999, a draft bill was introduced in Belgium, giving this country one of the most liberal euthanasia policies in the world. The bill gives adults with an incurable illness, unbearable and constant suffering, and a sound mind the right to ask for medical assistance in dying. The law also applies to individuals in a coma, if they have made their wishes not to be kept alive in such a state known to two witnesses within the previous five years. The law goes even further in that it creates a committee, or panel, of doctors and lawyers whose job it is to ensure that the law is being respected and applied appropriately. It is not anticipated that the passage of this law will significantly alter current practices in Belgium, since euthanasia is widely practiced in the country, despite the fact that it is technically a criminal act. The most significant impact of the law will be to protect doctors from prosecution under the current criminal code.

The passage of the law was staunchly opposed by the nation's Christian Democrat Party, principally on religious grounds. The Christian Democrats, who only recently lost their role in a power-sharing government for the first time in 40 years, argued that the bill opens the door to widespread abuse since it does not require the presence of a terminal condition.

The Christian Democrats had looked to Belgium's King Baudouin for support. In 1990, King Baudouin abdicated for 24 hours to avoid having to sign a bill liberalizing abortion in his country. King Baudouin cited religious convictions, based on Catholic doctrine, as the basis for his actions at that time. However, such an action in this instance is seen as unlikely, since the current King Albert II has a far more flexible opinion on this issue (DeathNet, Liberal Euthanasia Law, 2000).

CANADA

As of June 2000, Canadian law does not classify suicide as a crime, although physician-assisted suicide is considered a criminal offense. A 1995 poll of Canadian doctors (released in 1999) indicated that only 43% would practice euthanasia if it were legalized in Canada (Vollmar 1999).

Several medical cases have strongly challenged the extent to which this law should be applied to actual medical treatment decisions. The principal case was that of Sue Rodriguez, who asked the Canadian Supreme Court for formal permission to allow someone to aid her in bringing about the end of her life. Ms. Rodriguez argued that her life was no longer worth living as a result of amyotrophic lateral sclerosis, which had ravaged her brain and spinal cord and severely impaired her ability to walk, talk, and breathe. The court refused to issue the order in 1992 but, two years later, Ms. Rodriguez received the assistance of an unknown doctor and ended her life, in direct defiance of the court's decision (*The Economist,* 17 September 1994, 21). In addition to the public controversy generated by the Rodriguez case, the Canadian medical profession was forced to deal with the issue of euthanasia by the public statement of Dr. Tom Perry, a cabinet minister, and Dr. Peter Graff, an internal medicine specialist, both of whom admitted to treating dying patents with doses of morphine that may have hastened their deaths (Helme 1992, 8).

As a result of these public controversies, the Canadian Medical Association stated that, although it is not unethical for medical personal to withdraw heroic medical treatment from dying patients, the issue of euthanasia was one that must be decided by society itself and not the medical community.

In response to a number of high–profile cases, a 1995 Canadian Senate committee studied the issue but recommended that the national legislature make no changes in the national law pertaining to euthanasia at that time. The committee did, however, recommend the creation of a new category of crime, termed "compassionate homicide," to be used in cases of nonvoluntary euthanasia. In 1997, the Canadian Justice Minister suggested changing the law covering second-degree murder so as to allow a lower level of punishment for individuals convicted of the crime when euthanasia was involved.

In March of 1998, the Canadian Senate overwhelmingly rejected a proposal to reopen the issue for study. As of 1 February, 2001 no significant change in Canadian law has taken place (Robinson 1999).

COLOMBIA

On 20 May, 1997, the efforts of a group that strongly opposed the "right to die" went terribly awry when their actions inadvertently led to the legalization of a limited form of euthanasia. In an effort to eliminate all references to euthanasia in Colombian law, an individual brought a lawsuit before the Colombian Supreme Court. After examining the arguments in the suit, the court made a 6 to 3 ruling that, in effect, spelled out the rights of a terminally ill person to engage in voluntary euthanasia. The ruling gave Colombian lower courts the power to produce written guidelines and make rulings on the appropriateness of euthanasia on a case-by-base basis (Robinson 1999).

GREAT BRITAIN

The history of efforts to legalize euthanasia in Britain predate those in America by several decades, yet efforts have been far more successful in the United States. For all practical purposes, the American euthanasia societies followed the leads of their British counterparts, but simply found more fruitful ground than have England's Voluntary Euthanasia Society (founded in 1935 and now known as EXIT) or any of its predecessors. As a result, euthanasia in all its forms is still illegal in Britain, and Parliament has yet to take even the preliminary step of recognizing the legitimacy of "living wills."

Despite the long history of strong debate on the subject, few believe that the possibility of meaningful change exists. In the past, any effort to legalize even the most passive forms of euthanasia were met with strong resistance from the "anti-abortion lobby," a pro-life group of peers who have vowed to fight any legislation seeking to change Britain's present stance on euthanasia (Helme 1992, 10). Today, even under a revised system of governance that removes the system of hereditary peerage, Great Britain's parliament seems unwilling to seriously entertain meaningful changes in this area.

This lack of legislative action notwithstanding, the issue of euthanasia in Britain is not at a standstill. Several institutions within the British government and in the private sector have taken substantial steps to address the rights of

British citizens to free themselves of unwanted medical treatment, even when to do so would result in death. The most important instance of such an occurrence came as a result of a 1993 ruling by the British House of Lords, which has some functions equivalent to the U.S. Supreme Court, in the case of Tony Bland, who was left in a persistent vegetative state as a result of injuries experienced in a crowd pileup at a British football stadium. The House of Lords recognized Bland's right to be free from unwanted medical treatment and allowed the removal of his feeding tube, resulting in his death 20 days later (*The Economist*, 1 September 1994, 21).

Similarly recognizing the "right to die," Britain's Royal College of Nursing and the British Medical Association have both made recommendations that British doctors and hospitals make every effort to determine and follow the wishes of their dying patients. In addition, polling data collected by the *British Medical Journal* clearly demonstrated that almost half of Britain's doctors were willing to follow the request of a dying patient and hasten their death, provided the act were legal. Even more significant was the fact that a substantial number of doctors reported participating in such an act despite its illegality (*The Economist,* 17 September 1994, 22), thereby illustrating that while Britain formally regards euthanasia as a criminal act, its society has tacitly accepted the proposition of a limited "right to die," and the practice is being carried out behind closed doors, beyond the aegis of government regulation and without any formal mechanism in place to protect patients from potential abuse.

Despite the fact that recent polling in Great Britain indicates that up to 80% of British citizens and 64% of Britain's general practitioners favor the legalization of some form of voluntary euthanasia, Parliament has staunchly refused to legalize such actions (DeathNet, Four in Five Vote, 2000; Sofres 2000). Along these lines in 1997, in a 234-89 vote, the British Parliament resoundingly defeated the seventh attempt to legalize euthanasia in the last 60 years (Humphry 1999). Much of Parliament's opposition is religiously based. The Anglican Church in Great Britain has declared that physician-assisted suicide is incompatible with the Christian faith and should not be permitted by civil law. However, church leaders were clear in their position that the use of pain medication that hastened the death of a terminally ill person should not be considered a form of euthanasia (*Sydney Morning Herald*, 6 August 1998).

While the British Parliament has not been willing to legalize euthanasia, it has also shown little desire to weaken a patient's right to refuse medical treatment. On 14 April, 2000, the BBC News reported that the *Medical Treatment Bill,* which was designed to prevent passive euthanasia through the withdrawal or withholding of medical treatment, food, or hydration, was virtually dead. The bill was strongly opposed by the nation's medical establishment, who feared it would lead to widespread prosecution of medical staff. At present, the British Parliament seems highly resistant to pressure from either side of this issue (BBC News, 14 April 2000).

FRANCE

France is another country in which there is sharp contradiction between the declared state of the law and actual medical practice. Technically, French law makes no distinction between assisting in a suicide, which is illegal, and aiding a terminally ill patient in facilitating his or her own death. In addition to the illegality of the act, the French National Ethical Committee formally opposes the legalization of euthanasia, fearing that it will give doctors "an exorbitant power over the life of an individual" and that economic considerations might improperly play a role in the decision to terminate life (Helme 1992, 8).

For all practical purposes, it would appear that euthanasia does not occur in France; however, it is reported that French doctors commonly give terminally ill patients a "lytic cocktail," a mixture of sedatives that is intended to produce death. Once again, we find that practice flies in the face of the apparent illegality of the act of euthanasia.

GERMANY

Germany is one of the few countries that has a law specifically making active euthanasia a crime. Acts of mercy killing, or "killing on request," are punishable under German Penal Code Article 216 as low-level homicide, and those who are found guilty can be sentenced to up to five years in prison. Passive euthanasia, on the other hand, is widely accepted and is legally regarded as a matter to be determined by consultation between the individual patient and his or her doctor (Helme 1992, 9).

In September 1994, the German constitutional court extended the right to all citizens to use passive forms of euthanasia by ruling that doctors could not only withdraw life-sustaining treatment from patients who were in the process of dying, but could direct the removal of such treatments from all terminally ill patients (*The Economist,* 17 September 1994, 14). In addition to this expanded access to passive euthanasia within the medical community, Germany has no laws forbidding assisted suicide. It is, therefore, permissible to provide another with any aid necessary to bring about his or her death, provided the actual act is willingly and knowingly performed by the individual wishing to die. So open is this event that Deutsche Gesellschaft Fur Hummanes Sterben (DGHS), Germany's equivalent to the American Hemlock Society, openly provides advice on how to commit suicide and will even provide those who wish so to do with the necessary drugs (Helme 1992, 9). Despite this apparent openness concerning the "right to die," it is unlikely that euthanasia will ever be formally legalized in Germany. Distaste for the Nazis' use of euthanasia in their programs of racial hygiene is still quite strong (Shevell 1992, 2214-2219).

JAPAN

Despite the fact that the first international conference on voluntary euthanasia was held in Tokyo in 1996, like most Eastern cultures, Japan is still very much opposed to the idea of legislation that would legalize euthanasia.

Japanese doctors frequently follow the practice, once popular in the United States, of not informing the patient when he or she is terminally ill (*The Economist*, 17 September 1994, 21). On those rare occasions when it is publicly revealed that a doctor or some other member of the medical profession has taken an affirmative act to bring about the early death of an otherwise dying patient, Japanese society reacts with shock (Helme 1992, 7). Despite this fact, a 1990 survey conducted by the Japanese Medical Association indicated that three quarters of the doctors responding believed that the provisions of a patient's living will should be respected. However, even in the face of such support, in 1992 Japan's Society for Dying with Dignity did not believe that Japanese society is ready to consider legislation to legalize active euthanasia (Helme 1992, 7). This position changed somewhat in 1995, when a Japanese district court in Yokohama established a four-part test to determine whether or not a particular act of mercy killing would be considered murder in Japan. The test indicated that the act would not be considered a crime if:

1. the patient was suffering from unbearable pain,
2. the death of the individual was inevitable and imminent,
3. all alternative measures had been taken to relieve the pain, and
4. the patient made a clear statement of his or her desire to shorten his or her life or hasten death.

In making this ruling, the district court found Dr. Tokunaga guilty of murder, because there had been no clear expression by the patient concerning either pain or the desire to hasten death (Robinson 1999). This ruling has opened the door for Japanese doctors to treat pain aggressively, even if such treatment hastens death.

NEW ZEALAND

While euthanasia is clearly illegal in New Zealand, as in many countries, the will and desire to prosecute and punish those who aid in the deaths of others for humanitarian reasons is quite weak. A strong case in point is the 1999 prosecution of an 87–year–old man who aided his wife in her desire to die by helping her take sleeping pills and then placing a plastic bag over her head. In this particular case, while the husband was prosecuted, he was charged with the low-level crime of manslaughter, rather than premeditated murder and, in the end, received a sentence of only two years' supervision. Prosecutors in the case were clearly influenced by the fact that the defendant's wife was suffering from constant pain and that he was clearly motivated by his desire to show her compassion. While this ruling does not condone euthanasia, it has been cited by New Zealand's Voluntary Euthanasia Society as a decision that will likely encourage others to engage in similar acts.

NETHERLANDS

The Dutch have long followed a formal policy of "legal prohibition and practical tolerance" with respect to active euthanasia (Reeves 1985, 36). For a long time, such policies allowed both passive and active euthanasia to be practiced behind the closed doors of hospitals and doctors' offices, out of purview of the state. In 1984, the Supreme Court of the Netherlands ruled that voluntary euthanasia was permissible if specific conditions were met (Docker 2000). In response to this ruling, in 1985, a State Commission on Euthanasia voted to recommend a change in the Penal Code applicable to assisted suicide (Sections 293 and 294), thereby creating a limited exception in the rule for doctors (Gevers 1987, 160).

While this recommendation by the State Commission on Euthanasia was considered by many to be an important step toward the legalization of euthanasia, in reality the commission only sought to recognize practices that had become accepted as a result of a 1984 court action (Vervoorn 1987, 19-20). The ruling stated that acts of euthanasia could escape prosecution if:

1. the act of euthanasia was performed by a doctor,
2. there was evidence, either verbal or written, that the patient had requested euthanasia,
3. the patient's decision was free of coercion and was lasting in nature,
4. the patient was familiar with alternative methods of treating his or her condition and was capable of making an informed choice between those alternatives,
5. the patient was suffering from unbearable physical or mental suffering of an ongoing nature for which no reasonable relief is available,
6. there was evidence of a careful decision-making process on the part of all parties concerned. (Vervoorn 1987, 19-20)

Because of these rulings, the Dutch government estimates that instances of active euthanasia resulted in more than 2,000 deaths in 1990. They also estimate that at least an additional 1,000 deaths resulting from euthanasia were never reported and thus escaped official review. It is believed that in the majority of these unreported cases, the individuals either were too weak or were otherwise medically unable to make the necessary request for euthanasia to satisfy government standards, and doctors simply performed the act of euthanasia without reporting it (*The Economist,* 17 September 1994, 23).

In 1994, the Dutch parliament voted to formally legalize doctor-administered euthanasia for the terminally ill in Holland. Critics of this action challenged the idea that euthanasia can be administered in such a way as to protect the lives of those not wishing to be put to an early death. Alternatively, proponents of the act point out that less than one third of those patients who requested euthanasia received it and, that in most of those cases in which doctors took affirmative actions to bring about a premature end, the patient's existence had been shortened by only hours or days at most (*The Economist,* 17 September 1994, 23).

While the 1994 act of Parliament decriminalized voluntary euthanasia, it created a set of strict rules for establishing a patient's "explicit request" for such services and for determining when a patient could be categorized as experiencing "intolerable suffering without prospect of improvement." As a result of the strict nature of these rules, it has been charged that many Dutch doctors routinely violate these safeguards (*The Sunday Times* [Britain], 12 May 1999).

These claims have left many Dutch doctors in a state of uncertainty as to whether their actions are criminally prosecutable. In an effort to clarify this area, a bill was introduced into the Dutch Parliament on 12 July, 1999, that would officially decriminalize physician-assisted suicide (Vollmar 1999; Robinson 1999). The bill passed the lower house of the Dutch Parliament by a vote of 104-40 (Hemlock 2001). The bill passed its final hurdle on April 10 with a 46-28 vote in the national Senate making the Netherlands the first country to pass a national law allowing euthanasia (*Augusta Chronicle,* 11 April, 2001, 10A).

SOUTH AFRICA

In a speech made to her nation's Parliament, Health Minister Mantombazana Tshabalala-Msimang characterized euthanasia as an "equal constitutional right to life and to human dignity" (DeathNet, Parliament Opens Debate, 2000). Under South African law at the time of her statement, physician-assisted suicide is clearly a criminal act; however, the South Africa Law Commission has introduced proposals that would allow doctors to withdraw life support from dying patients or prescribe pain medication at levels that are likely to hasten death. The commission, however, stopped short of recommending the legalization of active voluntary euthanasia. The proposal to legalize euthanasia in South Africa has been strongly apposed by the African Christian Democratic Party, who take the position that such a law would be not only unethical but dangerous and unconstitutional (DeathNet, Parliament Opens Debate, 2000).

SWITZERLAND

Switzerland traditionally sought to deal with the dilemma of legalizing euthanasia by varying the potential penalties for homicide in accordance with the motivation of the actor who brings about the death. As a result, mercy killing was illegal in Switzerland, but if the court determined that the actor was motivated by the good intentions of bringing about a requested death for the purposes of relieving suffering, then the punishment for the crime could be significantly reduced (Lacampagne 1983, 533, 538-539, 547). To qualify for leniency in sentencing, the actor had to prove to the court's satisfaction that the victim was capable of understanding his or her situation and had "earnestly" requested death. For a request to be considered earnest, it had to be repeated several times and be of a sincere nature (Silving 1954, 350, 384).

This approach resulted in euthanasia remaining a criminal act, the punishment for which might be mitigated if the court determined the motives of the actor to be pure. Switzerland thereby avoided the necessity of having to legalize an action that many of its citizens may have opposed, but allowed leniency for those who were compelled to acts of euthanasia by the pain and suffering of others.

The reality of this arrangement was that, while euthanasia was illegal, few individuals were ever prosecuted for engaging in the act. The Swiss legal system, in effect, looked the other way and allowed the unsupervised practice of euthanasia for almost 60 years (Schaer 2000). Finally, in the 1970s, physician-assisted suicide was legalized and doctors were allowed to prescribe lethal doses of drugs for the purpose of aiding patients in their stated desire to die (*The Sunday Times* [Britain], 12 May 1999).

Today, Swiss law allows not only doctors but also private citizens to assist in the planned deaths of others. In fact, the Swiss Academy of Medical Science has taken the position that it is better that nonmedical personnel provide such assistance. Under Swiss law, the individual providing death services must be motivated by humanitarian concerns and stand in a position where they will receive no personal gain from the death of the client. The Swiss organization EXIT has stepped forward as the principal provider of death services in Switzerland. EXIT requires that all its clients be Swiss citizens, at least eighteen years of age, mentally competent, and be suffering from intolerable health problems. In addition, the individual must personally apply for the services and demonstrate that the application has not been made as a result of coercion or the undue influence of a third party (Schaer 2000).

CONCLUSION

While the debate surrounding euthanasia has clearly existed in many cultures for hundreds of years, it is an issue that has been dragged to the forefront of modern society by the advent of technology. Industrial development brought with it not only the technical and medical advancements necessary to artificially prolong life but also a society sufficiently affluent to afford those procedures. In conjunction with these factors, the individualistic nature of such countries as the United States led to a heightened sense of autonomy and the right to privacy.

Out of the conflict between the opposing ideals of preserving all life and giving individuals the ability to choose nontreatment or even death, a debate has arisen over whether we are discussing the emergence of new rights or simply the recognition of old ones that never before faced serious challenge. This conflict manifests itself in the contradictory legislative and judicial treatments of the problem. Judicial authorities have been much more willing to view the controversy over the existence of a "right to die" as one involving the recognition of a preexistent right, while legislatures have been simultaneously pushed to legislate both for and against the nascence of what many view as a modern creation.

The net effect of this controversy is that many countries have chosen to avoid becoming enmired in it and have followed an intentional policy of legal prohibition and practical tolerance. Within such passively permissive systems, euthanasia is publicly condemned by the law but socially recognized and tolerated, provided it stays out of the public's eye. The difficulty, then, becomes that in denying the practice of euthanasia as a common event, society relinquishes its authority to regulate its application and so its ability to protect those most vulnerable to the misuse of euthanasia.

Only in a few countries have governments been willing to accept the status of euthanasia as a modern conundrum that will not go away but must be dealt with. In these countries efforts are being made to come to grips with the reality of a technological age that promises only to make the issue of euthanasia an increasingly complex problem that cannot be ignored. Thus, these countries have opted to give limited recognition to the "right to die," while doing the best they can to give full protection to everyone's right to ongoing life.

Chapter 4

Anatomy of a Right

Before we can enter into any form of rational discussion about what has come to be known as the "right to die," we must first develop some basic understanding about what it means for one to assert that one has a "right." Even further, we must develop a common understanding of what it means to claim a right either to act or to refrain from acting in a way that will result in our own death. To many, the very idea that someone could claim a "right to die" runs counter to their understanding of what it means to have a right.

The term "right," though commonly used in Western society, is an elusive concept that lacks any one precise meaning. Taken in the abstract, the word is closely aligned with the concept of justice, inexorably linked to those abstract moral principles that serve as the foundation for all laws and rights. Conversely, in its more literal sense, the concept asserts a relationship between actors in which one actor has a claim of free action with which the other is bound not to interfere. Though distinct and separate, both senses of this term are conjoined, in that both refer to those sets of claims or rights that belong to human beings by virtue of their birth, rather than by membership in a particular society. In this way, such rights are said to be antecedent to, or in existence prior to, their recognition by positive law. Thus, legislatures are said not to create such laws but merely to have formalized their existence by backing them with the authority of the state (Nolan and Nolan-Haley et al. 1990, 1323-1324).

While both of these senses of the word "right" leave room for debate about what does and does not constitute a legitimate right, neither definition embraces the diverse connotative variations on the meaning of the word. When most of us make reference to a right, our vision is not one in which we make recourse to some theoretical principle of human nature or to an abstract concept of justice. On the contrary, we think of our rights as absolute, practicable claims to free action made possible not by some mystical force, but by the fact that the state has agreed to use force to compel compliance. Strictly speaking, then, the word "right" can be applied only to those principles and actions that the state has specifically authorized and agreed to uphold (Nolan and Nolan-Haley et al. 1990, 1324).

The difficulty with this conception of a right is that, despite the apparent need for a sensible approach to defining an elusive concept, it fails to encompass the variety of meanings that have played and continue to play an important role in the arena of American constitutional law. The classical conception of a right in constitutional law places rights in three different categories: natural, civil, and personal.

Of these three, natural rights are most akin to the theoretical conception of rights that have been discussed; they consist of the entitlements that all men and women have simply by virtue of their nature as human beings, including the right to life, liberty, and privacy, and are distinguished from those rights that are created and maintained by the goodwill of society. Thus natural rights are quite different from our second category, civil rights, which belong to all members of a particular society by virtue of their citizenship in a particular state and exist only when that state is willing to enforce them. Taken this way, the definition of a civil right is arguably most consistent with the popular conception of a right.

The third category, personal rights, though used in constitutional law, lacks any precise definition. Instead, the phrase is used to describe a person's right to be secure in person, body, life, and limbs. These rights are also akin to the right to privacy but are less precisely defined. In some cases this phrase has been used in a more expansive way to give protection to a person's reputation, as well as the personal liberty of action (Nolan and Nolan-Haley et al. 1990, 1325). This sense of the word "right" often applies when the freedom being asserted does not fit well within any defined civil right but is nevertheless traditionally recognized as a personal freedom, one that deserves protection.

Despite these discrepancies among the several definitions of the concept of a "right," a common ground exists upon which all definitions agree. In order for any right to be recognized, at least three elements must be present. First, there must be a claimant to some possession or entitlement of free action. Next, the subject of that claim must be considered by the claimant to be of positive value or a good. Third, there must be some secondary institution or individual who seeks to deny the claimant the entitlement to this perceived good. Put succinctly, in order for a right to be recognized, it must first be asserted and denied. In the absence of conflicting claims, there is no need to distinguish a right from a positively fulfilled request.

When these definitions are applied to the concept of a "right to die," opponents will raise several challenges to the idea that someone can assert such a right. The most straightforward of these objections is that when someone asserts a "right to die," the claimant is not asserting an entitlement to some good but, rather, is requesting permission to do what most individuals would consider to be evil. This objection cannot be overcome simply by arguing that what is evil to one person can be good to another, because such claims cannot be supported by our categorization of rights. This is true because if this entitlement is said to be a natural right, then it can no longer depend upon individual perception but must be a right that flows from the very nature of human existence. Further, if the claim is to be categorized as a civil right, it must be an entitlement created by some legislature and backed by the coercive power of the state. Finally, while the claim might possibly be asserted as a personal right, such rights are traditionally viewed as something that benefits the individual, while death, in and of itself, has never been seen as a general benefit. It is for this reason that our society generally supports the prohibition of suicide (Beschle 1988-89, 320).

A second objection that can be made based on these definitional requirements is that the assertion of a right must seek an entitlement to that which some other institution or individual has the power to deny. Despite all wishes to the contrary, it is commonly maintained that one of the traits that distinguishes human beings from lower orders is that we are aware of our own mortality and, thus, are aware that no man or human institution has the power to deny death (Beschle 1988-89, 320).

Proponents of the "right to die" often counter that such arguments are nothing more than a game of semantics and would point out that, while an abstract desire for death may, in fact, not be considered good, the ability to control the time, place, and manner of one's death is more clearly a claim for good. Further, it is equally clear that while the inevitability of death cannot be denied, control over its timing and manner can be denied and frequently is. It is this that distinguishes a claim for a "right to die" from an act of suicide, in that when an individual seeks to commit suicide, the asserted desire is simply for death, while the claim of a "right to die" is most frequently made in the face of impending death and only seeks to control the circumstances of that death so as to make the dying party more comfortable. When envisioned in this way, the claim of a "right to die" may, in fact, fit the definitional requirements of a right.

Those who intimately assert that there is a "right to die" are often infuriated by those individuals who seek to deny them this right. They see such efforts as attempts to interfere with what they consider to be the most personal of decisions. The difficulty with this assertion is that, by their very nature, rights are not entirely personal things. Quite to the contrary, the existence of a right implies a relationship between two actors that is characterized by conflict. This conflict is caused by the fact that when a right is either created or recognized in one party, it automatically creates a duty or obligation in some other party (Finnis 1980). In this sense, it must be understood that rights are not simply possessed by an individual, but are held as a shield against the actions of some other person, institution, or perhaps even the majority. Thus, it should be noted that rights are not actually ever recognized or even created, but merely serve as the justification for creating a duty in others not to interfere with another's freedom of action. In this way, a right is not created, while a duty is, and the right can be viewed as a consequence of the duty. Thus, an assertion of the right to free speech is in reality a claim of a duty on the part of the government and others not to interfere with someone's speech. In this way, a right cannot be seen as involving only one party because it necessarily limits the permissible range of activities of others. Therefore, the rights of one individual are necessarily tied up with the duties and obligations of another.

While this relationship between rights and duties might at first seem to promise to provide some foundation for understanding what rights we all can legitimately expect to claim, in reality it has only served to widen our circle of uncertainty. The reason for this growing ambiguity is that while legal scholars agree that there is an important relationship between rights and duties, they have not been able to develop a generally accepted method for distinguishing one from the other, and so have done little to aid in our understanding of what rights we actually have, if any at all (Hinchman 1984, 7).

What scholars can agree on is that when we talk about where rights came from, there are three potential sources. Alasdair MacIntyre identifies these three sources as:

- Contractual rights—which consist of rights that are the product of a mutual agreement with consideration, or some benefit being passed from one party to the other. In essence, such rights are the product of an exchange relationship where the first party receives certain entitlements, or rights, as a result of a transfer of something of value to the second party. This transfer of value could be in the form of corresponding entitlements or could be monetary in nature. Rights of this nature are enforceable in a court of law and generally create entitlements only in those individuals who are parties to the contract.
- Created rights—which come into existence as a result of legislative enactment. Such acts of positive law are designed to create entitlements for identified groups of individuals or all citizens within a society to act in particular ways and to have this right of action protected by the coercive powers of the state.
- Natural rights—natural rights are said to proceed from natural law and include such entitlements as are derived from inherent rights and inalienable rights. These rights are neither created by acts of positive law nor brought about by mutual agreement between contractual parties. In fact, such rights are said not to be created at all, but rather to have simply been officially recognized as existing. Thus, such rights exist independently of any government or association of people, though it may well take the cooperation of one or the other to give them practical force within society. Such rights are believed to exist as a result of a rational understanding of human beings' relationships with the natural world and with each other (McMullin 1978, 75).

It is important to note that while all legal scholars agree that these first two categories of rights provide us with a valid understanding of the source of rights, substantial disagreement exists about the validity of the natural rights concept. Alasdair MacIntyre, in his article, "The Right to Die Garrulously," rejects any conception of natural rights, stating that "nobody has ever given us the slightest reason for believing" that there are natural rights and that "such rights are at one with unicorns, witches, and Meinog's glass mountain." To support this claim, MacIntyre cites the words of the utilitarianist Jeremy Bentham who, when asked about natural rights, referred to them as "nonsense" and went on to condemn "imprescriptible, inalienable rights" as "nonsense on stilts" (McMullin 1978, 75-76).

Despite MacIntyre's and Bentham's condemnation of the concept of natural rights, and identification of positive law, or created rights, as the only legitimate source of societal entitlements, substantial debate exists as the validity of the concept of natural rights. This debate has its importance to those who advocate a "right to die" because of the nature of the right that many such advocates assert to be in existence. While all advocates of the "right to die" would be willing to admit that such an entitlement can be created by legislative acts, many would maintain that such a right exists even in the absence of a right created by positive law. They would argue that the right of an individual to rationally control the time and nature of his or her death is part of what it means to be a free and autonomous human being; it thus need not be created by positive law, but rather need only be recognized by the courts as one of our natural or inalienable rights. Therefore, legalistic arguments over the "right to die" involve a threshold issue concerning whether or not natural rights exist at all—a question that is not easily answered.

The difficulty in resolving this disagreement over the validity of natural rights is made even more difficult when it is viewed as a part of the historical evolution of Western legal philosophy that culminated in the creation of the American legal system. Within this tradition, any viable theory of law must be able to account for why it is considered necessary to treat human beings differently from the way we treat simpler forms of life or physical property. In addition, within American legal philosophy we should be able to explain why humans not only have "fundamental rights against the state's interference [civil liberties] but also rights to its help and support in securing goods now deemed indispensable to a genuinely human existence [civil rights]" (Hinchman 1984, 8). The challenge for those who would seek to debunk natural rights concepts is to come up with a theory of positive law that can explain each of these categories of law while not departing from American political traditions. Such a task is made difficult because of the historical development of both Western and American legal thought.

Early theories of legal practice did not include the concepts of the individuality and personal dignity that are so familiar to Americans today. In the ancient world, a person was not conceived of as an individual but rather recognized as a member of society. Thus, the classical philosophies of Plato and Aristotle viewed the state as being both teleologically and temporarily superior to the individual in that it was only through membership in the state that an individual became truly human, and it was life within the regulated structure of the state that enabled citizens to maintain this status.[1] In this way, rights were conceived as the constructs of custom, tradition, and religious beliefs and not as individual entitlements. Under such philosophy individuals are said to have rights only as a result of their relationship to the state. While this concept of society would strongly embrace the legal positivists' position that the only rights that exist are created rights, it is a theory of rights radically different from the legal/political theory that would serve as the foundation of American government so many centuries later.

Under American political philosophy, one of the primary purposes of government is to protect the individual from the arbitrary interference of the society as a whole. This protection is so strong that it can be invoked by a single individual, even against a majority of our society. Commenting on the significance of this change, Susan Ford Wiltshire, in her book *Greece, Rome, and the Bill of Rights*, states that "[w]hen the Bill of Rights became part of the United States Constitution on December 15, 1791, notions of human liberty and the civil status of the individual took a form unprecedented in the history of political governance" (Wiltshire 1992, 3). This new conception of rights recognized the unique nature of the human being and placed within his grasp a right to human dignity and individuality unknown to the classical world. The significance of this fact is that the only way to account for the slow emergence of the individual as an independent political entity is by an appeal to the concept of natural law, a concept with which our founding fathers were intimately familiar and eventually incorporated into our constitution.

When Thomas Jefferson wrote the Declaration of Independence and referred to the "Law of Nature," "self-evident" truths, and "unalienable rights," he was, in fact, incorporating into American political thought the theories of natural law that found their origins even before the development of Roman law and eventually shaped all the major political institutions of the Western world (Wiltshire 1992, 3). He was making reference to those natural law theories of individual freedom and equality that made the American and French revolutions possible (d'Entr'eves 1970, 18). The American acceptance of the idea that the individual has rights distinct and separate from his or her relationship to the state is the direct result of a series of philosophical developments that depend entirely on the theory of natural law. Thus, it was only through the emergence of natural law theories that the slow transformation from a state-centered society to an individual-centered political theory was made possible (Wiltshire 1992, 4-9).

The significance of this fact is reflected in the development of "right to die" claims being made in the United States today. Early movements concentrating on euthanasia and the "right to die" were couched in terms of positive law, in that they frequently sought to pass legislation creating such rights within society. However, as "right to die" claims have become more personal, the legal nature of the cases has shifted from attempting to obtain legislative permission to seeking the recognition of a constitutional right. Thus, prior to the court cases of Karen Ann Quinlan and Joseph Saikewicz, the right to die was discussed only in terms of the common law tradition of prohibiting unconsented touching. However, since the advent of these cases, almost all courts base their findings in "right to die" cases on the constitutional right to privacy, which, by its nature, emphasizes the right of the individual to exist independent of society (McCarthy 1981, 169). Thus, if we are to have a clear understanding of the nature of "right to die" claims as they are made today, we must first understand the role of natural law in developing the foundation for such a right.

Chapter 5

Opposition to the "Right to Die"

The "right to die" is an issue that often ignites strong passions and perhaps produces extremists on both sides of the debate. Certainly Dr. Jack Kevorkian can be said to be a "pro-right" extremist, while the "right to life" movement has produced several extreme positions of its own. Others prefer to take a more moderate approach, arguing that the focus should not be on the "right to die" but rather on such issues as the right of rational, mature individuals to choose the timing of their own death so as to avoid suffering and achieve what they may deem a dignified death. However, it is clear that not even this moderate position is sufficient to calm the concerns of many who oppose recognition of a "right to die."

While the largest portion of our population is willing to consider the legalization of some aspects of the "right to die" movement such as living wills, medical directives, or even health care proxies, some perceive even these steps as inherently wrong. In an effort to categorize the arguments against the "right to die," we can see that most nonreligious opposition to the "right to die" falls roughly into three categories: the wedge or slippery-slope argument, the need to protect innocent life, and the incompatibility of the act with the medical profession's view of a rational life. Of these three arguments, as variations on the wedge argument are probably the most common, this is where an investigation into opposition to the "right to die" should begin.

THE WEDGE AND THE SLIPPERY-SLOPE ARGUMENTS

These arguments generally begin by raising a question about what fundamental values we want our society to reflect and, more particularly, what do want our society to reflect about the value of human life. The argument asserts that any social tolerance for the "right to die," even with procedural safeguards, represents the beginning of a slippery slope that our society will slide down or, conversely, the thin edge of a wedge that will slowly widen the gap between our moral beliefs and practices and eventually result in a wholehearted erosion of our societal respect for life. Such an argument is based upon the widely held belief that the right to continued life is one of the most fundamental values of our society. Proponents of this view argue that the importance of this value is reflected in such culturally sacred documents as the U.S. Declaration of Independence and the United Nations Declaration of Human Rights (Cole 1989, 393, 402).

Thus, those who use the wedge and slippery-slope arguments to oppose any support for a "right to die" reason that any socially permissible act of mercy killing is inherently dangerous to all human life, because what may very well start out as an innocent agreement upon the acceptable boundaries of such an act exposes our society to the inevitable pressure to expand such acts to situations that, at one time, would have been unthinkable. In essence, the argument views any permissibility in the area of the "right to die" as the beginning of an incremental devaluation of human life that can only lead to terrors reminiscent of the Nazi Holocaust. Under such a perspective, the legalization of physician-assisted suicide is nothing less than a warped perception of self-control that, in truth, is nothing but societally condoned murder and thus, a weakening of our respect for human life (Cole 1989, 405).

In response to this argument, advocates for the "right to die" have made several points, the first being that the slippery slope and wedge arguments raise important questions that need to be taken seriously. In essence, both sides recognize that there is danger and that when such a fundamental right as ongoing life is involved, we must consider the possibility of future abuses and mutations of what is presently conceived of as a rational policy. However, advocates for a "right to die" are quick to point out that many of the fears that are raised by the slippery-slope argument can be nullified by guaranteeing procedural safeguards that can only serve to reinforce the societal importance of the "right to life," rather than erode it.

Chief among the safeguards protecting the societal importance of life is the requirement of voluntariness, a procedural guarantee that the "right to die" can only involve individuals who have voluntarily requested an end to their lives, and that this is all that is needed to altogether deflect the slippery-slope argument of those who appose the existence of a "right to die" (Dickinson 1996, 107). Others go farther and say that, in order to avoid the dangers raised by the slippery slope, additional safeguards must be included, such as requirements that only licensed providers be allowed to assist in such deaths and that the wishes of relatives be considered in some formal way before a final decision is made (*The Economist*, 17 September 1994, 14).

Another challenge that is frequently made in opposition to the slippery slope argument is the idea that opponents to the creation of a "right to die" are simply trading one slippery slope for another. While forbidding any form of euthanasia may protect the value of human life, it opens up an even more terrifying dilemma, namely the slippery slope of allowing society, or more precisely, government, to limit the personal liberty that citizens have to decide what will happen to their own bodies. Proponents of the "right to die" also argue that it was the loss of personal liberty and the personal right of bodily integrity that led to the deplorable deeds of Nazi Germany, and that a loss of respect for human life is most likely in a society that is willing to allow others to destroy the autonomy and human dignity of others in the name of societal good (Kotch 1994, 100). In keeping with this argument, the only role for government, in any mechanism for providing individuals with an option to exercise their "right to die," is in assuring against abuse. Ultimately, however, those who favor the creation of a "right to die" argue that the only true protection against abuse is self-responsibility.

The final argument against the wedge and slippery-slope arguments is perhaps the most straightforward. It simply argues that line drawing, in even the most difficult of situations, has long been one of the principal jobs of the American judiciary and that it has served our nation well as a tool for distinguishing between permissible and forbidden behavior (White 1994, 141). The argument can be extended to demonstrate that if we, as a society, were to abandon all social reforms simply because they presented the danger of a slippery slope, we would rarely be able to make any significant public policy decisions. Almost all reforms, from the creation of welfare to social security, were once opposed by slippery-slope arguments (White 1994, 141).

In response to these defenses, opponents of a "right to die" would likely respond by saying that such defenses are based on a hopelessly naive faith in the goodness of human nature, pointing to the fact that several times important American figures have embraced the concept of involuntary euthanasia as a tool for eliminating socially undesirable individuals. Principal among these examples is Joseph Fletcher, who in a 1968 article in *The Atlantic* openly advocated the use of euthanasia as a way of treating children with retardation and Down's syndrome. "Right to life" supporters might claim that Fletcher's arguments are not all that dissimilar from those heard today in support of a "right to life" in that he urged that not all lives are worth living and that euthanasia was the only merciful way of dealing with such children (Dedek 1972, 133-134).

In addition to this well-known example, opponents would point to the statements of the Euthanasia Society of America during its general meetings in 1939, in which it openly stated that its goal was to pursue the legalization of voluntary euthanasia only because that was all that present public sentiment could be expected to support, but that the society hoped that one day compulsory euthanasia would also be possible (St. John-Stevas 1964, 46). Although this was many years ago, it must be noted that exactly such sentiments led to the ease with which Nazi Germany was able to implement its policies of racial hygiene, allowing them to institute such laws as the *Gesetz zur Verhutung Erbkranken Nachwuches* (the Law for the Prevention of Genetically Diseased Offspring, widely known as the "Sterilization Law"), as well as the *Reichsausschuss zur wissenschaftlichen Erfassung von erbund anlagebedinster schwere Leiden* (the Committee for the Scientific Treatment of Severe

Genetically Determined Illness), which eventually oversaw the termination of over 70,273 individuals' lives (Shevell 1992, 2214-2219).

While it is easy to say that such events could not happen in the United States, it should be noted that the eugenics movement in the United States actually convinced several state legislatures to implement legal procedures for the forced sterilization of the mentally incompetent and those considered to be habitual criminals (*Skinner v. Oklahoma*). In addition, opponents recognize that several well-known American physicians supported the principles of racial hygiene. Among them were W. G. Lennox and Foster Kennedy, who advocated involuntary euthanasia as late as 1942 (Shevell 1992, 2215). While many of us may be willing to dismiss all this as little more than ghosts from our past, opponents argue that our growing societal fear of becoming dependent upon others and our insistence upon unrestricted personal freedoms and personal liberties can cause us to "want to rid ourselves of those who mirror our own dependency or place high demands upon our capacity for care-giving; [and that] this is true even though we may simultaneously feel love for those of whom we wish to be rid" (Meucci 1988, 18). Such arguments must be seriously considered. It was only January of 1995 when a Los Angeles Mensa chapter (for people with IQs of 132 or higher) published two articles in its newsletter advocating the propriety of killing off "the old, weak, the stupid, and the inefficient," as well as the elimination of the homeless, "like abandoned kittens" (*U.S. News & World Report*, 23 January 1995, 12). In the end, they echo the words of University of Michigan law professor Yale Kamisar, who urges us to remember that "Not all people are kind, understanding and loving. Yet they will be making decisions about the elderly and the helpless" (Ubell 1992, 24).

THE DANGERS OF A COST-BENEFIT ANALYSIS

Many who oppose the "right to die" movement believe that legalized euthanasia, even in its voluntary form, will begin to push both social institutions and individuals toward the adoption of a cost-benefit analysis that will result in the denial of medical care to those whom society deems too old, too ill, too needy or simply as not having a life worth preserving.

Opponents of the "right to die" point to such "death-with-dignity" advocates as Daniel Callahan and Derek Humphry, who call for the legalization of euthanasia by touting its cost efficiency (Meucci 1988, 11). The appeal to a cost-benefit analysis might depersonalize death decisions and thus allow institutionally, rather than morally minded individuals to define and objectify those in need of medical care in such a way that human compassion and individual freedom will be replaced by a governmental equation that determines whether a person is entitled to live or die.

In addition to expressed fears of a totalitarian state seeking to cut expenses, even at the cost of human life, opponents of the legalization of euthanasia can point to the apparent contradiction between the concept of voluntariness, which those who support legalization hold out as so important to their argument, and the frequency of cost-benefit analysis in the literature supporting euthanasia. It can be argued that as society begins to concentrate on the need to save money through the use of such principles as "utility" and cost-worthiness, it begins the process of institutionalizing the principle that not all lives are equally worth living. As a result, many individuals may be compelled to view death as the only socially responsible choice they have, or as the only choice that will save their families from the burden of growing medical costs. Under such conditions, the concept of a voluntary decision to die is, at best, little more than an illusion or, at worst, a convenient mechanism of relieving our guilt for allowing someone to die, who may have wished to live (Dickinson 1996, 107).

In the end, the ultimate fear is that euthanasia will not be viewed by society as a voluntary option to be taken only as a last resort, but will be viewed instead as a social duty. In support of exactly such a conclusion, opponents point to Charlotte Perkins Gilman, a supporter of euthanasia, who left a note at the scene of her self-euthanasia stating that "when all usefulness is over, and one is assured of an imminent and unavoidable death, it is the simplest of human rights to choose a quick and easy death." It is ironic that despite that note's appeal to free choice, the title, "A Last Duty," clearly communicates Gilman's state of mind (Glick 1992, 137). Advocates have even gone so far as to suggest that individuals who are willing to contractually refuse expensive end-care might even be able to enjoy lower insurance premiums (Dickinson 1996, 107). For opponents, this is clearly little more than being forced to make "the devil's bargain" of trading human dignity for human sustenance.

In response to these charges, supporters of the "right to die" point out that over the last two decades the many advances in medical technology have increased the expense of treatment tremendously, but when these technologies are applied to end-care patients they produce very few positive results, at a significant cost. In addition, for many these technologies are not only financially burdensome to themselves and their families but are also physically intrusive and unpleasant. Consequently, we all should have a choice whether such procedures should be performed on us. Such arguments are bolstered by research that suggests that the ease and profitability of caring for the elderly and debilitated within nursing homes provides a ready economic incentive for such institutions to prolong the lives of their clients as long as possible (Almgren 1992, 25). In essence, proponents of euthanasia argue that the undesired and artificial prolonging of life is an evil just as dangerous as the involuntary removal of life. The key is to create a system that prevents both.

Finally, in response to the charges of cold and unfeeling cost-benefit analysis, many supporters of the "right to die" are forced to point out that, while few individuals want to be responsible for deciding how and upon whom our national resources will be expended, current conditions leave us very little choice. In the ideal world the expense of medical treatment would not be an issue, but the world is far from ideal, and it is clear that such decisions must be made (Callahan 1987). In addition, it is foolish to assume that such issues are avoidable. It seems clear from the anecdotal evidence received from numerous physicians that such cost-benefit decisions are already being made and probably have been for some time (*The Economist*, 17 September 1994, 22). Indeed, even the "Declaration on Euthanasia" issued by the Vatican Congregation for the Doctrine of the Faith on 26 June, 1980, recognizes that as a long-standing principle the "cost" of a medical procedure is one of the acceptable standards upon which to base a decision to receive or refuse medical treatment (Vatican Congregation for the Doctrine of the Faith 1980, Sect. 4).

PRESERVATION OF THE MEDICAL PROFESSION

The last of the three most common arguments against the "right-to-die" attempts to tie the integrity of the medical profession to the issue of killing. Opponents argue that the physician-patient relationship is one that necessitates a high degree of trust that would be impossible if our medical professionals were allowed to play any significant role in determining who will live and who will die (Cole 1989, 393). In addition, they argue that even if individuals are said to have a right to end their own lives, nothing in this right could possibly be interpreted as to allow them to demand that their physician participate in this act. Also, they argue that such an act is inconsistent with the physician's oath "to do no harm" as well as the Principles of Medical Ethics of the American Medical Association (AMA), which dedicate a doctor to the "prolongation of life" (Cole 1989, 393). Opponents warn that it is this very dedication to life that has led the medical profession to discover new cures for diseases that were once considered to be terminal and that if doctors are no longer dedicated to extending human life, the impetus to discover new cures through the use of experimental drugs and procedures will be seriously weakened.

In response, advocates argue that the Hippocratic Oath was designed to prevent the early practitioners of medicine from using their knowledge to enable others to engage in murder or political assassination (Dedek 1972, 120). In support of this position, they point to the growing hospice movement, which was once itself thought to violate the Hippocratic Oath, but is now gaining wide acceptance within the medical field (Gentile and Fello 1994, 4). In addition, there is by no means any clear consensus of opinion within the medical establishment itself. Medical journals regularly carry articles debating the acceptance of and the ethical considerations concerning euthanasia (Godley 1992, 608-610). As a result, advocates see any opposition based on the position that euthanasia is inconsistent with medical practice as both fallacious and premature.

GENERAL OPPOSITION

In addition to the more well-defined arguments just considered, there is a general argument against the legalization of euthanasia that adopts as its basis the contention that any recognition of a "right to die" would constitute an unjustified elevation of individual rights over community interests. Advocates maintain that, while every case in which a decision must be made about the termination of medical treatment involves the obvious interests of the patient, such cases also involve important interests of the state. They argue that, while several state interests are involved, the most important are the preservation of life, the prevention of suicide, and maintenance of the ethical integrity of the medical profession (Horan 1981, 147, 168), with the most important of these being the preservation of life.

It is asserted that, while individuals clearly do have some rights regarding their medical treatment, these rights are not sufficient to override community interests in preserving life and our society's respect for life. To charges that the "right to die" is based in the Constitution, opponents to the "right to die" counter that no such right has ever been found to exist by any authoritative judicial body and that attempts to legalize euthanasia constitute an attempt to unconstitutionally withdraw the protection of life. It is further asserted that, even if there were a constitutional basis for a "right to die," such a right by its very nature would be personal, and so, at the very least, it would be impossible for a third party such as a parent or guardian to request the removal of life support from an unconscious individual (Horan 1981, 152, 169-171).

In opposition to this position, advocates of the "right to die" propose that the U.S. Constitution does provide what is necessary to support a "right to die." Several constitutional principles are raised in endorsing this assertion. The first and most important of these sources is the constitutional right to privacy (*Griswold v. Connecticut*). This right has been found to include the right to bodily self-determination, as found in common law. In reaching that decision, the Supreme Court of the United States stated that "no right is held more sacred, or is more carefully guarded, by the common law, than the right of every individual to the possession and control of his own person, free from all restraint or interference of others, unless by clear and unquestionable authority of law" (*Union Pacific v. Botsford*). It is argued that this right is the foundation of both the doctrine of informed consent and the patient's right to refuse medical treatment and that, by extension, such protections create within all citizens a "right to die" (White 1994, 145-147).

In support of this contention, advocates can now point to the ruling of the U.S. Supreme Court in the case of *Cruzan v. Director, Missouri Dept. of Health*, in which the Court ruled that there was a constitutionally protected interest in refusing life-sustaining treatment.[1] Many state courts have similarly addressed this issue and have found that the constitutional right of self-determination does support the right to refuse even life-sustaining medical treatment.

RELIGIOUS OPPOSITION

Thus far, only those arguments against euthanasia that can be said to be primarily secular in nature have been outlined. However, it would be a serious oversight not also to include those opposition arguments that take religious belief as their principal base of objection. Within the controversy surrounding the potential existence of a "right to die," it is clear that religion and religious beliefs play an important role in the development of both personal and organized opposition to the concept. It is equally clear that religious institutions within the United States, particularly the Roman Catholic Church, have played important roles in opposing the legalization of a "right to die."

As the movement for the official recognition of a "right to die" gained steam during the 1960s and 1970s, opposing interest groups began to form whose principal goal was to block any governmental endorsement of such a right, including the adoption of living will legislation. The Roman Catholic Church played an important role in the formation of this opposition, using its large congregations and political contacts to form public opinion and spearhead such efforts by linking legislation advancing the "right to die" with the dangers of involuntary euthanasia of the mentally retarded, the old, and the infirm (Glick 1992, 38, 58). As a result of this organized opposition, the state Catholic Conferences quickly became the most powerful interest group opposing the legalization of euthanasia. Henry R. Glick, in his book *The Right to Die: Policy Innovation and Its Consequences,* observes that "no other interest group has been as concerned with these laws as the Catholic Church, nor have they had nearly the impact" (Glick 1992, 202). He notes that, in an attempt to continue these efforts, the Roman Catholic Church created "The National Right to Life Committee" as a secret lobbying organization for the purpose of carrying on the fight against the legalization of euthanasia without endangering the Church's tax-exempt status and that this organization has been very successful in influencing the wording and limitations placed in many pieces of living will legislation. Glick attributes the success of the Catholic Church's efforts to influence legislation to the fact that the American Catholic Church is not itself conceived of as a predominantly conservative institution like many of the Protestant Evangelical organizations within the Republican party that also oppose the legalization of euthanasia, but who have not had the same level of success (Glick 1992, 21).

The principal foundation of religious opposition to the "right to die" is twofold. The first is that life is good, in and of itself, and must be understood as a gift from God that does not belong to individuals to do with as they see fit. Suffering is not an absolute evil but often provides opportunities for spiritual growth and the atonement of sins by sharing in Christ's passion (McMullin 1978, 1). The Roman Catholic Church recognizes the necessity of relieving needless suffering and the seriousness of questions pertaining to when an individual should be resuscitated or placed on extensive technological support (St. John-Stevas 1964), but ultimately it asserts that life is sacred and must be treated with a reverence that forbids anyone, either personally or by the acts of a second party, to terminate human life before it naturally comes to an end (Vatican Congregation for the Doctrine of the Faith 1980).

The second basis for the Church's opposition to the "right to die" can be found in what it perceives as a growing danger to "innocent life." It is the position of the Roman Catholic Church that no statute that allows for termination of human life will sufficiently protect themselves: the mentally ill, the retarded, those in a state of unconsciousness, and children. As a result, it maintains that any statute legalizing a "right to die" would unjustly injure our society's respect for innocent life and contribute to the moral decay that threatens the maintenance of a good society and our security within it (St. John-Stevas 1964, 50). It is argued that we have moral responsibility to protect life and that, although individuals may wrongly choose to turn away from this obligation, as a society we must never institutionalize the acceptance of ending innocents' lives.

Those who support the "right to die" argue that religion should not dictate law in the American constitutional system. Therefore, to allow religious sentiments to block the individual rights of others would be a violation of our constitutional guarantees. Ultimately, while religion may play a role in our personal decisions, we must be free to follow the sentiments of Nero, who stated that "[t]here is this blessing, that while life had but one entrance, it has exits innumerable, and as I choose the house in which I live, the ship in which I will sail, so will I choose the time and manner of my death" (Ingersoll 1895, 17).

SEARCHING FOR A MIDDLE GROUND

Despite the clear difference of opinion between those who advocate the legalization of euthanasia and those who oppose it, there may still be room within our society for a significant agreement about how the terminally ill should be treated. If we take the many and varying opinions about euthanasia and conceive of them as other than irreconcilable positions, we can then begin to recognize a rich and continuing debate concerning the use of medical technology and the appropriateness of life shortening and life-prolonging procedures. Given the nature of the questions to be answered, this is a debate that is not likely to end soon.

Ultimately, the questions that must be answered in order to produce a clear standard for future action are themselves cloaked in a veil of ambiguity. This lack of clarity, or perhaps presence of complexity, can be found in the very terminology of the questions being asked. When we begin to discuss such terms as "euthanasia," it quickly becomes clear that the word has not one meaning, but several. To some the term is equivalent with mercy killing, while to others it can represent little more than a decision not to aggressively treat. Are we referring to "active" or "passive" euthanasia? This problem becomes even more complex when we further add such modifiers as "voluntary" and "involuntary." Thus, we are left not with one question but with several, and begin to experience a blurring of the ethical dimensions of the question. If euthanasia is active and voluntary and self-administered, is it suicide? If it is active and voluntary but administered by another, is it murder? If it is passive but involves the removal of life-sustaining technology from an unconscious person, is it voluntary? Where is the dividing line between an act of commission and an act of omission?

The difficulty is that the vast majority of cases involving some question of euthanasia fall into some gray areas of decision making. This problem is exacerbated by efforts to develop religious standards that can be clearly applied to what is largely a secular society. As a result, many religions and denominations recognize the right of their members to "die with dignity," while asserting the necessity of providing medical care to all who desire it. What we are left with is a balancing act. We recognize the right of the ill not to have their lives prolonged beyond the realm of reasonable personhood, while demanding that those who wish to be sustained are kept alive through the receipt of all the benefits that medical technology can provide.

As a result of these tensions, many religions have an implicit understanding that the involuntary prolongation of an existence that offers no true chance of recovery is equivalent to an act of violence against an already-suffering individual. However, the difficulty is in determining what treatments may be removed and which treatments are essential for the preservation of moral conduct. In order to understand the complexity of this question, one must understand that each and every case is different. In one instance, conditions may call for the provision of any and all treatments that offer reasonable hope of improving the individual's condition, while in others the provision of such basic elements as food, water, and air may necessitate the type of invasive surgery that, in the end, will do little other than prolong the suffering of the victim. Thus, most religious groups are faced with certain realities that make the promulgation of clear guidelines difficult; as follows:

1. The provision of care in some instances can be an act of a lower moral quality than the removal of care.
2. Care decisions will largely be made in secular institutions with only passing concern for the individual standards of its patients.
3. In the majority of the cases in which such issues arise, the victims of illness or injury are no longer competent to actively participate in the decision-making process.

As a result of these realities, many have focused their attention not on specific rules of conduct but, rather, on the question of how to show love for the terminally ill and suffering, while fulfilling the other ethical obligations of their religion. Along these lines it may be possible for all sides to agree that no action should be taken to intentionally cause harm, that we do all that is in our power to relieve suffering and protect the dignity of the dying, and that when there is little hope that the dying process can be halted, the obligation to sustain life is brought to an end. At such a time, the provision of heroic medical efforts does nothing to further our obligation to care for the ill but, rather, becomes a form of violence against the physical body of the dying and perhaps against the will of God.

However, once the death of the individual is recognized as inevitable and efforts to sustain life have been halted, a new obligation arises that requires us to provide love, dignity, and comfort for the dying. This requirement is based on the goal of providing the dying individual with those attributes of care that are necessary for experiencing a meaningful personal existence even if for only a short period of time. Those decisions about the removal or withdrawal of medical care must be based on an understanding of whether those measures heighten the recipient's comfort or ability to interact with his or her world. Going even deeper into the religious viewpoint, it our obligation to surround the dying person with a loving environment. In order to do this, we must respect the wishes of the dying while at the same time resisting the modern tendency to dehumanize those who no longer meet our standards of self-care and productivity. Thus, we must never fall into the trap of using our own conceptions of what constitutes a meaningful life to determine who has a right to live; rather, we must assume that all have a right to live while recognizing that some may choose to exercise their right to die. Within that individual struggle our obligation is to provide the comfort of human interaction and affection that is necessary to enable them to depart from this world in a state of comfort, peace, and love.[2]

Chapter 6

Roman Natural Law Theory

The function of political philosophy has always been to explore the basic questions concerning the appropriate relationship between the individual person and society and the rights and obligations of that person within the ideal society. Thus, political philosophy, from its humble Socratic beginning, has dealt itself the task of attempting to answer such questions as What is justice? What form of government is best? Who should rule? What rights and obligations befall the citizen? It has even asked such basic questions as What is a human being?

Great questions like these have long been the intellectual playground of such thinkers as Plato, Aristotle, Aquinas, Hobbes, Locke, and Marx. For more than twenty-three centuries, political philosophers have proposed various answers to the human political dilemma, some advocating totalitarianism, others democracy; some basing their theories upon the rule of man, others upon the authority of God. However, over this entire period, only one theory has continually been present. This theory, through various incarnations, served as the catalyst for the transformation of a collection of legal principles and philosophical schools of thought into the legal system that formed the foundations of the Roman Empire; it was the driving intellectual force behind the power and authority of the Catholic Church in the political affairs of the medieval state; it was one of the foundational principles of the Protestant Reformation; it served as a cornerstone for the development of social contract theory; and it played a decisive role in both the French and the American revolutions. Throughout the entire history of political thought, only one doctrine has experienced such longevity and diversity of political effects, and this is, of course, the doctrine of natural law.

Over the 2,300 years of its existence, the doctrine of natural law has served as a criterion for the evolution of international law, and natural law theory has served as a yardstick against which the positive enactments of man could be measured and as a theoretical foundation for many of the legal norms of the Roman Empire. The theory of natural law has indeed been one of the mediating theories for many of the significant historic events that have shaped Western civilization. Despite this long and colorful history, some will still ask why we are bothering to speak about natural law theory today, given the clear predominance of positivism within our legal structure, and more particularly, why we have included this subject in a book dedicated to exploring the question of whether there is a "right to die." To be sure, natural law has not been a widely held theory since the seventeenth and eighteenth centuries. Since its last intellectual heyday, natural law theory has been harshly criticized by positivists and was, at one point, considered to be in such a state of disrepute that few self-respecting political scientists or philosophers would admit to adhering to its tenets (Voeglin 1997, 268-276). [1]

This distaste for natural law theory is nothing new. It was a strong rejection of its principles and the principles of natural rights that led Bentham to refer to it as not just simple nonsense, but "nonsense on stilts" (Bentham 1843, 501). Despite great efforts to repudiate natural law theory, it represents a collection of ideas that cannot be driven from the political landscape, leading Oliver Wendell Homes to refer to it as a "brooding Omnipresence in the sky" (*Southern Pacific Railway v. Jensen*). Today, this situation has changed somewhat; once again, a growing collection of theorists see natural law as a useful concept which to draw (George 1992). This, of course, is not to say that any theorist who makes reference to its principles will be free from attack; this is far from the case. Natural law, despite its philosophical tradition, is still a controversial theory that many wish to avoid.[2]

If, indeed, natural law theory is so controversial, why bring it up at all? The answer is that it is painfully relevant to the topic of whether the "right to die" exists. It would be difficult, if not impossible, to adequately discuss the evolution of rights theory, particularly within the United States, without discussing the role that natural law theory played in the development of this concept. In addition to its relevance to questions about the existence of individual rights, natural law has a special relevance to questions that fail to fit tightly into political, legal, or moral categories.

The following two sections demonstrate not only that natural law has played an important part in the development of a theory of rights, upon which an argument for the "right to die" can be based, but also that its principles are of such a nature that they provide a vehicle for blending legal and moral considerations into one theory, thereby proving to be a particularly useful tool for addressing difficult ethical questions such as those involved with the "right to die." However, before launching into an application of natural law theories to the present question, it is first advisable to provide an explanation of the historical significance of natural law theory, both to the questions of the "right to die" and to the evolution of rights theory within the United States.

Today, if one were to ask the average American "Do individuals have rights?" one would be inviting a look of bewilderment, as if the listener had just stumbled upon some extraterrestrial who was obviously ignorant about the state of the Earth. Our average American would unthinkingly reply, "Of course, individuals have rights." In fact, the vast majority of those living throughout the world today would answer similarly (see Appendix C for the U.N. Declaration of Human Rights and the International Declaration of the Rights of Man). Indeed, such a question would seem absurd to the average listener, particularly in the United States, where the theory of rights plays such a central role in our ideology of government. However, such a widely held acceptance of the existence of individual rights is a fairly recent phenomenon in the history of Western civilization.

To have talked about individual rights within the ancient world would have to been to talk nonsense, because, within the paradigm of the Greek city-state, the individual was not seen to exist as a separate identity from the state. Within Greek political thought, the state was viewed as being both morally and teleologically superior to the individual. As Aristotle argues in the *Politics*, he who is without a *polis* is either a god or a beast (1253 a3). Thus, the teachings of Plato and Aristotle both view the individual as part of the state and, as such, in some way belonging to the state and not capable of possessing rights against it.[3]

A review of the history of the rights of man must begin with an understanding of the slow transition that took place from the ancient Greek conception of the state-centered understanding of man to an individual-centered understanding of society that allowed for the evolution of a theory of rights. The significance of this understanding to the present question is that, to a large extent, this transformation from a state-centered to an individual-centered understanding of mankind was made possible by the emergence and development of the concept of natural law (d'Entr'eves 1970, 18).[4]

However, we should not downplay the importance of Greek political theory to the evolution of rights. It was, after all, the Greeks who, through their philosophy, created the idea that human beings were capable of collective self-rule, although it took more than 1,000 years of Roman legal development to put this idea into practice. The idea that the individual has rights distinct and separate from his or her relationship to the state was a later development that, by its nature, was directly dependent upon the foundation laid by this aspect of Roman legal tradition. The single theory that binds this progression of legal developments together is the influence of natural law (Wiltshire 1992, 9).

THE ORIGINS OF NATURAL LAW

Unfortunately, it is not possible to give precise definitions to the various versions of natural law that have existed throughout history. Precise dates for their creation or rise to prominence are difficult. The process of change is more evolutionary than revolutionary and at many times in history, multiple interpretations have vied for superiority or different interpretations have been prominent within different sectors of society, such as the clerical and the secular. It is unlikely that philosophers, theorists, and jurists of the past recognized clear distinctions between the various interpretations of natural law. Most conceptions of natural law are either highly theoretical or vaguely stated, and clear conflicts may have been difficult to identify. In other cases, several interpretations may have been simultaneously operating in a blurred state of confusion, competition, and agreement. However, with historic hindsight, trends in the development of natural law theories can be identified so that different schools of thought emerge.

The question of the nature of law in early primitive societies can be addressed in one of two ways. Either it can be asserted that law did not exist at all and what maintained primitive clans or groupings was a form of competitive authority (or the principle of might makes right), or it would have to be maintained that laws were created as a result of positive enactment. This positive enactment would need to include the promulgation of a law by some recognized authority or lawgiver and the availability of some mechanism for enforcement of the law against those who would break it.[5]

Regardless of what the earliest societies of man looked like, it is clear that, as Western society developed, law came to be preserved as a positive act. Law was created by lawgivers and handed down for all to obey. It was not until the creation and popular use of the Greek alphabet that citizens began any participation in the practice of law. By the fifth or sixth century B.C., the vast majority of Athenians would read and actively participate in the lawmaking process (Burns 1981, 371).

This increased use of the written language brought with it not only the earliest foundations of popular sovereignty, but also the earliest known references to a theory of justice that challenged the predominance of positive law. The earliest two recorded references to ideas that can be seen as the beginning of a theory of natural law can be found in the pre-Socratic works of Heraclitus (d. 478 B.C.) and Sophocles' *Antigone* (441 B.C.). Heraclitus introduced the idea of the eternal principles of nature when he wrote that neither the "gods or man" made the world, but that "it always was and is and shall be." With this thought, Heraclitus introduced the world to the idea that all things are subject to systematic explanation (Havelock 1978, 3). Then, in *Antigone,* a theory of justice is proposed that resembles the principles of natural law in that it asserts the idea of an eternal and immutable justice. In this Sophoclean tragedy, Antigone defies the commands of the mortal Creon that her brother should be left unburied. In defence of her actions, Antigone cites the authority of an "unwritten and unshakable" law of the gods. She speaks of this law as a form of justice that human authority has no power to set aside and that all mortal commandments must express, or ought to express, if they seek to do justice. Thus, she argues that human laws that fail to express this eternal sense of justice forfeit their authority and power to command (Fagles 1984, 82).

These ideas helped raise one of the central questions of Greek philosophy: What is the nature of justice? This question raises the issue of whether all law is properly viewed as a matter of convenience, tradition, or social convention or whether there are laws that exist as a result of man's relationship with the natural world. One of the primary debates of Greek political thought concerns the relationship between *physis* and *nomos*. The Greek Sophists generally distinguished between *nomos* (νομos), or the process by which man creates rules, and *physis* (πhysis), the universal laws that were the product of the gods (Myres 1927, 270; Vinogradoff 1922, 26; Ostwald 1986, 260-273).

This notion that law and justice are two separate concepts and that, in order for a law to be fully binding, it must meet some external standard did not end with one Sophoclean tragedy. It was an idea that came to be reflected within all of the great works of Greek political philosophy. Perhaps this is the greatest contribution of Greek society to the Western world: a philosophy that did not merely accept the world as a sphere controlled by mysticism but sought to answer such questions as. What is the nature of man? What form of government is best for the human animal? What is the nature of justice? These ideas, along with an appeal to some external authority, can be found in the works of Socrates, Aristotle, and Plato. Each of these great thinkers in some way recognized the existence of eternal truths and their binding nature on man.

Socrates recognized that ethical knowledge was conceptual, universally true, and unchanging (Nelson 1982, 18). Plato, on the other hand, attributed a distinction between natural law and positive, or man-made, law to Hippias and saw the principle as dangerous to social order (Barker 1918). While Plato rejected this distinction, Aristotle to a great extent embraced it and, as will be shown later, attempted to apply these ideas to the political world.

It should be noted that the term "law of nature" failed to have any one consistent meaning for the ancient Greeks. However, its principal meaning for that time was in reference to a set of laws that were considered fundamental and in accordance with ancient customs and the nature of man. The law of nature was seen as clearly distinct from legislative enactment, the primary function of which was not to seek justice but, as much as possible, to foster human convenience.

As was stated previously, Aristotle embraced this distinction between the two types of laws and incorporated it into his *Nicomachean Ethics*. Aristotle maintained that there were two distinct types of justice. The first was a type of justice that was in accordance with both the rational principles of man and a natural rule of justice and so was considered intrinsically the best of all possible laws and consequently was everywhere and at all times valid. The second type of justice was of a simpler nature, needing only to be rational for a given locality, and thus was conventional. Laws that fell into this second category were not considered as being necessarily good laws. Such laws could be either good or bad, as they were the product of imperfect human reasoning and pertained only to a particular people (Aristotle 1984, 1294 a7-9). While Aristotle saw the need for both types of justice for the ruling of a city-state, he clearly saw the latter as representing the positive enactments of man for the convenience of a particular people and the other, natural justice, as something that was binding on all, everywhere. In this sense Aristotle asserts the superiority of natural law and maintains that all positive enactments of man must either find their origins in its principles or be in accordance with its dictates (Aristotle 1962, Bk. I, 1098 a7-8, and Bk. V, 1134 b18). Aristotle clearly recognizes the need for man's written laws to be in accordance with natural justice, which was unchanging and applicable to all peoples, in all places, for all the ages of man. Aristotle maintained not only that natural law was superior to positive law, but that the dictates of natural law could be used as a defence against the local laws that violated its principles (Aristotle 1927, 1373 b4 and 1375, a 27).

While the Greek conception of natural law was not precisely defined, it did provide a standard by which positive laws could be judged. The Greek legal system was thus structured in such a way as to protect laws that were considered to be fundamental. These fundamental laws, along with long-standing customary rules, were recognized as being different from ordinary positive enactments in that changes within their makeup were considered to be of particular importance to the citizenry. In fact, these categories of law carried with them such importance that citizens were deemed to have the right to challenge any changes that were made in them as being either inappropriate or unallowable (Calhoun 1923; also see Goodell 1893).

The Greek legal system recognized a dualism within its sense of law and justice. The first consisted of superior customary and natural law, and the second consisted of local, or conventional, law. This same distinction would later be echoed in the medieval church's distinction between divine and civil law. However, with the conquests of Alexander the Great came the demise of the Greek city-state, upon which Greek legal structure had built its theories of justice. As a result, it would fall to the Stoics, not Aristotle, to do the work that would be necessary to popularize an understanding of natural law.

From this humble beginning and from the works of Heraclitus, Sophocles, and Aristotle, the foundational elements of the natural law theory were developed. However, it was the Stoics who used these rudimentary beginnings to develop a theory that could serve as the foundation for both legal and political institutions (Wright 1962, 4-5), a theory that would serve as a cornerstone for much of the development of Western civilization, from the Stoics of the Hellenistic age to the American Revolution of 1776.

The Stoic Philosophy and the Roman Empire

The Stoic school of philosophy was founded in approximately 300 B.C. by Zeno of Citium. The most historically important theory to be developed by this school of thought was the theory of natural law. The Stoics took from Aristotle his theory of a superior law and chose to emphasize its ethical nature. They considered natural law to be a principal guiding force for human action and maintained that its dictates were immanent in the natural universe and could be discerned by the use of human reason. While the Stoic philosophy of natural law still lacked the definition that would be necessary to make it a useful theory on its own, its main contribution to the development of legal thought was that it offered a challenge to the traditional conception that law was nothing more than the codification of tradition or the making of positive laws for human convenience (Wiltshire 1992, 13).

The importance of this development in natural law theory to the question of the "right to die" is that, from its earliest beginnings, natural law took up as one of its principal building blocks the idea that it is a natural tendency for man to seek to preserve himself. In this sense, the Stoics adopt Aristotle's proposition that man's basic drive for self-preservation is one of the key tools by which the human race learns to distinguish between good and evil, that which contributes to the preservation of human life being good and that which is destructive of human life being bad. Through the development of these distinctions, eventually rules of law and ethics were promulgated. Thus the Stoics saw man's drive to preserve his own life as one of the important building blocks of all ethical and legal codes. However, this should not lead us prematurely to the conclusion that natural law can be used to support only one view of the debate about the "right to die." In fact, the Stoic philosophers themselves had an advanced conception of the virtue of a merciful death and believed that such a death was ethical so long as it was in keeping with reason.

For the Stoics, natural law, the authoritative guide to all acts, is to be found in the application of reason to a clear understanding of objective reality. The Stoic philosophy maintained that the natural world was constructed through divine powers and, as a result, to live in accordance with its nature is to live in accordance with the divine principles embedded in it. In addition, they proposed that man could chose to live in accordance with nature or to live against it, but that to live in accordance with reason is to choose to act morally and in keeping with the universal laws of nature (Long 1974, 164-65, 192). Under this philosophy, a virtuous act is determined not by its outcome or its effect on the world but instead by the degree to which the act is in keeping with a rational understanding of nature.

Within the Stoic conception of natural law, there is little room for a theory of rights. Instead, natural law is seen as a set of restrictions that limit the permissible bounds of human action. However, it is important to note that while the Stoics adopt Aristotle's conception of two distinct types of law or justice, *jus gentium,* or universal law, and *jus civile,* or civil law, unlike Aristotle the Stoics recognize for the first time the existence of the autonomous individual, an individual freed from the identity of his society or community and seen as possessing full self-ownership and therefore free to make his or her own moral choices. Of course, this newfound freedom should not be overstated, for while the individual had been carved out from the common identity and restrictions of community, these restrictions were simply replaced by the bondage of natural law (Wiltshire 1992, 17). While the Stoics reinvigorated the theory of natural law, the Romans forged the Stoic philosophy into the practical legal structure that became the foundation of the modern legal system. It is the Romans' use of the Stoic philosophy of natural law in combination with the emergence of the individual that gave birth to the earliest developments of individual rights.

In the hands of Rome, the use of law was transformed from a collection of disconnected local legal codes into a unified legal system capable of handling the growing complexities of both social and commercial life. The Romans were an eminently practical people, not given to excessive creativity; however, their use of law demonstrated a keen ability to examine the laws of newly captured territories and adapt their most productive rules while rejecting all others. Indeed, the Romans were so adept at this process that they were even willing to reject their own legal norms in favor of new ones that had been demonstrated to be more productive (Nicholas 1962, 1-2).

The importance of the influence of Roman law on the Western world should not be underemphasized. The modern state or nation as we know it spends an inordinately large amount of its energy making and enforcing laws, and it is through this act of creation, recognition, and enforcement that the rights of its members evolve. As a direct result of the influence of the Roman legal system, we understand the importance of law to the structure of a society. It is from studying the Roman legal system that political scientists take their understanding of "society," or *societas*, as a collection of peoples organized by private law. Similarly, when political science came to understand government as an authoritative entity that derives its authority not from its own merits but from the people, it simply recognized the Roman concept of *mandatum*.

Rome was a nation possessed by law. Just as in the United States today, Rome ordered all of its social and political relationships through the use of law. It was in Rome that the force of law and those inevitable practitioners of law, the lawyers, first seized the lives of man.[6] Much of our present-day legal system has been influenced by Rome and, as we shall see, the theory of natural law is to a great extent a product of Rome's legal system.

It is clear that the Roman doctrine of natural law was borrowed from Greek philosophy, particularly from the Stoics. The earliest Roman use of a universal law doctrine can be found not in civil or commercial codes, but in the Roman understanding of international law or *jus gentium* (the law of nations). However, Roman use of natural law concepts drastically changed in the hands of the Roman jurist Cicero (106-43 B.C.). Under the influence of Stoic philosophy, Cicero became the leading Roman advocate of the use of natural law principles as a source of civil law principles (Carlyle and Carlyle 1903, 6). He saw natural law as "right reason agreeing with nature and diffused among all, unchanging, everlasting" (Cicero 1965, 20-21). Under Cicero's urging, the *jus gentium* gradually grew to encompass an ever-growing sphere of ordinary civil life. Stoicism provided Cicero with the necessary foundation to impose the "rule of reason," or the force of Roman law, over all the conquered territories of Rome.

By the fifth century A.D., the role of natural law within the Roman legal structure had grown to such an extent that it was recognized as an established part of the legal code. The prevalence and influence of natural law concepts on Roman law was reflected in Emperor Justinian's *Digest* of legal codes (Myres 1927, 309). By this time, natural law had come to represent a collection of idealized standards and principles accessible by human reason and applicable to our daily lives so as to guide us in our efforts to pursue justice (Dickinson 1920, 16-17).

Justinian's *Digest* recognized three distinct sources from which law could be derived. The first was *ius civile*, the law of the state, which were laws of convenience for a particular locality; the second was *ius gentium*, the law of nations, created for international commerce and exchange; and, finally, there was *ius naturale*, the law of nature, which was considered to be the expression of the higher principle, equity (Wiltshire 1992, 21). The Romans developed a legal principle of *ius civile* tempered in its applications by the recognized dictates of *ius naturale* (Haines 1965, 8). For the Romans, natural law provided a mechanism by which they could condense established Roman law and the divergent laws of various captured territories into one coherent standard of justice.

Roman Law and the Development of Rights

Cicero saw natural law as the force of reason that compelled not simply the private citizen but also that citizen's government to recognize given truths and to conform its actions in keeping with its provisions. For Cicero, the binding force of natural law represented the convergence of ethical and legal considerations, dedicating all human affairs to the principle that it is in this realm that justice must be found. Natural law theory provided the meeting place where the universal principles of morality and the temporal existence of human affairs collided and reached agreement. This view of natural law committed the Roman legal system to the proposition that some laws were fundamental in their nature and that they could not be changed by human action. Cicero described this aspect of natural law when he stated that "it is impossible to abolish it entirely. We can never be freed from its obligation neither by the Senate nor by the People" (Cicero 1965). He expressed this view by asserting that positive law was by itself insufficient to govern human affairs. Mankind was seen as too variable, too given to self-interest, too likely to change laws to fit the will of the majority. While there was clearly room for democratic principles within Cicero's ideology, it is also clear that he believed that concepts of justice are not subject to democratic determination. The majority does not determine what is ethically correct or morally just, and therefore some laws are to be held beyond the control of the majority. This point is of particular importance because it is only through the development of this understanding of universal law that the concept of rights can be born (Wiltshire 1992, 24-25).

As stated earlier, the incorporation of natural law principles into the rational structure of Roman law aided in the further emergence of the autonomous individual. As this concept of individuality grew, the idea that individuals possessed rights, not as a part of the community but by virtue of their human birth, also grew. This growth in the concept of rights was not achieved by an extension or grant of privilege from the common community to the individual but rather by an expansion of the idea of laws beyond the broad concept of citizenship. As the power of the Roman Empire spread and its laws took on greater importance and asserted greater influence on the world, the authority of law began to shift from the community to the individual. However, this, in and of itself, did not create what we in the modern world would conceive of as an individual right. Quite to the contrary, Roman law recognized no such rights. Such a concept would have seemed quite odd even to Cicero, because Roman law viewed *iuris civilis* as an outgrowth or consequence of *jus naturale*; one was not seen as superior to the other, but rather both were seen as coequal in their binding forces (Wiltshire 1992, 25-26).

This is not to say that the influence of natural law did not have a significant impact upon the evolution of rights. One of the important by-products of the mixing of Roman law with the Stoic philosophy of natural law was the recognition of the semi-autonomous individual and a dedication within the Roman legal code to the principle of equality. Cicero maintained that natural law mandated the equality of man be held in the highest esteem. He stated that "no two things are so alike one another, so exactly its counterpart, as we all are to one another. Nay, if bad habits and falsehood did not distort weak minds and send them in different directions, no one would be so like his own self as all men would be to all other men. . . . Now all men have received reason and so all men have received justice" (Cicero 1966, I, x, 29; xii, 33). This recognition of the equality of man as one of the basic tenets of natural law came into direct conflict with the Roman practice of slavery despite the fact, as stated earlier, that natural law was not sufficient to overturn the dictates of ordinary civil law. However, as Roman law progressed, later Roman jurists did indeed recognize that slavery was contrary to the *jus naturale* (Haines 1965, 10, n.4). Thus, natural law principles could not override positive law, but could be used as tools to allow jurists to change and adjust the positive law. This was the principal way in which Cicero and, later, Seneca viewed the function of natural law. They saw the *ius naturale* as appealing not to that which *is* but to that which *ought* to be (d'Entre'ves 1965, 23).

Geifferet Samule outlines three historical stages in the evolution of legal rights. The first stage of legal rights has to do almost entirely with physical property, which was what determined an individual's sovereignty within society. The only true subjective right in private law is located in Roman laws of property, that is, between persons and things. The second historical stage, the inductive, was concerned with moving away from the relationship between subject and property and toward the relationship between subject and subject. The third, or deductive, historical stage in the process culminates in such claims as "I have a right to vote" or "I have a right to free speech" (Wiltshire 1992, 28).

In this final stage, the subjective right is freed from the artificial constraints of institutional society and, instead, becomes a means for understanding what constitutes a human being and ultimately for bringing morality and politics together. Despite the great advances within the Roman legal system that were made possible by the incorporation of the Stoic theory of natural law, it would be incorrect to conclude that developments in the Roman legal system brought us into this third stage of the evolution of rights. The true significance of natural law theories within Roman law is not to be found within the creation of right or even within the doctrine of natural law itself but within its function. It allowed the Roman Empire to assert its law into its expanding empire, based on the principle that its laws were believed to have intrinsic value in and of themselves and therefore should be obeyed, not because of Rome's power to compel obedience, but because to follow its laws would be to produce "*quod semper aequum ac bonum est,*" that which is always just and good for all (d'Entre'ves 1965, 30-31).

In review, we can ask, "How does the Roman use of natural law seek to inform us concerning the modern-day questions of individual liberties and rights such as "the right to die?" To be certain, it can not be said that the Roman natural law tradition created such a right; however, it can be argued that it has informed us, to some extent, about a way of exploring the justness of any positive law that would seek to regulate such actions. Roman natural law tradition clearly recognized that self-interest and prejudice made the use of positive law alone insufficient to address some of the most important issues of human life. In this regard, it recognized the proposition that morality and law are unavoidably interconnected and that laws concerning issues of rightness or justice should not be determined by the popular will of the people but by the operation of reason. The Roman tradition of natural law also guides us in the use of that reason, in that it directs our thought not to the factual situation of what practices actually exist in the world but focuses us on our rational understanding of what practices ought to exist. Finally, this natural law tradition is dedicated to the proposition that some laws are held as fundamental to justice and, as such, are beyond the interference of either the government or the majority. In essence, they are issues of justice that pertain to human beings, not by virtue of community membership or citizenship, but by virtue of being human. It is clear that many present-day positivists would attack the proposition that any area of legislation is beyond the power of the majority to address or that natural law principles have the authority to affect the course of the positive law. But such propositions clearly ignore the fact that the Roman natural law tradition never maintained an authority to override positive enactments. Instead, the function of natural law within the Roman legal tradition was to serve as a source of guidance, an appeal to a base rationality or set of fundamental guidelines about what rules are in keeping with human nature and what laws *ought* to apply.

Chapter 7

Natural Law Theory through the Middle Ages

Throughout history the theory of natural law has varied greatly in interpretation, but the main stream has, for the most part, maintained its roots in Greek and Roman philosophy and law. This is clearly the case with the theory of natural law that predominated during the decline of the Roman Empire and the advent of the Middle Ages. As the authority of the Roman Empire began to collapse, it created a power vacuum that needed to be filled. Slowly at first, and then with greater speed and momentum, the Catholic Church expanded its influence and displaced the Empire as the center of authoritative rule-making.

To a large extent, it was the church's incorporation of the natural law theory of the Stoics and Roman law that made this transition possible. Natural law theory provided Christianity, just as it had earlier provided Rome, the necessary vehicle to ethically justify its legal and social structure and its authority. Stoicism provided for an universe that was divinely ordered (d'Entr'eves 1965, 35), and the Roman interpretation of natural law provided a tradition of looking to this divine order for guidance in making the laws necessary for the worldly governance of man. All that was necessary was for the church to give identity to this divine order and add to man's understanding of the universe not only a worldly element but also a heavenly one. Having done so, the church could easily position itself as the arbiter of both worldly natural laws that ordered mankind's earthly existence and divine law that led mankind into a heaven. In essence, the medieval church took the Greek and Roman philosophies of natural law and Christianized them (d'Entr'eves 1965, 34); or, as stated by Wiltshire, "Stoicism was ready for baptism," and "The body of citizens, *corpus civium*, . . . was transformed into the body of Christ, *corpus Christi*" (Wiltshire 1992, 30, 32).

In today's society, many individuals who have any familiarity with the concept of natural law identify it with the variety that became widely accepted during the Middle Ages. This interpretation maintained a correspondence between natural law principles and "higher law," as handed down by God through revelation or scripture. Unlike the pure Roman law doctrine, medieval natural law was viewed as absolutely binding and capable of overruling all other laws. The medieval mind viewed natural law as prior to civil law in existence and authority (Friedberg 1876, I, v, I, sect. 1, I, viii, 2).[1] In its simplest form, the medieval interpretation recognized God as the source of natural law.

As the ideas of Cicero and the Roman jurists were Christianized, their predominance within the Catholic church was further aided by the writings of the Roman jurist Seneca (c. 4B.C.-A.D.65), who originally introduced the theoretical relationship between natural law and "a state of nature" (Carlyle and Carlyle 1903, I:23). The works of St. Ambrose, St. Jerome, and St. Augustine popularized the theories of natural law, as did the work of St. Isadore of Seville, who formulated the statements of natural law that became a part of canon Law (Carlyle and Carlyle 1903, I:104-105, 106). The medieval church's conception of natural law reincorporated the Roman distinction between *ius gentium, ius civilis,* and *jus naturale* was blended into canon law; however, as the theory passed through this translation process, it was unmistakably changed to depart from the Roman and Stoic interpretation in several significant ways. First, the Stoics, just as they rejected Plato's appeal to some transcendent reality, would have found themselves completely at odds with the Catholic Church's introduction of the eternal realm into the natural law equation. For the Stoics, natural law was to be found in the natural world, and to look for it elsewhere would be to pervert the theory. Second, the Stoics viewed human nature as basically good, eliminating any need for an authoritative interpreter of the dictates of natural law (Wiltshire 1992, 33). This contradicted the Christian view that human adherence to natural law principles, as interpreted by the Catholic Church, was necessary to harness the fallen and corrupt nature of man on earth. Thus, while the Stoic interpretation allowed for popular access, the Christian view was necessarily restrictive (d'Entr'eves 1965, 36-37). As a result, the medieval canonists saw the *jus naturale* as being identical with God's law as revealed in the Gospel. It embodied the moral principles that God had implanted in human nature, which encompassed the essence of humanness; as such, it was immutable (Haines 1965, 13).

The difficulty with the Catholic Church's use of natural law theory is that, over time, it took on an increasingly less specific meaning, and eventually the term came to be used as a catchall category used to justify whatever principle the church deemed appropriate at any given time. Consequently, the influence and authority of natural law doctrines began to lose much of their ethical authority (Watson 1971, 235).

As the power of the Catholic Church began to come under attack, St. Thomas Aquinas took on the task of redefining natural law and bringing it back into line with the teachings of Aristotle. This necessitated once again recognizing the importance of the state to the full development of mankind and elevating its role to the top of the authoritative hierarchy. Under such a design, natural law was again viewed as the source of rules that are necessary for the state to attain justice (d'Entr'eves 1965, 38-39; Gierke 1922, 74). Aquinas's suggestion that the state, not the church, should be at the center of law-making was fiercely criticized by many of his contemporaries. As it became inevitable that the church would lose its central role, despite all efforts to retain it, Aquinas's revitalization of natural law theory became the "most authoritative expression of the Catholic view of life" (d'Entr'eves 1965, 39).

Aquinas maintained that natural law was the best source of guidance for man's efforts to attain justice here on earth. He viewed natural law as a reflection of man's human nature and his relationship to God's universe, describing natural law: "As though the light of natural reason, by which we discern good from evil, and which is the Natural Law, were nothing else than the impression of the divine light in us. So it is clear that the Natural Law is nothing else than the participation of the Eternal law of rational creatures" (Aquinas, Ia, 2ae, quae. 91, art. 1 and 2). However, while St. Thomas so idealized natural law, he maintained that it alone was insufficient for the operation of the Christian state. While the dictates of natural law were sufficient to create a functioning state, justice needed the assistance of grace, which could be provided only by God through his church (Wiltshire 1992, 36). Thus, Aquinas distinguished eternal and divine law from natural law, the first emanating from God and the latter representing man's rational application of God's universal laws, which allows him to distinguish between good and evil (Haines 1965, 13). Therefore, for Thomas Aquinas, the proper division of law includes four separate categories: eternal, divine, natural, and positive.

Under such a scheme, eternal, divine, and natural law principles were all equal in authority to the positive proclamations of the civil state. Natural law was seen as having authority independent of the state, and the proper role of the state was to pass only those positive laws that were in keeping with the dictates of natural law. Any government that failed to do so was acting illegitimately and was subject to having its authority challenged (Aquinas, Ia, 2ae, quae. 95, art. 2). Aquinas is the first to say that while the state is a necessary condition for our existence, if it operates in violation of the natural law, we may have a duty to disobey it. It should be noted, however, that this is far from the revolutionary doctrine that would latter be put forward by Locke (Wiltshire 1992, 39). For Aquinas, any government whose rulers tried to promote the common good of its citizens, even if they failed, was to be honored (Carlyle 1869, 126, 141). Without the natural law concept as a bridge, the medieval mind could not have conceived of the secular state as a good expresser of natural morality. However, it was Aquinas's Christianized interpretation of natural law and Aristotelian political theory that allowed for this shift.

While Aristotle saw man as good and government as the perfection of man, Aquinas saw God as the perfecter of man and government as one of his tools, made functional by man's natural sociability that caused human beings everywhere to enter into government. Therefore, natural law not only creates the state but also serves as a basis for judging it. As a result, even though the State may represent the highest expression of man's natural morality on earth, allegiance to it can at best be conditional, for any state can promulgate unjust laws; and, under the medieval interpretation of natural law as put forward by Aquinas, an unjust law is no law at all (Aquinas, 2a, 2ae, quae, 104, art. 6). As a consequence, Aquinas's assertion that a citizen should not obey any law that is in violation of the dictates of natural law validates the place of the individual as the determiner of good and evil. In doing so, he also validated the role of the individual within the authority of the state (Wiltshire 1992, 38). As a result, Aquinas allowed Aristotelian ethics and politics to be grafted to the Christian interpretation of life (d'Entr'eves 1965, 42).

NATURAL LAW IN THE MIDDLE AGES AND THE DEVELOPMENT OF RIGHTS

The natural law theories of Aquinas can easily be converted into a theory of human rights based upon the Christian view of human beings (Maritain 1944). Aquinas's theory of the state is principally a restrictive doctrine, stressing the duties of the secular state as opposed to the rights of individuals. Despite this fact, when we add to Aquinas's propositions that natural law principles are discoverable by the individual and that the state is obligated to obey such principles, we have a theory ripe for the creation of rights. Unfortunately, this medieval interpretation of natural law was not used in that way. Aquinas's theology may have reshaped the role of the Catholic Church in the Western world and provided for the ongoing influence of natural law within its structure, but its predominant influence was to strengthen institutions of power rather than individuals.

As the Roman Empire converted to Christianity in the fourth century, the merger of church law and Roman law led inevitably to the predominance of the monarchial political order, under which the monarch was to be seen as the hand of God supported by the authority of the church. This unsteady alliance between church and state worked remarkably well until the eleventh century, when Pope Gregory VII (1020-1085) sought to greatly expand his authority. As all sides scuffled for power, the study of Roman law and its use of natural law principles was reintroduced in Bologna, for the purpose of strengthening the Papacy, and in Ravenna, where Peter Crassus began using Roman law to try to defend the principle of the "divine right of kings" (Wiltshire 1992, 41-46).

As Wiltshire noted, "The reception of the Roman legal system has a special appeal to ambitious emperors, princes, and even clerics because it placed the state above all interests, both public and private. Roman law did not admit the feudal intermixture of public and private purposes, and, therefore, supported with great efficacy a descending theory of government, whether secular or sacred" (Wiltshire 1992). Within such a system, the individual is clearly a subject to be ruled, rather than a citizen capable of possessing autonomous rights (Wiltshire 1992, 47).

Under medieval church rule the individual cannot be said to possess the most basic of rights. Even property rights were alienated from the individual by church doctrines that placed true ownership of all things in the hands of the Lord

God Creator and recognized the church as the only institution on earth able to act with God's authority. In addition, the principle of human equality, which for Cicero so clearly flowed from the principles of natural law, became little more than a propaganda tool within the political doctrines of the medieval church. Pope Gregory the Great (540-604) had made clear the church's interpretation of the natural law theory of equality when he declared that, although under the dictates of natural law all human beings were clearly equal, to borrow an Orwellian phrase, "some people were more equal than others." Pope Gregory announced this doctrine through the almost mystic statement that "Nature created all men equal, but by a varying order of their merits, an occult dispensation ranked some behind others" (Wiltshire 1992, 48).

Although it may seem that the Middle Ages had no effect on the development of individual rights, in the long run, the effect was quite significant. While the glorification of monarchial rule seems far removed from the idea of individual liberty, medieval doctrines opened up the way for the theories that would one day undermine the authoritative basis for such royal hierarchial systems. Natural law theory in the Middle Ages led to the creation of a crack in the absolute power of "God's representatives on earth" or "the divine right of kings." This crack can be found in the most humble beginning of a theory of inalienable rights. While it is true that within the political structure of the Middle Ages no individual could lay claim to anything resembling an inalienable right, it is also clear that a theory of corporate entities was beginning to develop and maintained the existence of inalienable corporate rights that could be used to restrain even the king. This development is reflected in thirteenth-century Roman canon law, which recognized that the ongoing survival of corporate entities required the existence of guaranteed rights. Additionally, at the same time as the power of kingdoms was growing, the way in which the authority of the king was viewed began to shift from that of absolute dominance to that of guardian. As a result, the common good of the people came to be recognized as a collective inalienable right, which one day would be expanded to provide bases for the creation of individual rights (Wiltshire 1992, 48-49).

NATURAL LAW AND THE RENAISSANCE AND REFORMATION

The historical period of time known as the Renaissance (1300-1600 A.D.) brought with it many changes in the political philosophy of the West that are pertinent to an understanding of individual rights. It is during this period that the faint beginnings of individual rights, which were outlined in the previous section, begin to reach their full voice and ultimately reach their crescendo in the American and French revolutions. It is during this period that the political affairs of the West were once again separated from the religious, resulting in a secular view of natural law.

The evolution of English law raises a matter of subtle controversy when one begins to speak of natural law and the evolution of fundamental rights. One view of this subject would maintain that England was sufficiently isolated from

Rome by its geography and culture, so that the Roman doctrine of natural law had little to no effect on its legal development, and that English law developed primarily as a result of the recognition of customary practices (McIlwain 1910, 51-53). Others maintain that there is a clear connection between the evolution of English common law and the natural law theories of the preceding ages. Advocates of this position point to the heavy reliance of the common law on the use of "reason" as a standard of justice and the role of English jurists as advocates of natural law doctrines (McIlwain 1910, 51-53; Plucknett 1922). To be sure, both positions can be supported by strong arguments; however, close evaluation would suggest that, while the feudal English system did develop with a great deal of independence, its development was, to some extent, influenced by natural law theories and that its influence provided important support for the emergence of individual rights.

The evolution of the feudal system, to a great extent, not only allowed English law to develop in isolation but also allowed for the development of a multitiered system of authority that placed a great deal of power in the central ranks of authoritative structure. Within the feudal hierarchy the lord had a given number of vassals under him, upon whom he depended for the control of his lands. As a result, a form of mutual dependence evolved that empowered not only the lord but also his vassals. The traditional practices that arose concerning this relationship were slowly recognized as England's common law—a law that, from its beginnings, sought not just to protect the power of the lords but also to protect vassals from the monarchical tendencies of their lords. Thus, the first vestiges of political power were placed in a class of individuals, not as a community, but as individuals (Ullmann 1975, 53-62).

Under such a system, a vassal's oath of loyalty to his lord was considered to be a personal commitment that could be withdrawn at any time the lord failed to meet his obligations to the vassal or attempted to overreach his appropriate bounds of authority. Such an arrangement clearly supports the notion that feudal vassals conceived of themselves as holding rights as individuals, rather than as some loose community. It also demonstrates that the feudal system of monarchical rule was one of limited powers in which a balance, rather than a monopoly, on the right of political control predominated (Ullmann 1975, 68).

While it is clear that the beginnings of the English common law tradition occurred in relative isolation from natural law traditions, it is also clear that this isolation was not long lived and that natural law theories slowly began to creep into the common law. By the thirteenth century, the theory of natural law was clearly popular among the ecclesiastical chancellors (lawyers), who considered it to be an important part of the law of "equity." References to its authority can be found in the duties imposed by "reason," as well as "God's law" and the "law of nature" (Holdsworth 1922, 216). Thus, the influence of natural law doctrine over the development of the common law of England is to be found primarily in the influence of Roman Church clerics.

Robert N. Wilkin maintained that the influence of Roman law, with its underlying principles of natural law, was "so completely accepted in England that Englishmen thought it their own." He maintains that "it never was foreign after the twelfth, or early part of the thirteenth, century. It had an extensive influence on Bracton and, through him, on Cole. While we think of Cole as particularly a champion of the common law, his principles were the same as those of Roman and natural law" (Wilkin 1947, 228-229). The importance of Bracton's work is that he based his arguments for limiting the powers of the king directly on his understanding of the law of nature, as taken from the Roman law (Carlyle and Carlyle 1903, III:34). In any event, while it is clear that Roman law had influence over the development of the common law and the jurists who interpreted it, the extent of this influence is a matter of continuing debate. Written records show only rare references to "the law of nature," or natural law, within the historic development of the law of equity, while references within the development of mercantile law are slightly more frequent, but still uncommon (Pollock 1901, 11).

The true importance of natural law theories to this age is that they provided support for those traditions and customs that had been developed during the feudal period, thus allowing an argument for their fundamental charter to be put forward. It was this compatibility that established the necessary conditions for the emergence of individual rights that were to come. The events of the feudal age left fertile ground that would be seized upon by political thinkers, following the Reformation, and that would lead to the growth of natural rights theory (Ullmann 1975, 97).

The Reformation brought with it the force required to strip away the medieval religious content from natural law and open it up to become a revolutionary theory. As a result, political theorists were once again able to separate natural law from godly admonition and concentrate on a view of natural law that glorified human reason. One of the earliest glimmers of this separation of natural law from its medieval religious content came from the scholar Pietro Pomponazzi, who argued, in opposition to the orthodox view of the church, that human reason was a tool for the making of ethical decisions and that theology, while helpful, was not a necessary component of an ethical life. This theory represented the final victory of Aristotelian worldly philosophy, with its appeal to human observation and reason, over the Platonic need for access to some form of transcendent reality (Cassirer 1992, 66).

By throwing off the restraints of the medieval church, natural law theorists were once again able to concentrate on the rationality of mankind and the importance of the human being as an active player in the political and ethical realms of life. Under the mantle of the church, the ability of the individual to play any significant role in the political life of his community had been reduced to the level of obedience. Acceptance into the "Body of Christ" brought with it a loss of identity and independent political authority. However, the decline of political power within the Roman Catholic church as a result of the Reformation brought with it the emergence of a new conception of the individual. Unlike the past, this concept was not an individual whose identity was tied to community, citizenship, or church; it was an individual who had independent authority over the various affairs of life—an individual whose religious, political, and ethical decisions could be made independently of one another. In essence, we see an emerging understanding of mankind as an autonomous, rational individual rather than a subject (Wiltshire 1992, 67).

This resecularization of natural law theory became popular, not only among political theorists but also among many of the leading jurists of the period (Coleman 1914, 119-120). In fact, the secular interpretation of natural law became so ardent that, by the sixteenth and seventeenth centuries, Spanish jurists openly maintained that the principles of natural law were binding not only on mankind and his political institutions, but on God himself. While not all interpretations of natural law were so extreme that they sought to limit God or even maintained that natural law was part of the will of God, they all agreed that the principles of natural law were discoverable by right reason in accordance with nature and, as a result, its dictates were immutable. It was widely maintained that any laws that contradicted its principles were, by their very nature, without authority (Dunning 1905, 13, 132). Spanish jurists also believed that natural law began to concentrate upon the rights of man and the absolute duty on the part of the state to protect these rights. Such rights were held to be the product of the natural condition of equality, which has originally been posited as part of natural law theory by Cicero, some eighteen centuries earlier (Pound 1922, 82-83).

This secular foundation of natural law established the two necessary conditions for the emergence of a revised theory of natural rights. The first condition was the development of the rationalist theory of mankind, and the second condition was an understanding of a social order in which all men were governed by law, rather than by God's appointed rulers. The stage was set for a return to the Aristotelian and Stoic conception of natural law, but this time it would need to be modified to account for the existence of the autonomous individual. As a result, it would become necessary to develop a conception of natural rights upon which the existence of the individual could be based (Wiltshire 1992, 67).

Natural law theory of the eighteenth century is thus characterized by four primary shifts in the understanding of the underlying social order: Religious tenets no longer served as the central focus of social relationships; the communal conception of the individual gave way to the recognition and existence of autonomous individuals, each with the ability to effect public life; the development of an understanding of the human animal that recognized an innate ability to make moral choices based on a rational understanding of natural law; and the recognized existence of natural rights and their ability to overcome the acts of a corrupt government. In the end, the most important contribution of eighteenth-century natural law theory is that it sets the stage for the emergence of the individual as an autonomous political force. For the first time in history, the individual is elevated to the status of a being who possesses rights and powers that stem not from his or her community, nation, or tribe but rather from the virtue of human birth.

Chapter 8

The Development of Natural Rights Theory

While by the eighteenth century the history of political thought had evolved to the point that the individual was emerging from the protective shell of society, it would take the development of individual rights to bring the autonomous individual into political reality. Some historians have argued that political theory, since the time of Cicero, has inherently implied the existence of "rights" based on the Stoic conception of equality (McIlwain 1964). This position faces several obstacles.

First, when we examine political thought from the dominance of Rome to the eighteenth-century, we clearly find philosophic continuity concerning the appropriate relationship of man to society lacking. While Roman thought did not separate the individual from his or her society, Christianity viewed each individual as a distinct moral entity incorporated into the body of the church, thus removing any autonomy the citizen may have possessed. Both of these conceptions conflict with the eighteenth-century view of the autonomous individual, who is now freed from the constraints of church and community.

The second major obstacle to the continuity of rights theory is that different political theories conceived of human rationality differently. Although each of the major periods that we have reviewed depended in some way on natural law, along with its appeal to human reason, what each of these theories meant by reason varied widely. For the Romans, reason was not something exercised by an individual; rather, it was conceived of as something akin to the common experience of the community. Similarly, while natural law theory of the medieval period recognized the individual, rationality was not considered to be inherent in the human animal, but was a gift from God; the test of man's rationality was not common understanding, but conformity with the Church's interpretation of divine law. The eighteenth-century conception of individual rationality, freed from the constraints of community or church, departs radically from both of these conceptions. No longer was there a need for external conformation of individual judgments, and rationality was now considered to be a self-evident part of human nature.

One of the earliest advocates of natural rights based on natural law theory was Hugo Grotius (1583-1645), who authored *The Laws of War and Peace* in 1625. In this work, Grotius attempted to devise a completely secular theory of natural law, a theory of law from which the necessity of God and His divine law has been withdrawn. Thus, Grotius conceived of natural law as providing the basis for a theory of rights that are inherent to mankind as a result of his humanity alone. According to Grotius, such rights were said to belong to each person as a result of his individual birth and were considered to be inalienable. These rights were not thought to be separate from natural law principles, but were sanctioned or supported by natural law and therefore discoverable by the application of human reason and the conditions of human existence (Haines 1965, 50). In this sense, Grotius viewed natural law not as the dictates of Godm but as reflections of man's role in an ordered universe that, once created by God, incorporates particular immutable truths that cannot be changed, short of the destruction of this same universe. In this way, he maintained that natural law was based on a set of fixed principles, or conditions, and its dictates could be judged by virtue of their inherent cohesion and logical clarity. Grotius sought to anchor his theory of natural law to a set of immutable principles similar to mathematical truths, which, although they cannot be seen, are recognized as being as true and valid as those things that we perceive with our external senses (Grotius 1925).

While much of Grotius's theory is reminiscent of earlier works, particularly those of Seneca of Rome (Radin 1923, 288), his approach to the theory was unique. Grotius's approach to natural law problems was highly scientific. Although many theorists maintained similar views of the origin of natural law principles, Grotius was the first to argue that natural law should be viewed in the same sense as mathematics. He argued that natural law was capable of producing general rules of human conduct and was appropriately dealt with on the level of abstractions in the same way that mathematicians deal with numbers. For Grotius, natural law was not suited to answering specific questions concerning human history but produced only general principles of natural law (Wiltshire 1992, 69). Thus, Grotius' work had a tremendous influence on the political theory of the seventeenth and eighteenth centuries; his contention that, "The law of nature is a dictate of right reason which . . . has in it a quality of moral baseness or moral necessity; and that, in consequence, such an act is either forgiven or enjoined by the author of nature God" (Grotius 1925), has been echoed in the works of such political theorists as Pufendorf, Vattel, Leibniz, and even Montesquieu.

As a result of this transition, natural law theories became the fuel for revolutionary ideas that threatened the dominance of both church and state. Protestant philosophers began to systematically challenge the Catholic view of the state and its limited powers. The advocates of imperial rule used the law of nature, as divined by human reason, as a weapon against the papacy; and the church maintained that, while natural law may indeed incorporate ideas of freedom and equality, these conditions were soon destroyed by the fall of man and his ongoing sinfulness.

Indeed, natural law theory was important to the struggle for dominance between the church and secular kings and princes, and natural law soon fueled a strong philosophical debate concerning the "divine right of kings" (Gierke 1934, 37). This debate was expressed by the works of such influential political philosophers as Hobbes,[1] Spinoza, and Austin. As the debate grew, it eventually eclipsed the medieval conception of natural law, abandoning it in favor of a more secular version that identified the state, rather than the church, as the only legitimate source of law. It was largely this new interpretation of natural law, with its full recognition of the individual, that finally put to rest the medieval conception of the group identity of man. In its place, it left a radical theory of the state based on the precepts of natural law. As a result, a foundation was laid for the emergence of a theory of state supremacy that would eventually become one of the principal dogmas of the modern political age.

The work of Samuel Pufendorf was an important step in the development of the philosophic thought that shaped the politics of this new age. Pufendorf continued Grotius' efforts to detheologize the law of nature and to identify it as the product of right reason that could be used to identify human conduct as either right or wrong. It was through his work that natural rights theory gained its emphasis on the idea that individuals possessed rights, independent of either society or the state, and that these rights were part of man's inheritance from the state of nature (Coleman 1914, 311). It was this emphasis on the inheritance, as it unfolded from man's natural condition, that led to the development of social contract theory.

NATURAL RIGHTS AND SOCIAL CONTRACT THEORY

The emergence of social contract theory clearly delineates the full development of the individual within natural law theory. The concept of the social contract has, as its foundation, the idea that all human beings are autonomous individuals of equal political authority, who are free to enter into or abstain from entering into a mutually beneficial contract. In this sense, the development of contract theory can be seen as a necessary step in the evolution of natural rights. By incorporating individualism and the emerging theory of the modern state into the theory of natural law, social contract theory served as unifying theory for rights (d'Entr'eves 1965, 57-59).

Thus, contract theory is appropriately conceived of not as a theory of law or government but rather as a theory of rights that posits the existence of autonomous individuals—individuals who have value and political authority independent of any government, group membership, or the existence of some divine and involved creator. It implies that the human relationships that exist prior to the creation of a social contract are governed by the relationship of mankind to nature, while at the same time nothing in this theory demands that this human interaction will be harmonious or even comfortable. For this reason, human beings are said to enter into a contract so that the protection of the modern state could be brought to bear on, and into line with, the existence of natural rights (d'Entr'eves 1965, 59).

In the progression of contract theory, Thomas Hobbes and his *Leviathan* (1651) set the stage for the shift from political theories that favored the authority of kings to those that recognized the principles of popular sovereignty. Prior to Hobbes' political theory, strong debate existed concerning the nature of sovereignty. Some maintained a belief in simple or absolute sovereignty, which recognized an absolute right to authoritative power by either a king or the people directly. Other theorists advocated for the concept of double sovereignty, which recognized a limited right of sovereignty in the ruler but also continued to recognize the sovereignty of the subjects that limited the power of the king. However, with the triumph of social contract theory over rival theories of political order, the conception of political authority became so individualized that there could no longer be any debate about its source. It flowed from the individual to society through a social contract; the sovereignty of all government representatives, whether monarchy, aristocracy, or representative democrats, owed their authority to the collective agreement of those individuals who authorized its existence. Thus, Otto Gierke states that in the end it is

> a purely "collective" interpretation of personality of the people which really predominates in the natural law theory of the state. The people are made co-extensive with the sum of its constituent units; and yet simultaneously, when the need is felt for a single bearer of the rights of the people, it is treated as essentially a unit in itself. The whole distinction between the unity and the multiplicity of the community is reduced to a mere difference of point of view. (Gierke 1934, 46-47)

Gierke maintains that, in the end, the elevation of this living unity to the rank of a person (corporation) is little more than a legal fiction.

The importance of this shift in the understanding of sovereignty is that under Hobbes' social contract theory the concept of the common will was seen as little more than the agreement of individual wills. As a result, it was recognized that in order for any community to act with legitimate authority, it was necessary for every individual to participate positively in the decision-making process. While it could not be expected that such a standard of universality could be maintained for every decision, Hobbes argued that it could be maintained on two points: first, on the original agreement to create civil government and, second, on all alterations to the original agreement. Hobbes said that, on all other matters, a simple majority vote was sufficient (Gierke 1934, 47).

Hobbes proposed that when faced with the choice of living within the state of nature or entering into society, the autonomous individual would rationally choose to surrender all his natural rights to some common government. For Hobbes, mankind is to be understood as being dominated by a lust for power that so interferes with his social relationships that man rationally chooses to subjugate himself to government. In his view, life within the state of nature is so unpleasant, "nasty, brutish, and short," that "any government is better than no government." Although Hobbes rejected the necessity of natural law principles for a foundation of natural rights, John Locke (1632-1704) recognized human freedom as nothing less than mankind's knowledge of the law of nature. Locke maintained that the law of nature established a body of restrictive rules that limited the conduct of mankind within the state of nature. He argued that these principles of natural law were accessible to mankind by operation of reason and that reason dictated that the principles of equality and independence were the fundamental conditions of the state of nature. In this sense, Locke argued that natural law provided a group of binding principles, according to which mankind could stop acting, but against which mankind could never morally act (Locke 1970, 193). Thus, Locke distinguished between the principles of natural law and natural rights, but he saw the two principles as necessarily connected. For Locke, natural law represented a set of dictates or obligations, similar to the medieval conception of natural law with which Locke himself was most familiar. However, Locke maintained that, as a result of the existence of these restrictive conditions on human action, a set of opposing natural rights could be said to exist. In this way, Locke developed a doctrine of natural rights that recognized these rights as a part of man's pre-societal/political condition; principal among these rights were the rights to life, liberty, and property (Locke 1970, 9).[2]

Locke maintained that natural law, in conjunction with the state, by design serves the function of establishing and protecting the inalienable rights of the individual. While Locke's view of human nature is far more positive than that of Hobbes, he still alleges that human beings by their nature are inherently protective of their own rights and abusive of others and that it is to control this nature of man that civil government is formed by universal consent or social contract. Therefore, Locke saw the social contract as representing an of-all, between-all, to replace the war of "all against all." Thus, the main function of this contract comes to transfer to civil government the right to make and enforce positive law. However, the individual does not surrender those natural rights that are necessary to maintain individuality. For example, citizens do not surrender their right to the use of individual judgment or their right to revolt against any government that violates the dictates of natural law or the social contract (Wiltshire 1992, 79). Locke interpreted natural law as binding, not only on the individual in the state of nature but also on the legislature once society was formed under the social contract. Any legislative acts that violated the fundamental principles of natural law were, in his opinion, not properly to be considered as law (Locke 1970, 8-14).

In this sense, Locke can be seen as a philosophical descendant of the theories of Aristotle, rather than Plato.[3] Locke closely agreed with Aristotle's conception of fundamental law, recognizing it as immutable law that was either divine in origin or the product of right reason and was common to and binding on all of mankind and, indeed, the universe itself. Conversely, he maintained that there were practical positive laws that were made by man and necessary for an organized life, but that they were destined to be in continual conflict with this universal law. Positive law was thus an attempt to elaborate or apply the basic principles of natural law to the everyday world of the human animal. As such, positive law could not hope to meet the idealistic standards of the natural law but, at best, to approximate them (d'Entr'eves 1965, 22-23). In addition, Locke maintained that human beings were not capable of acquiring perfect knowledge and, therefore, could not determine absolute truth. The importance of this idea is that no authoritarian form of government can be justified by a claim of omnipotence or truth, since only basic moral principles are determinable (Wiltshire 1992, 77).

Even though the contract theories of Locke and Hobbes varied greatly, the basic elements of the contract remained the same. The contract represents the collective force of human will acting to establish a previously nonexistent relationship of mutual obligation, an obligation that does not exist simply by the force of natural law. The substantial elements of this contract represent the natural rights of the individual, which are either surrendered to society in exchange for a set of positive rights of equal or greater value, as in the theories of Hobbes and Rousseau, or continue to remain with the individual, in which case the only function of the civil government created by the contract is to secure these rights, which is the position that Locke maintained (d'Entr'eves 1965, 57).

The significance of this shift of emphasis for the development of American law should not be underemphasized. In his work, Locke advocates a revolutionary theory of popular sovereignty, constitutional limitations, and individual rights. In making this argument, he ties his theory to the principles of natural law and natural rights as discerned by human reason, maintaining that human beings are born naturally possessing rights by virtue of their relationship with nature. Locke does not make use of positive legislative acts, the common law, or tradition to provide the authority needed for these rights. Instead, he maintains that the existence of these rights is natural to the human animal.

Locke radically alters historical understanding of natural law theory so as to create a foundation for natural rights, creating a foundation by identifying the social contract as the central element for the recognition of natural rights. Susan Ford Wiltshire captured the spirit of Locke's shifting view of natural law, when she wrote that "Locke's accomplishment was that he moved from worshipping natural law as a static abstraction to affirming it as the moral infrastructure of tolerance and freedom, providing what we might call a pre-ethical proposition. That is, natural law now underlies rather than determines human freedom and worth" (Wiltshire 1992, 80).

For example, these ideas laid the foundation for the opinions expressed by American jurists that the arbitrary acts of a legislature may be void, even when not expressly prohibited by the Constitution, if they have failed to act within their appropriate legislative character (Haines 1965, 23). Locke's view of natural law demands that mankind never be enslaved by absolute government. Unlike Hobbes, Locke viewed individual freedom not as a historic fact of the state of nature, but as an essential moral right embodied by it. Therefore, when we refer to natural law, we do not refer to the law proper but to the rights that belong to each of us as a result of the foundation of that law, just as the right to act must be presumed before the rules of action can be laid down (d'Entr'eves 1965, 60-61).[4]

Locke makes it clear that the evolution of natural rights theory could never have taken place without the theory of natural law, and its acceptance is entirely dependent upon the Roman incarnation of the theory that so strongly emphasizes the importance of the rule of law. In this way, the Roman legal tradition was transformed by the humanists of the sixteenth century from a corporate legal theory into the theory of natural rights of the seventeenth and eighteenth centuries, whose main function was to sustain the individual against the corporate entity (Wiltshire 1992, 88). It was this radical conception of natural law and natural rights theory, so far removed from its original corporate nature, that traveled to America.

Chapter 9

The Evolution of Natural Law Theory and the "Right to Die"

While the makeup of natural law theory has varied greatly over the centuries, the foundational principles common to all interpretations find their origin in the human desire to discover some external, immutable yardstick by which we can determine the justness of mankind's particular opinions, theories, and acts. We seek this standard to determine which principles our societal norms should express and which our civil laws ought reflect. We seek this measure because we believe it represents the minimal standards of justice without which no government can rightly possess the authority to command.

This standard of justice has been conceived of as a higher law, alternatively finding its authority not in the majority opinion of man or in the use of force, but in God, right reason, or an understanding of man's relationship to the natural order of the universe and those rules that flow from his creation within it. This type of law is not made but discerned, discovered, or revealed. It is a law that is concerned not with the will of the majority, but with standards for ethics and politics. It was this inevitable movement of the human spirit that compelled the creation and recreation of the theory of natural law and sustains its existence over twenty-one centuries of human history. But now, before we move on to explore the uniquely American interpretation of the theories of natural law and natural rights, it is wise for us to pause, not to examine the broader implications of this theory but to explore how these ideas have historically affected the answer to the question that represents the main issue of this work: "the right to die."

The origin of the word "suicide," with all its negative connotations, as a way of describing the act of self-killing is a relatively recent development within the human language, seeming to date from approximately 1662 (Westcott 1885, 31). This should not be taken to mean that self-killing is simply a phenomenon of the modern age. Reports of self-killing can be found in the oldest written records of mankind. For example, references to such acts can be found in the earliest examples of classical Greek literature such as the Epikaste and the

Oedipus myth, the narratives of Homer and the Homeric poems (Mair 1921, 12, 26-27).

The phenomenon of self-killing is not new to the modern age; however, it may surprise modern readers to learn that our current debate about the propriety of self-killing, suicide, and euthanasia is also not a modern dilemma, but, in fact, represents an important issue within the entire history of the theory of natural law. Although the act of taking one's own life appears always to have been a part of human history, attitudes concerning such an act have been anything but constant and fixed. For example, during different periods of history, acts of self-killing have been either glorified as noble deeds or condemned as one of the darkest sins against the Creator. However, as attitudes have shifted and waned, one attribute concerning views on self-killing has remained surprisingly constant. In almost all cases, rules and attitudes concerning the propriety of self-killing have been influenced in some way by an appeal to an external standard of justice, either made a part of or directly related to natural law theory.

As mentioned earlier, there is no lack of references to acts of self-killing among the ancient Greeks; however, surprisingly, the contemporary literature conveys no condemnation of such acts. Quite to the contrary, there is a clear tendency within early Greek literature to elevate literary instances of self-killing to the level of heroic acts. Within this literary tradition, the act of taking one's own life is portrayed as an act of great bravery, sacrifice, or even virtue. Apparently, this attitude was not limited to the confines of literary works, for no evidence can be found to suggest that Athenian civil law considered such acts to be an offense against the community (Mair 1921, 12, 29-30).

The lack of civil condemnation of self-killing in Athenian law should not be taken to mean that there was universal agreement on the appropriateness of such acts. Early Western philosophical debate about the propriety of self-killing generally focused on the quasi-religious grounds that self-killing would be displeasing to the gods, and so it was with Socrates when, in the *Phaedo,* he states:

> There is a doctrine whispered in secret that man is a prisoner who has no right to open the door and run away; this is a great mystery which I do not quite understand. Yet I too believe that the gods are our guardians, and that we men are a possession of theirs. . . . Then, if we look at the matter thus, there may be reason in saying that a man should wait, and not take his own life until God summons him, as he is now summoning me. (Plato 1927, 54)

In this passage, and the lines that follow, Socrates expressed a belief that mankind is a possession of the gods and that to take one's life prematurely will result in some form of punishment, perhaps in the afterlife, if there if one. It is interesting to note that Socrates concluded that his taking of the executioner's poison was permissible since he believed that he had been called by the gods to do so. In this way, Socrates leaves us with the proposition that while self-killing is generally wrong, not all acts of self-killing can be condemned.

The difference between the two categories seems to be whether or not one has been called home by the gods, a determination that is ultimately personal.

Similar to Socrates, both Pythagoras and Plato condemned self-killing, Pythagoras on purely religious grounds and Plato because he saw such acts as violating man's essential nature, as well as being acts against God. Aristotle also objected to acts of self-killing, but on entirely different grounds than Plato and Socrates. Aristotle, whose theories were heavily relied on by John Locke (Locke 1970), maintained that it was part of mankind's nature to seek pleasure and to preserve himself and that it was this human attribute that served as one of the important tools in distinguishing between good and evil (Aristotle 1962, A4). Therefore, if man rationally follows his true nature, he should be inclined to preserve himself. However, Aristotle's main objection to self-killing was not that it violates man's nature, for the avoidance of pain could justify such an act, but rather that such an act is a threat to the authority of the community. As cited previously, Aristotle did not conceive of human beings as possessing any clear sense of self-ownership. For Aristotle, the citizen belonged to the state; as such, any citizen who took his own life was guilty of taking that which rightly belonged to the community (Aristotle 1984, 1337a 8-29).

While those philosophers who established the early foundations of Western political thought clearly disapproved of self-killing, principally on religious grounds, this attitude took a radical shift with the introduction of the Stoic philosophy. Unlike their predecessors, the Stoics evolved a positive philosophy of self-killing that left decisions of life and death in the hands of the individual (Lecky 1938, 76). Within the Stoic philosophy of natural law, the individual was seen as the sole authority in determining the time and manner of his own death. As was shown earlier, this philosophy of natural law viewed each human being as free and equal and, therefore, in full possession of his own life. For the Stoics, possession of one's life meant not only the right to be treated equally, but the right to determine the course of one's existence, even to the extent of determining when that existence will end. Hence, the Stoic morality of self-killing was not a matter for public dispute. If an individual found himself in an intolerable state of existence, the option of terminating one's own life was not only free of stigma, but was acceptable (Mair 1921, 12, 31).

The Stoics thus inherited an atmosphere of civil ambivalence but philosophic/religious disapproval of self-killing from their Greek predecessors. However, simultaneously, the cultural and governmental structures that served as the foundations for the Greek understanding of the nature of man were being destroyed. The process that had begun with the Peloponnesian wars (431 B.C.–404 B.C.) and had continued under the hands of Alexander the Great swept from existence the social structure of the Greek city-state that so defined the Greek conception of man and community. As the dominance of Rome grew and the authority of Roman law expanded, philosophical understandings of the nature of man radically changed. While the Stoic philosophers of the Roman age were not quite ready to herald the emergence of the autonomous individual, neither were they willing to conceive individual human beings as something that was owned by the community. Under Stoic philosophy the human being had become an individual, but an individual who was bound by the dictates of natural law as embodied in the Roman legal system. Therefore, the Stoics conceived of the individual not as free from all constraints, but as free to form one's own judgments concerning those personal matters of life that were not rightly subjects of positive law; even then, the constraints of natural law applied.

Under these constraints, the Stoics saw the human being as an entity capable of making his or her own decisions regarding matters of personal destiny. While the state had the right to protect itself from extreme peril or to force military service for the protection of its existence, it was seen as having no authority over the issue of personal existence. For the Stoics, the state would have been acting beyond its proper authority if it were to try to interfere with an individual's decision to continue living or to die, because to enter into such a realm would be to remove from mankind the freedom that natural law dictated he must have.

Although this attitude was widely accepted among Stoic philosophers, Seneca (4 B.C.–65 A.D.) became its principal advocate. The Stoic philosophy of self-killing is embedded in their understanding of natural law. They viewed mankind as an animal with a noble existence, an animal possessing the physical embodiment of the soul, which is of great value in the whole of the physical universe, distinguishing mankind from lower animals and giving us liberty and dignity, which set us apart as free and equal creations. However, it is important to understand that while the Stoics recognized the existence of a soul, they did not recognize it as a distinct entity from the body; therefore the soul, like the body, was viewed as something ruled by those natural laws that govern the physical universe. As a part of the physical world, the Stoics viewed mankind as an animal gifted with the ability to use reason, and each individual was free to use his or her reason to determine the propriety of life or death.

Under this philosophy, self-killing was free from any negative social stigma, and the right of an individual to determine the time and manner of his or her own death was unquestioned. Thus, under Roman law, the morality of suicide was not an issue of dispute. Seneca recommended that the aged should feel free to take their own lives once their age and health had left them with little to face other than undignified decay. Old age, painful or chronic illness, or malignancy all served as clear justifications for taking one's own life. Under such conditions, the Stoics maintained that self-killing could not be considered inappropriate.

When we examine the acceptance within Stoic philosophy of acts of self-killing, we discover that they did not believe that death was good or in any way preferable to a healthy existence. Quite to the contrary, the Stoics frowned on what they would have seen as cowardly acts of self-killing to avoid one's responsibilities in life (van Hooff 1990, 125). For the Stoics, the main justification for ending one's existence was directly tied to questions concerning the quality of life, conceiving mankind as an animal that was intended to lead a healthy existence that allowed him to use his rational capabilities to understand the universal laws of nature. If at any time persistent ill health or old age interfered with these important qualities of life, it was permissible, but in no way mandatory, for one to terminate one's existence (van Hooff 1990, 124).

In this sense, the Stoics did not see rational acts of self-killing to avoid the degrading experiences of illness or disease as an offense against the gods, but did see irrational acts of self-killing, akin to what we mean by "suicide" today, as sacrilegious events to be prevented. The distinction between the two categories of actions rests with a distinction between rationality and irrationality. If a person rationally views his or her life and, after drawing up a balance sheet, sees that death is preferable to life, then, in a free and rational act, one may end one's own life. However, self-killing out of irrationality, depression, or fear of responsibility was to be avoided. For example, Seneca saw self-killing as a act of individual freedom, an act that could liberate the individual from the oppression of illness or government, and so he maintained that the old and the ill should take it upon themselves to release the soul from the body once illnesses or status in life had rendered them or seriously threatened to render them incapable of fulfilling their functions as rational human beings (van Hooff 1990, 190).[1]

The Roman justification for the authority of law was strongly influenced by the Stoic philosophy of natural law. Under early Roman law, self-killing was generally considered to be permissible, with only a few types of suicide deserving the attention of the state. For example, Roman law clearly saw acts of self-killing prior to being officially brought to trial as an admission of guilt that resulted in the confiscation of the defendant's property, as well as a denial of ordinary burial rights. It is important to note, however, that this punitive action was taken not because of the suicide but because of the assumed guilt of the actor (van Hooff 1990, 167-168).

Similarly, Roman law viewed self-killing among the armed forces as an acts of desertion. If a soldier was unsuccessful in his attempt to kill himself, he faced a possible punishment of death upon his recovery. However, in practice the emperors and jurists recognized many mitigating circumstances that softened such actions. For example, if a soldier could demonstrate that his act had been motivated by unbearable physical suffering, disease, or mourning, among other excuses, his punishment could be severely moderated or vacated all together (van Hooff 1990, 172).

Under Roman law, acts of self-killing by the average citizen drew little attention. While one's passing may have been noted, normal succession rights were permitted to the relatives left behind. All that was necessary was that the aot be attributed to any number of permissible factors, including, but not limited to, tedium, sickness, grief, insolvency, or madness (Masaryk 1970, xxviii). However, it must be understood that the Roman state and its jurists did not view themselves as moralists. Their job was not to rule on the moral rightness of an act, but to determine whether it fit into to the dictates of Roman law; under the Roman jurists' interpretation of natural law, it clearly did. After all, under Roman law, even slaves were considered to have the natural right "to rage against their own body" (van Hooff 1990, 171).

The influence of this Stoic philosophy extended not just to its followers, but into the very heart of Rome (Burns 1984, 1:187). Seneca's philosophy of death is reported to have permeated not only the legal profession but the medical profession as well. Roman doctors did not view assisting in the act of taking one's life as contradictory to their function or oath of service. Rather, they saw assisting with rational acts of self-killing as a normal part of their function (van Hooff 1990, 158). While it is clear that, during the early period of Roman society, frivolous acts of self-killing resulted in a loss of *dignitas*, justifiable and rational suicide was viewed as clearly acceptable and in keeping with the natural law (van Hooff 1990, 124).

Although early Roman law seems to have taken the route of minimal attention toward acts of self-killing, this attitude was not universal. Among Jewish scholars, Flavius Josephus argued that acts of self-killing were not in accordance with man's nature, and thus he condemned those Jews who took their own lives while hiding from the Romans in the cavern under Jatapata and on Masada. Flavian argued, "Suicide is alike repugnant to nature which all creatures share, and an act of impiety toward God who created us. Among the animals there is not one that deliberately seeks death or kills itself; so firmly rooted in all is nature's law—the will to live" (van Hooff 1990, xiii). While Josephus spoke eloquently about the need to preserve one's life, there is no indication that his work represented a common opinion among the Jews of his time.

The Christians of the first century seemed to follow the Roman traditions concerning self-killing and showed very little interest in the ethical issue of suicide. Early Christian writing contains no indication that taking one's own life was considered to be a sinful act, and early Christians responded pastorally, rather than condemingly, to instances of self-killing. In fact, it was not until the fourth century that Christianity began to systematically disapprove of all acts of self-killing (van Hooff 1990, 26, 183).

As the Christian church began to grow, it adopted an expanded version of the Platonic view of self-killing, maintaining that such an act was an offense against the authority of God. At the same time, many of the members of the early Christian Church participated in acts that can clearly be categorized as self-killing. Within the early Christian Church there are many examples of deliberately invoked martyrdom, toward which the church demonstrated great ambivalence (O'dea 1882, 70).

The Christian rejection and characterization of self-killing as a sin did not come until late in the third century, and, even then, its disapproval was still largely based in neo-Platonic terms. The church argued that God had created the body as a temple for the soul to rest in while here on Earth (*temporale corporis habitaculum*) and that it was not appropriate for any human being to force the soul to leave this resting place unless called to do so by God Himself. In addition, the church clung to the Platonic conception of the individual as an entity that possessed something less than self-ownership. In essence, the church rejected the Stoic conception of man in favor of the older Platonic conception of mankind as the property of God, and thus argued that taking one's own life would be contrary to man's true nature.

The Christian attitude concerning self-killing was ambivalent until St. Augustine (A.D. 354–A.D. 430) established a clear doctrine concerning such acts. Augustine maintained the absolute sinfulness of every voluntary act of self-killing by analogy to the act of murder. He argued that taking one's own life was self-murder, bringing the concept even closer to what we today characterize as suicide. Augustine also made the first appeal to Biblical writings in an effort to lay a foundation for the disapproval of all forms of self-killing. This move was largely motivated by the theological teachings of the Donatists who claimed that the Old Testament, through Saul and Samson, legitimated certain types of self-killing, particularly killing oneself to avoid sinfulness. In response, Augustine made great efforts to distinguish between simple acts of self-killing, which were never desirable, and genuine martyrdom. To make this distinction, Augustine appealed to the New Testament, citing Jesus's refusal to throw himself from the Temple's pinnacle as well as the Ten Commandments as rejections of self-killing. Augustine made it clear that the Christian martyr could kill himself only to avoid being forced into sin (van Hooff 1990, 195-196).

To a great extent, the shifting and competing attitudes within Christianity can once again be accounted for by shifting conceptions of the nature of mankind. An examination of the Jewish conception of man, as contained in the Old Testament, reveals the belief that God is responsible for breathing life into His creation and making man a living being (Genesis 2:7 RSV). Thus, God was conceived of as the creator and sustainer of all human life. However, under Jewish teaching no dichotomy existed between the body and the soul. For example, the ancient Hebrews had no specific word for body as distinct from the soul. Within this ideology, the individual was considered to be an indivisible whole. It is only among the later writings, such as the *Wisdom literature* and *Deuterocanonical books* (Apocrypha), that we find references to a body/soul distinction (Sena 1981, 5-6).

Within the Old Testament, the principal word for the existence of life within a human being is *nepes,* which refers to the throat or breathing substance that makes up an individual. In this sense, it was the act of breathing that constituted a human being as a living individual. In addition to *nepes,* the word *ruah* directly meant breath, wind, or spirit; however, *ruah* had a distinct meaning that referred to "the vital influence of God upon human beings. . . . A human being's life principle." Thus, *nepes* lives and dies, while *ruah* does not. *Ruah* is God's living force communicated to human beings, but belonging to God. Therefore, *nepes* conveys life while *ruah* conveys the gift of God's sustaining power.

Hence, the ancient Hebrews conceived of mankind as simply a living body, not an incarnate soul that was affected by death. This conception of man's nature predominated until the second century B.C. Under such a belief, death offered nothing other than some vague existence within the shadow world that was largely considered to be less than desirable. However, New Testament theology fully adopted the vocabulary of a body/soul distinction, thus reinterpreting the nature of man. Now, death was no longer to be considered an end to existence, but merely a shifting state of being (Sena 1981, 7-15). The importance of this distinction is captured in the work of Anton van Hooff, who maintains that, as a general historical rule, wherever a strong distinction is made between the body and the soul and a totalitarian conception of society prevails, the individual is denied the right to take his own life. Van Hooff states that dualism and totalitarianism are the two constant elements in the undercurrent of philosophical disapproval of *mors voluntaria* in the ancient world (van Hooff 1990, 167). Of course, Christianity eventually developed to provide not only the philosophical body/soul distinction but also the totalitarian political structure needed to result in the condemnation of self-killing.

With its new authority, founded securely in a new understanding of the nature of man, the Council of Arles (452 A.D.) ruled that suicide was an act of diabolical inspiration. In addition, in 562 A.D., the Council of Braga disallowed religious burial rights for all who died by an act of their own hands. The medieval Christian Church translated these dictates into civil law, resulting in harsh penalties for those who took their own lives. For example, as a punishment for a sinful act condemned by religious authorities, the body of an individual who had killed him or herself was reportedly defiled in various ways, such as burying the body where two roads crossed and driving a stake through the body (Ingersoll 1895, 21). In France, bodies of suicide victims were dragged through the streets and then hung upside down (Lecky 1869, 2:61). Similarly, in England suicide was made a crime against the state, resulting in the confiscation of the offender's property. Surprisingly, such laws were often said to be based on the Roman law, which in fact rarely required such forfeitures (van Hooff 1990, 172-173). Laws of this nature remained in the English statute books as late as 1869 (Lecky 1869, 2:62).

While Augustine is the principal church father responsible for establishing almost all acts of self-killing as a sin, it was St. Thomas Aquinas (1225-1274) who fully embedded the position within modern Christian interpretation of natural law. Aquinas was the most influential Christian philosopher of the middle ages. His theology combined the philosophical understanding of Plato, Aristotle, Roman law, and the Stoics with the emerging concept of the modern state and, by so doing, reconstructed a basis of authority for the continued political influence of Christianity. Aquinas was aided in this endeavor by the twelfth-century revival of the study of Roman law in Bologna, which was quickly used to lay the legal foundation for the divine right of kings.

Aquinas's greatest gift was the ability to synthesize varying political and theological thoughts into one cogent ideology, and he used natural law theory as one of the principal pillars of his work. In Aquinas's view, all creatures had a natural inclination to preserve themselves, and natural law consisted of those things that aided in the preservation of life and condemned those things that sought to destroy it (St. Aquinas 1948, Ia, IIae, 94, 2). Hence, Aquinas's contribution of bringing natural law theory solidly into the Christian fold continued the church's strong condemnation of self-killing.

It was through this doctrine that Aquinas supported the principle that acts of self-killing and euthanasia constituted "the killing of the innocent" and condemned such acts as clearly contrary to the dictates of natural law (Aquinas 1948, Ia, IIae, 94, 5 obj. 2). Aquinas clearly states that the act of taking one's own life is wholly wrong for "everything naturally loves itself, and as a result of that love naturally seeks to preserve its life and to avoid all things that would detract from it. . . . Therefore, all who take their own life have committed a mortal sin because they have violated this natural law" (Aquinas 1948, IIa, IIae, 64, 5).

Aquinas's Christianized interpretation of natural law leaves little leeway concerning the propriety of self-killing. However, this does not mean that Aquinas believed that human beings were obligated to do everything possible to sustain their lives. As will be discussed later, Aquinas argued that, while we were all obligated to take advantage of ordinary medical practice, there was no need to take extraordinary measures to preserve one's life. While Aquinas clearly opposed actively taking life, there is room within his theories for passive activities that can lead to a quickened natural death. Despite this possible flexibility within modern interpretations of Aquinas's theory of natural law, his influence strengthened the authority of the medieval Christian Church; as a result, political theories concerning the potential propriety of self-killing all but disappeared from Western philosophy.

With the advent of the Renaissance, the authority of the Catholic Church began to wane and secular philosophy began to work against the traditional religious attitude concerning self-killing. Under the control of the Christian Church, the power and authority of the state merged with the church's dualistic conception of man's nature. Under such conditions, there was little room for the emergence of any philosophy respecting the right of an individual to terminate his own life. However, the rise of the secular state opened the way for such philosophy to emerge. While the church saw man as consisting of a distinct body and soul and saw itself as having authority over both, the secular state saw only a unified individual or, at best, maintained that it had authority only over the physical matter that made up the human being. As a result, the secular state found itself with a view much closer to that held by the Stoic philosophers than that of the Christian Church.

In addition to the reemergence of a unified conception of the nature of man as he related to the makers of positive law (the state), sixteenth-century man was conceived of in other terms that were radically different than anything before. As stated earlier, the sixteenth century marked the emergence of a conception of human nature that viewed mankind as a collection of autonomous individuals who possessed not only liberty over their own bodies but also natural and inalienable rights. The emergence of this conception of man's nature brought with it a panoply of individual rights, as well as the rejection of totalitarianism.

As a result, the question of the "right to die" could once again be raised.

The advent of the Reformation not only brought with it profound challenges to the authority of the Roman Church but also ushered in a new emphasis on the importance of the individual as a possessor of individual rights and liberties. The emerging natural rights theories often took as their foundation the Roman and medieval interpretation of natural law and frequently maintained not only that these natural rights limited government but also that government had a positive obligation to protect such rights.[2]

Along these lines, John Donne (b.1573) appears to be the first modern philosopher to have constructed a sympathetic view of self-killing. For example, his work *Biathanatos* consisted of a discussion of the various acts of self-killing that could be found in antiquity and contained a strong defence of the right of the individual to engage in a rational act of self-killing. While Donne did not maintain that all acts of self-killing should be permissible, he attempted to use examples from antiquity and the Christian martyrs to argue in favor of particular categories of self-killing (Donne 1648). Donne's work was never published during his life and so was not made available until his son brought it to publication in 1648. Even then, the work was subjected to harsh criticism. The Western world was still under the spell of Aquinas's religious interpretation of natural law, but the political tide was shifting.

The best example of this shift can be found in the work of John Locke, whose contribution to American political thought has already been mentioned. Locke was deeply intrigued by natural law, not only as it pertained to government and the state of nature but also as it related to ethics and moral obligation. Locke wrote a series of essays on natural law that were later bound into a collective work (Locke 1970) exploring the proposition that the obligation of self-preservation is the first law of nature.

Throughout his work, Locke seems to be pulled in contradictory directions. As a theorist and moralist, Locke was extremely indebted to the works of Aristotle and Thomas Aquinas. Locke was clearly a religious man; however, his theories led him to reject the proposition that self-preservation is the principlal, or first, law of nature. This is not to say that Locke approved of acts of self-killing; rather, Locke saw the rule of self-preservation as advantageous rather than obligatory. This was quite different from his view of other human actions that Locke strictly held out as forbidden by natural law. For example, among these forbidden deeds were the acts of theft and murder (Locke 1970, 101, 181, 193). In this way, Locke appears to have rejected the arguments of the Christian Church, which attempted to equate acts of self-killing with murder and to forbid both through the authority of natural law and scripture.

Locke did, however, seem to maintain that self-preservation was a natural instinct and that those things that generally contributed to the preservation of life were probably virtues. Thus Locke writes that man "has not liberty to destroy himself. . . . For man being all the workmanship of one Omnipotent, and infinitely wise Maker lives and dies at His pleasure not our own" (Locke 1970, 9). For Locke, life was not something to be held on to at all costs. He expressed this sentiment in a literary eulogy he delivered as a part of his professorial duties:

> To endure a life burdened by so many ills is pitiable enough, to love it is surely more pitiable. And to desire not to leave the prison and convicts cells, though so many doors are open on all sides, shows that we are pitiable not only on account of our condition but also our own will. . . . What folly indeed is this that anyone should purposely deliberately, and gladly preserve a life which he enters at nature's bidding tearfully and unwillingly and that he should respect, and cherish whole heartedly, a gift of nature which he could not receive without grief and lamentation! Thus on the threshold we linger like fools and lament, but once in, dance as if there was nothing disagreeable in prison except the entrance. . . . Farewell, then, to the trystfull pleasures of life; the world has nothing to give that is worthy of our prayers except the grave. (Locke 1970, 227-229)

While Locke would never have advocated the propriety of self-killing, neither would he elevate its prohibition to the level that Aquinas and Hobbes attempted to give it (Aquinas 1948, Ia, 2ae, 94, 2; Hobbes 1994, 79).

Later in the eighteenth century, the right of an individual to take his own life would be defended by such theorists as Montesquieu (1689-1755) and David Hume (1711-1776). Montesquieu used natural law theories to argue in favor of a set of natural rights that were considered to be inherent in the individual and possessing sufficient authority that they could limit governmental authority (Haines 1965, 50), thus placing many individual decisions beyond the control of government. Similarly, Hume argued in favor of the Stoic philosophy of man and maintained that an individual should not be forced "to prolong a miserable existence, because of some frivolous advantage which the public may perhaps receive from him" (Hume 1783, 19).

Therefore, while the neo-Platonic and Christian conception of the duality of mankind prevented them from entertaining any question about the right to die (van Hooff, 1990, 188), sixteenth-century philosophers saw man as a free individual having the right to make his own decisions concerning the personal matters of life, whether it be his choice of occupation, his religious beliefs, or the end of his life. Any interference with such choices on the part of the state, beyond what was strictly necessary for its self-preservation, was seen as an invasion of the autonomous individual's rights. Under such conditions, the individual was considered to be the undisputed master of his own life. Decisions concerning his desire to live or die were held out as matters of personal choice.

Chapter 10

The American Interpretation of Natural Law

As can be seen from the preceding historical review, for most of its colorful history the concept of rights has not played a major role in the theory of natural law. The Greeks, who were largely responsible for developing the foundations of natural law theory, had only a limited understanding of rights beyond those pertaining to property, and though natural law theory did begin to introduce the concepts of individual freedom and equality upon which the concept of rights would one day be based, only a limited conception of rights would develop.

The Christianization of natural law theory changed little in regard to a development of rights theory. Under its Christian interpretation, natural law was viewed as a set of personal obligations that had been made immanent in the world and in man's nature. Nevertheless, some of these duties were not simply for personal utility, but were for the benefit of other persons and, as such, did create a primitive set of rights. However, these rights were not conceived of as existing independent of God's will.

While some theories prior to the seventeenth century did develop a philosophy of rights, their impact was limited. It was not until such theories were embedded within the theory of natural law that they began to strongly influence actual political practices (George 1992, 279). It fell to John Locke to transform the theory of natural law into a theory of rights that would serve as a justification for revolution and shape the political arrangements of a continent. Under Locke's theory, natural law was transformed into a set of positive standards which empower the individual and obligate government, and it was from the writings of Locke, among others, that Americans were introduced to the conception of natural rights (Locke 1970, sec.135). For example, it was Locke's understanding of natural rights that would find its way into the second paragraph of the Declaration of Independence, "We hold these truths to be self-evident, that all men are created equal, that they are endowed by their Creator with certain unalienable Rights, that among these are Life, Liberty, and the pursuit of Happiness" (Jefferson 1776).

To a great extent, the creation of the modern state and the development of an understanding of individual liberties was the product of those ideas unleashed by the forces of the Protestant Reformation. It was only as a result of this historic shift that the citizen came to be viewed as an independent entity capable of holding rights against the state. In addition, the Reformation helped redefine the conception of the citizenry from that of a collective mind to that of an association of autonomous persons, each with an individual conscience capable of making independent personal and political choices (Gierke 1934, 6). The importance of this shift to the American conception of natural law is the role that it played in bringing natural law theories to colonial America.

During the early colonial period in America, one of the principal sources of natural law theory was the religious teachings of Puritan clerics. It was through the religious tenets of New England's Puritan communities that the concept of natural law first found its way to the American colonies. As the Puritans immigrated to New England, their objective was religious rather than political. Early Puritan settlers were not concerned with the development of individual rights or autonomous individuals; their aim was to develop a "city upon a hill" where all governmental decisions would be made as a part of their religious rather than their political lives, resulting in the outgrowth of few new concepts. Although unplanned, Puritan thought still played a significant role in evolving the American theory of natural law because as its foundation was the principle that the only source of true law was the authority of God and that human ordinances that were not in keeping with this will did not deserve the status of laws. For the Puritan, the only way for a law to be valid was for it to be in keeping with God's teachings. Early Puritans firmly maintained there was a perfect synthesis between divine law and natural law concepts, and they possessed the absolute conviction that natural law was fully recognizable through the holy scriptures (Wright 1962). In this way, the Puritans were philosophically related to the medieval interpretation of natural law.

This view of natural law was so strong among early Puritans that even John Winthrop, a civil rather than a religious official, maintained the view that society should be ordered in accordance to the dictates of natural law. Winthrop believed that the fundamental laws used to govern the ideal civil state must be derived from the "perfect rule and reason" of God's will (Winthrop 1864-1867, 2:440). This emphasis on God's law was prevalent throughout the religious writing of the early colonial period in New England and is reflected in many of the earliest political colonial documents. For example, the Fundamental Orders of Connecticut stated that the colonial government "shall have the power to administer justice according to the laws here established, and for want thereof according to the rule of the word of God." Similarly, the New Haven governmental body agreed that Holy Scripture contained all that was necessary for the direction of civil government (Wright 1962, 32).

While the early Puritan writers on the nature of law aligned themselves closely with the religious nature of medieval natural law theory, this strictly religious interpretation of natural law concepts was not long lived. Within the span of a single generation, religious leaders in New England began to broaden their interpretation of natural law to include influences from beyond the religious spectrum. As the colonies stabilized, their religious leaders increasingly came under the influence of earlier interpretations of natural law as implied by the writings of Aristotle, Plato, and Cicero. In addition to these ancient thinkers, the influence of seventeenth- and eighteenth-century political philosophers such as Locke, Pufendorf, Milton, Montesquieu, and Blackstone began to drift into the sermons and written works of the Puritan clergy (Tyler 1963, 1:132). This broadened interpretation introduced an increased emphasis on individual conscience as well as the theory of rights and, in so doing, helped in the development of a set of ideas that would serve as the foundation of the American Revolution. As a result of these new influences, with the emphasis on natural law remaining, the sermons of eighteenth-century Puritans could easily be mistaken for a political oration on the rights of man rather than a religious exegesis of the Bible (Barker 1948, 274).

As the Puritan view of natural law came to include nonreligious sources of authority, the doctrine of natural law began to shift from the purely restrictive doctrines found under the medieval interpretation to a more liberal doctrine that placed a greater emphasis on the rights of man as dictated by nature. This change in emphasis began a process of philosophical change that eventually led to the development of an independent and purely secular interpretation of natural law that frequently, though not entirely, excludes any reference to the law of God. For example, Jonathan Mayhew writes, to his followers, of the importance of natural law by stating that the authority of such law is so great that even God is limited by law; not the law of man, "but by the eternal laws of truth, wisdom, and equity, and the everlasting tables of right reason" (Mayhew 1976, 46).

Similarly, John Wise based his arguments in favor of congregationalism on the dictates of natural rights, placing particular reliance on the writings of Pufendorf (Parrington 1954). Wise was also the first American to clearly assert that "the end of all good government is to cultivate humanity, and promote the happiness of all and the good of every man in his rights, his life, his liberty, estate, honor," thus helping to lay a foundation for Jeffersons similar use of natural law principles in the Declaration of Independence (McLaughlin 1932, 71-72).

As can be seen, many of the legal codes of early America were heavily influenced by the religious teachings of the day, as a result, many of these codes came to be based on the theory of natural law and/or natural rights, as it later developed. Law was a common course of study among the upper classes in America, and its importance to the emerging American nation was substantial. With the broad influx of different nationalities to the American continent, many areas found themselves without any common history or any traditions of nationality to bind them together as one people. As a result, law became the glue that began to bind the American people together and to define our common character.

The study of law began to expose our national leaders to a common universe of ideas, and at the center of that universe was the theory of natural law. For example, during the eighteenth century, Vattel wrote *The Law of Nations*, which was read throughout the Continent and in America. Vattell's work made extensive use of the theory of natural law to develop a basis for the existence of individual rights of an absolute and universal quality. Vattel argued that, without question, "Liberty and independence belong to man by his very nature, and that they cannot be taken from him without his consent [and that any] nation, whose common will is but the outcome of the united wills of the citizens, remains subject to the laws of nature, and is bound to respect them in all its undertakings."

In addition, Vattel strongly advocated for the propriety of a written constitution that could clearly enumerate such rights and maintained that the fundamental rights that would be embodied in such a document could not be changed by simple legislative act because they did not represent ordinary law, but rather were to be considered "fundamental" (Vattel 1916, 51).

Vattel's work, along with the work of Grotius, Pufendorf, and Burlamaqui, became part of the formative influence on the development of the early American legal theory. Each of these writers advocated for the existence of natural rights as brought from the state of nature. Such texts introduced the American lawyer to a far different education than would be received today. Young American lawyers of the time would not have been exposed to the many volumes of positive law and precedents that consumed the time of English lawyers. Instead, the American would have spent as least as much time studying the philosophical concept of rights as studying the dictates of positive law. Indeed, even Blackstone, who had a strong influence on the development of American legal theory, demonstrated an understanding of Pufendorf and Burlamaqui in his commentaries (Barker 1951).

While it is true that the many colonists who came from England brought with them an understanding of the traditions of common law, these ideas were quickly enlarged, as, within the colonial environment, statutory law was scarce and the judicial process was for the most part informal. The lack of precedents and clear judicial standards left American colonial judges with little guidance. At the same time, expanding colonial settlements had a growing need for judicial rulings to organize their affairs. As a result, early American jurists frequently appealed either to the Bible or to commonly held beliefs about what was appropriate and right under the dictates of natural law.

The relative isolation of colonial authority from the influence of organized government, as well as the relative independence with which it operated, allowed for the development of a limited, but strong, concentration on personal rights. Speaking of the early American jury system under colonial rule, Forrest McDonald states that "juries exercised all but absolute power on a case-by-case basis. In an everyday sense, juries were the government, and it was upon them that the safety of all rights to liberty and to property depended" (McDonald 1985, 40). Furthermore, he states that the jury found its legal authority "in nature and in principles of natural justice and disregarding, if they saw fit to do so, the instructions of the judge as to what the law was and, for that matter, even the plain language of an act of Parliament or of a colony or state legislative enactment" (McDonald 1985, 40-41).

Under such conditions, the American colonial jury lost, or simply disregarded, any distinction between natural law and natural rights. The two concepts came to be regarded either as synonymous or so closely related to one another that no distinction was seen to be necessary. Thus, many of the decisions of colonial judges appear to have been based on an understanding of natural law that mandates that, in order to be valid, all positive laws must coincide with the dictates of natural law and therefore must reflect its eternal and immutable principles.

This unique nature of American legal theory resulted in the development of a dichotomy within the law that was particular to America. Within American legal theory, two distinct arenas of law came to be recognized. The first was that body of law that governed property interests as well as civic responsibilities; the second body of law concerned itself with those ideas and principles that would eventually be embodied in the Constitution. Such law was not concerned with the obligations of the citizen but, rather, concerned the duties of the government. No analogous distinction could be found in the English law of the eighteenth century, and it was upon this distinction that colonial lawyers would come to base their challenges to the actions of Parliament. The American colonial spirit would denounce the actions of the English Parliament as violating natural law and the rights of all Americans who lived under its authority (Barker 1948, 283-285).

While there are many examples of American resistance to English authority based on the grounds of an individual colonial charter or even on the principle of the English constitution, it is clear that, by the time of the American Revolution, the doctrines of natural law/rights had become the foundation for continued resistance. Throughout the colonial period, the theories of natural law and natural rights became the principal justification for revolution, and an appeal to such theories can be found even among those arguments that advocate other bases for resistance.

When colonial Americans appealed to the dual theories of natural law and natural rights, they appealed to more than could be claimed under any simple interpretation of English law or colonial charter. They appealed to a standard of law that outlined what the ideal society ought to look like; not to those rights that they knew existed, but to those rights they believed ought to exist and to those ideas that had become part of the philosophical and political legacy of the seventeenth and eighteenth centuries, the ideas of Pufendorf, Burlamaqui, Vattell, and Locke (Becker 1966).

As American writers began the transition from their theological and legal theories to a revolutionary political philosophy, the secular principle of natural law took on increasing importance. While the previous era of American history was more concerned with the need for unity and survival than with the development of political philosophy, by 1760 the American continent was flooded with political essays, tracts, papers, and constitutions. These documents circulated widely, not only in America but also on the Continent, and natural law concepts played an important part in the majority of them. By 1773, natural law concepts had become a standard part of American political thought (Tyler 1963; Adams 1922).

This justification for the growing revolutionary impulses of colonial statesmen was furthered by the development of two distinct appeals to natural law theory. The first appeal took the English constitution as its basis, but then argued that its principles were not simply the developments of tradition but were, in fact, the recognition of natural law principles and, as such, must be applied equally to all men, whether in the colonies or in England. At their bare minimum, these principles guaranteed fundamental rights and free government. The second argument, which became far more popular than the first, maintained that the dictates of natural law created a guarantee of individual liberty, regardless of what the English constitution maintained (McIlwain 1923, 152).

Thus, by 1774, when the first Continental Congress was called into session, it is no surprise that their thoughts and tongues turned to the theory of natural law. For example, one of the first points of business of this Congress was to create a committee whose main task was to draw up a statement of "rights, grievances, and means of redress," as well as to agree on an understanding of the source from which their authority flowed. It did not take long before Richard Henry Lee, the representative from Virginia, proposed four points upon which American resistance could be justified, namely, natural law, the British constitution, the charters of the several colonies, and tradition (McDonald 1985, 57).

Almost immediately, upon the suggestion that natural law should be used as a basis for the authority of colonial resistance, both James Duane of New York and Joseph Galloway of Pennsylvania strongly objected. Both Duane and Galloway recognized the development of natural law theory as the foundation of a theory of natural rights. However, they also recognized that the contemporary use of natural law theory in this context would lead to an argument against the sovereignty of the crown, and revolution was, as of yet, undesirable for either man. Both men clearly saw that to use natural law as the foundation of resistance would in essence constitute an argument that, because of the abuses of the English crown, the American colonies had somehow slipped back into the state of nature and, in doing so, had gained their independence. For many colonialists, this was a far too radical step to be taken at that time (McDonald 1985, 58). In the end, their opposition resulted in only a passing reference to the "immutable laws of nature," out of fear that anything stronger would unnecessarily damage those good relations that still existed between England and the colonies.

Despite this opposition, the popularity of natural law theories among early

American political activists provided a common basis of agreement from which America could claim authority. As a result, by the time of the Declaration of Independence, the theory of natural law had been systematically developed and redefined a theory of natural rights that was reflected in most of the important writings of the period. For example, Alexander Hamilton published his first tract in defense of natural law concepts at age 17 and went on to publish a second tract one year later. In *The Farmer Refuted* (1775), Hamilton urged Americans to "[a]pply yourself without delay to the study of the law of nature," and he recommended such authors as Burlamaqui, Grotius, Locke, Montesquieu, and Pufendorf, whose theories involved a purely secularized interpretation. This secularization of natural law concepts reached its peak in Ethan Allen's "Oracle of Reason," in which he states, "They may keep their alleged manuscripts of God's eternal law, it is sufficient for me to possess the deistical Bible, reason, by which I judge that even the commandments of the Decalogue would not be binding upon any rational being unless they coincided with the law of nature" (Wright 1962, 161 n.3). We should note, however, that while this passage suggests a possible hostility to the religious sources of natural law, most early American works do not share this tone.

Examples of a more religiously based appeal to natural law can be found among the revolutionary writings of James Otis. A Boston lawyer, Otis wrote several pamphlets encouraging resistance to the crown that appealed to the authority of natural law in support of such acts. In his pamphlet "A Vindication of the Conduct of the House of Representatives of the Province of the Massachusetts Bay," Otis states that it was God who "made all men naturally equal," and that it was upon this authority, as laid down by the law of nature, that man is entitled to resist those who seek to remove his rights (Tyler 1963, 1:42, 48). In support of his assertion that government must be limited, Otis cites Locke's *Discourse on Government*, as well as the authority of the law of nature and God.

In historical retrospect, it was said that Otis' "little fugitive pamphlet" represented the collective understanding and spirit of the Continental Congress of 1774 and the Declaration of Independence all rolled into one. However, Otis's (1764) most influential work was probably his pamphlet entitled "The Rights of the British Colonies Asserted and Proved." In this work, Otis argues in favor of the concept of limited government and bases this concept on the unchanging will of God, whose laws never vary.

While it is beyond argument that Otis, as well as many other founding fathers, made continual use of the concept of natural law and natural rights, it is also clear that they did so not in a philosophical manner but rather as an exercise in practical justification. In this sense, the common appeal to natural law theory that is so frequently found in early American writings should not be viewed in the same light as the carefully analyzed philosophies of previously covered natural law theorists. Instead, the American use of natural law must be recognized as an appeal to an emerging philosophy of individual rights and governmental limitations that was conveniently tailored to meet their special needs, particularly as it was interpreted by Locke (McDonald 1985, 60). Under these conditions, there was little need for close philosophical justification, as the American interest at that time was in liberty and, on an ever-increasingly, independence and revolution.

With the passage of the Stamp Act, the amount of revolutionary literature produced that claimed natural law as its authoritative base for opposition dramatically increased. For example, Samuel Adams, who as a Harvard College graduate had received his education in an environment largely designed as a training ground for ministers, had been exposed to the concepts of natural law that were inseparable from the religious tenets of the day and used these ideas in his political writings. Adams (1765) was moved to write that the Stamp Act violated the rights of all colonists, which "are founded in the law of God and nature and are the common rights of mankind." Going further, he stated that "no law of society can, consistent with the law of God and nature, divest the inhabitants of this province of those rights" (Barker 1948, 276; Wells 1865, 1:16-23, 70-77).

Similarly, John Adams wrote of the theory of natural rights in his many pamphlets, believing that these rights were immutable and therefore not subject to change or challenge by any of the dictates of positive law. In this vein, Adams wrote, in one of his early works, that no act of positive law could "wrest from the populace, the knowledge of their rights and wrongs, rights, that cannot be repealed or restrained by human laws—rights, derived from the great Legislator of the Universe" (Adams 1865, 3:449). In this use of natural law theory, Adams demonstrates a clear understanding of natural law as providing a basis for the existence of natural rights, rights that, unlike the Stoic or medieval conception, are beyond the power of positive law to restrict. As such, Adams' work represents part of the growing American understanding that some rights are, by their nature, fundamental.

John Dickinson carried this concept of fundamental rights, as justified by natural law, forward in his address to the Committee of Correspondence in Barbados (1766). In this address, Dickinson characterized the rights of man as being "created in us by the decrees of Providence, which establish the laws of our nature. They are born with us; and cannot be taken from us by any human power, without taking our lives. In short, they are founded on the immutable maxims of reason and justice" (Wright 1962, 77). It is interesting to note that, despite Dickinson's strong use of natural law theory in the quoted passage, his use of the theory was infrequent, most probably because of his desire to avoid a revolutionary separation from England and perhaps evidenced by his refusal to sign the Declaration of Independence, believing it to be act of premature separation. However, in the end, it was indeed the philosophy of natural law that carried the American founding fathers into that final act of revolution, and it was the principles of natural law and natural rights that they embedded in the document that declared their independence.

When Thomas Jefferson prepared to write the Declaration of Independence, there could have been little doubt in his mind about the propriety of embedding the principles of natural law into the language of this historic document. By the time of the American Revolution, the theories of natural law and natural rights were standard philosophical fare of American political ideology. Surprisingly, however, Jefferson himself did not previously make broad use of the philosophy in his writings. This is not to say that Jefferson was unfamiliar with the theory or that he rejected it as a foundation for inalienable rights; quite to the contrary, on those occasions when he did refer to the principles of natural law, it was generally for the purpose of supporting the existence of fundamental rights (Wright 1962, 86).

Jefferson asserted that the rights of Americans were based on "the immutable laws of nature, the principles of the English Constitution, and the several charters or compacts" of the colonies. In addition, Jefferson reaffirmed his belief in the importance of natural law to the foundation of rights during his service as Secretary of State and President, stating at one time, "The evidence of this natural right [expatriation], like that of our right to life, liberty, the use of our faculties, the pursuit of happiness, is not left to the feeble and sophisticated investigations of reason, but is impressed on the sense of every man" (Haines 1965, 56). It was in this way that Jefferson came to be regarded as a champion of the doctrine of natural rights, and it was this sense of natural law that Jefferson wove into the Declaration of Independence.

In 1776, when Jefferson wrote the Declaration of Independence he unmistakably used the theories of natural law as the foundation for revolution against the arbitrary authority of the English Crown. In stating "When in the course of human events, it becomes necessary for one people to dissolve the political bands which have connected them with another, and to assume among the Powers of the earth, the separate and equal stations to which *the Laws of Nature and Nature's God* entitles them" (emphases added), he clearly places natural law at the center of American philosophical authority to challenge the acts of the English Crown. By going on to state, "We hold these truths to be self-evident, that *all men are created equal*, that they are *endowed by their Creator* with certain *unalienable Rights*, that among these rights are Life, Liberty and the Pursuit of Happiness" (emphasis added), Jefferson aligns himself with the entire history of natural law from the time of the Stoics to that of the seventeenth- and eighteenth-century advocates of natural rights theory. It is clear that Jefferson's statements did not introduce any new theory of government or law to America. Instead, he simply applied to the American situation those ideas that had become accepted principles of government among the colonial leaders of his day. A review of the laws of the colonies, the public documents of the time, the writings, the constitutions, and literature of the era clearly demonstrates that the theories of natural law and natural rights had a substantial impact on the development of the American conception of rights. The theory of natural law not only allowed for the justification upon which to declare all relationships with Great Britain dissolved but also served as the basis for the construction of a new constitutional form of government.

Chapter 11

Natural Law and the Post-Revolutionary Era

The period of American history following the American Revolution is marked by the legal and political disorder that came with the dissolution of authority. As the colonies recognized their independence from English authority, based on the dictates of natural law, many ex-colonists came to view themselves as having slipped back into a state of nature in which all previously recognized authority was now void. For example, Patrick Henry declared exactly such sentiments at the first Continental Congress by stating that "all Government is dissolved and we are now reduced to a State of Nature." All previous governmental boundaries had been removed, so that he no longer considered himself a Virginian, but an American (McDonald 1985, 146).

The difficulty with this position was that many of the inhabitants of the former American colonies took the statement much too literally. For example, in 1777, the government of Maryland contended that the large tracts of unsettled land, originally granted to Virginia by the English Crown, were now open to all the inhabitants of the American continent; the authority that had originally made the grant had been stripped of all control of the land. Similarly, the residents of the Kentucky tract of the State of Virginia petitioned the Continental Congress in 1782 for separation from Virginia and admission as a new state, citing that the Revolution had dissolved the authority of any government over it and, as a result, that it had the right to bring itself out of the state of nature as an independent state subject to its own authority (McDonald 1985, 146).

Adding to the confusion caused by these claims, several other former colonial states also viewed themselves as being in a state of nature, maintaining the right to emerge as independent nations. It was along these lines that the residents of northeastern New York declared independence and claimed the authority of natural law to form the independent State of Vermont. Likewise, the inhabitants of western North Carolina fought a small civil war in an unsuccessful attempt to assert their natural law rights to form the State of Franklin. The people of Pittsfield, Massachusetts, closed the city's courthouses, declaring that all governmental authority had been dissolved and that residents were now in a state of nature in which the old civil authorities had no power to collect debts or render judgments. At one point, the national state of affairs became so bad that one of the delegates to the Continental Congress from the State of South Carolina stated that "the inhabitants of every colony considered themselves at liberty to do as they pleased upon almost every occasion" (Egerton 1931, 124).

The relative infancy of the American situation lent itself, in some cases too well, to the theory of natural law. However, the break from English authority had left the American judges with a need to make judicial determinations without the availability of statutory law and at least a theoretical break from the precedents of English common law. To resolve this difficulty, American jurists simply returned to the principles of natural law, as well as to the biblical principles that had been so important during the colonial period. Using natural law as a tool helped stabilize the development of American law and keep it consistent with developing the constitutional principles (Pound 1922, 44).

From this beginning the American legal system evolved, building upon the principles of natural law, complete with its conception of inalienable rights inherited from its revolutionary period. These concepts were then translated into constitutions maintaining that individuals possess rights by virtue of their existence and that these rights were superior to those of society or even the government itself. From this principle came the concept of limited government, an important aspect of American government. In this way, natural law served as one of the principal backbones of the development of the doctrine of civil liberties and limited social and political control of the individual. Thus, Edwin Borchard states,

> The constitutional doctrine of the seventeenth and eighteenth centuries, working with the tool of natural law, erected constitutional limitations into legal obligations founded on unimpairable contract, . . . enforceable, if necessary, by the right of resistance, and posited for every state an implied constitution founded on the natural law right of the individual and having as much force as a written constitution. (Borchard 1927, 794)

Clear distinctions can be drawn between American and English legal philosophy of the eighteenth century, distinctions that caused the American legal system to embrace natural law concepts while its English counterpart, for the most part, ignored them. While some natural law theorists did, in fact, claim that English law had been influenced by the theories of natural law, by and large most English legal scholars saw law as either positive or as the evolution of traditional practices into binding obligations. In contrast, natural law theory is accepted in America as the eternal and immutable force of justice that government, whether or not it does, is called to obey. It is a sense of justice that seeks to guide us in determining what values government *ought* to express through its positive laws, while recognizing that no legitimate government can seek to change or set aside these laws.

Therefore, American legal and political philosophy began by recognizing two distinct realms of law. The first is positive law, which may consist of legislative enactments or the recognition of tradition. The second is the realm of natural law, which represents reason and identifies those laws that ought to exist, as well as designating those rights created by them as fundamental. In this way, while the use of positive law slowly became embedded in our actual legal practice, the concepts of natural law became a part of our overarching legal, governmental, and constitutional philosophy. As a result, while positive law governs the majority of our daily actions, when its provisions come into conflict with the fundamental dictates of natural law, the latter clearly wins.

The fact that natural law is, by and large, an unarticulated background philosophy of the American political and legal structures both (if the two can be separated) makes developing a strictly American interpretation of natural law difficult at best; this has led many to deny the authority of natural law within the American structure. However, one sense of natural law theory that can be clearly identified as having a profound affect on the development of American history is that sense of natural law that identifies which laws must be considered as "fundamental." It is this conception of natural law that finds its way into our constitutions and distinguishes American constitutional law from ordinary civil law. This understanding of natural law is expressed by Vattel's writings, an understanding that under the guidance of natural law, which makes fundamental law, a legislature can make only civil law and that the latter is clearly to be considered inferior to the former.

It is this set of distinctions within American political ideology—natural law versus positive law and fundamental law versus civil law—that so decisively distinguishes American government from all other governments of the eighteenth century. Essentially, this distinction is a recognition that, under the American conception of rights theory, the legislature is limited in two ways. First, it is limited by fundamental law as expressed by the Constitution; second, it is limited by natural law, so that even within the arena of civil law its rulings must conform to those standards. However, this still leaves us with the need to identify the principles of natural law, which, under their American incarnation, are for the most part philosophic rather than clearly articulated guidelines.

The resolution of this dilemma can be found in the actions of our founding fathers. When the political leaders of the American Confederation came together to bring into existence the United States, they created a constitution that not only provides for the basic structures of government but also a document that, aided by its first ten amendments, sought to express the American understanding of natural law and rights theory as the fundamental law of the Constitution. This merger of natural law theory and the expression of fundamental laws within our Constitution and its Amendments has had a substantial influence on the evolution of American history. In this sense, the founders sought to bring into existence a political entity unique among mankind. They sought a union between the principles of what ought to be and what was, a union between the theories of natural law and practical government.

Almost immediately upon declaring independence from England, the American colonies set about the process of drafting state constitutions; to a great extent, natural law theory informed their understanding of what an appropriate government should look like. For example, in 1776, a New Hampshire tract was published with the title, "The People are the Best Government: or a Plan of Government Founded on the Just Principles of Natural Freedom." This tract demonstrated a heavy reliance on the theory of natural law to justify the need for democratic government. In addition, similar pamphlets circulated through the colonies, each emphasizing the importance of natural rights and the need to create a civil authority that would be limited by principles of natural law (Wright 1931, 105-109).

Between 1776 and 1780, eleven states had undertaken the task of adopting constitutions, and several of these states included a declaration of rights promoting a common understanding of what natural, or fundamental, rights were incorporated into their constitutional guarantees. It was this common agreement that served to stabilize many of the state governments following the Revolution and, to a significant extent, it was this unifying effect of natural law theory that made the American Revolution successful (McLaughlin 1932, 87-93).

The first constitution with a declaration of rights came from the State of Virginia, and its unique contribution to the history of American government is considerable. A product of the efforts of James Madison, George Mason, Edmond Randolph, and Patrick Henry, among others, the Virginia Declaration of Rights and the Constitution of the Commonwealth of Virginia was officially adopted on 6 May, 1776. It came to be one of the principal patterns upon which the national Bill of Rights would be patterned.

George Mason was responsible for drafting Virginia's Declaration of Rights as well as the first Virginia constitution. In doing so, Mason used as the foundation for these documents not the English common law but rather the principles of natural law, which he held as the principal source of individual rights. It was on the authority of natural law that the first religious freedom provision was introduced into the historical stream of American political ideology. The Virginia Declaration of Rights directly influenced the creation of the bills of rights for the states of Pennsylvania in 1776 and Massachusetts in 1780. However, its most important contribution was its influence over the emerging national Constitution or, more precisely, the Bill of Rights that would later be attached to it (Wiltshire 1992, 90-91).

Surprisingly, despite the strong traditional emphasis placed on rights within the American interpretation of natural law, delegates to the constitutional convention unanimously defeated the first proposal to attach a bill of rights to the federal Constitution. The difficulty, however, was not a disagreement about whether Americans had rights or even so much what rights American had, but whether the Constitution was the proper place to attempt an enumeration of those rights. Eventually, the issue of a bill of rights became an obstacle to the adoption of the Constitution. Martin Luther argued that an explicit statement of recognition was the only way to protect the natural rights of man from the interference of government. Similarly, George Mason strongly objected to the lack of a "declaration of rights," and Thomas Jefferson, one of the most important supporters of the Constitution, greatly desired the inclusion of a bill of rights so that it recognized the natural rights of man. Finally, in 1788, the State of Virginia adopted a bill calling for a national bill of rights "asserting and securing from encroachment, the essential and unalienable rights of the people." Echoing this call, North Carolina and New York each demanded a summary of the natural rights of man, asserting their inalienable qualities (Wright 1962).

In response to these pressures, Madison addressed the tenth Congress and informed them that he was preparing to propose amendments to the new Constitution for the purposes of creating a bill of rights. By and large, in drafting the Bill of Rights, Madison used the Virginia Declaration as a pattern and, in December of 1791, ten of the original twelve amendments were approved for submission to the states and were ratified. One important point that should be noted about the Bill of Rights is that in enumerating the rights of its citizens, Madison chose not to follow the proposals of Massachusetts, South Carolina, and New Hampshire, which concentrated on delineating the rights of the member states. For the most part, he chose to enumerate a list of rights that would be considered to pertain to citizens by virtue of natural law rather than to the states themselves, rights that were to be held not by the community, but directly by individual citizens. Furthermore, Madison recognized that one of the greatest dangers to individual liberties came not from the mechanical body of the national government, but from majoritarianism. Madison maintained that one of the principal functions of the Bill of Rights would be to protect the minority from the overbearing will of the majority that would seek to use the dictates of positive law to remove their rights (Hunt 1904, 5: 389-390).

Thus, with the advent of stability within the various states and the creation of a national government, the ardent appeal to natural law, as transformed into an appeal to fundamental law, was embodied in American constitutional theory. This ideology still distinguished between rights that are held out to be inalienable and the ordinary dictates of positive civil law, but there was no longer any need for the revolutionary spirit of eighteenth-century natural law theory. Instead, natural law was appealed to as a standard to which government was to be held, a standard that government ought to uphold, and a standard that was placed into the Constitution through its identification of fundamental rights.

The significance of this role of natural law was that it identified constitutional law as being clearly superior to positive law and by so doing set the stage for the advent of judicial review, first in the State of Virginia and later by the U.S. Supreme Court. In this way, the founding fathers not only recognized the sovereignty of the American people through their republican government but also recognized the sovereignty of the constitution as a common understanding of the principles of natural law and the fundamental rights that flow from it. Thus, the principle of fundamental law took on a new importance in the national constitution, and natural law allowed America not only to justify its revolutionary acts but also to achieve popular approbation for a set of rights that were commonly held out to represent those fundamental laws that properly delineated the appropriate relationship between man, society, and government.

Chapter 12

Natural Law and the Constitution: Then and Now

In the eighteenth century, the American incarnation of rights theory was inextricably bound up with the conception of natural law. It accepted, as a given, the idea that legitimate governments must recognize the limits imposed by the fundamental dictates of natural law as discovered and applied through right reason. However, American ideology put a twist on the theory of natural law by combining it with a fully developed theory of the emerging individual. As a result, American natural rights theory recognized the importance of the individual within governmental processes, while at the same time recognizing the need to guarantee those individual rights that are necessary for the maintenance of human dignity. Thus, one of the major influences of natural law theory was that the national constitution came to embody the eighteenth-century conception of natural law and natural rights. Consequently, natural law theory has played and continues to play a vital role in the evolution of American judicial thought.

Surprisingly, the idea that natural law concepts have, in some way, been incorporated into the Constitution is strongly contested by American positivists. English opponents of natural law theory have a decided advantage in making declarations that natural law can not be deemed superior to the positive enactments of a legislature. The reason for this is that, under the English system of law, there has never been any significant acceptance of the concept of fundamental law, while in the United States our initial constitutional philosophy of rights is based upon it. This leaves the ardent American positivist with the problem of having to deny the authority or, more often, the existence of any theory of natural rights, while having to find some way to justify the existence of fundamental law concepts that are widely accepted as restrictions on the national legislature.

This unique role of natural law and natural rights theory within American constitutional law creates within our legal theories a type of dualism in which we recognize the importance of positive law, while still holding some areas of human action as being beyond the authority of and interference from even the national legislature. For example, the expression of law found in the Declaration of Independence and the Bill of Rights represents a type of law that empowers man to resist the efforts of arbitrary governmental authority by holding up, as a barrier to such acts, the fundamental principles identified by natural law. In this sense, the American Revolution can be seen as a revolution of the mind as well as a war for independence, a war that brought into focus a set of ideas that reshaped the world by bringing about not only the creation of the United States but also the French Revolution and, eventually, the advent of European liberalism.

While it seems clear that the dual theories of natural law and natural rights played an important role in the development of early American history, many legal positivists have challenged the notion, arguing that its impact provided little more than a momentary justification for revolution (Spencer 1915, 347). American positivists maintain that while natural law is concerned with morality and therefore is locked into the world of religion and myth, law is reality and is concerned with custom, efficiency, and the dictates of the majority. Thus, making law little more than an act designed to promulgate the state (Gray 1909, 94).

However, an examination of American legal history demonstrates not only that natural law principles played an important role in the development of America's political philosophy, but that they have always been an important part of our judicial history. For example, the passage of the national Constitution, with its accompanying Bill of Rights, represents a point of historic transformation of the theory of natural law. While seventeenth- and eighteenth-century political theorists had long written about the relationship between the theory of natural law and the existence of natural rights, the American Constitution represented the first instance where the theory of natural rights becomes real and natural law is made synonymous with the constitutional principles of fundamental law, due process, and judicial review.

The transformation of natural law principles into the fundamental law principles of the Constitution has become an integral part of our present system of constitutional law. This process of incorporation was aided by three elements of American political theory that were, by and large, accepted at the time that the Constitution and the Bill of Rights were adopted and have continued to influence judicial politics throughout American history. The first attribute of natural law theory that lent itself to incorporation into American constitutional law is its compatibility with the that individuals possess certain inherent rights which government has an obligation to discover and protect. In this sense, American political beliefs are strongly influenced by Locke's social contract theory, which accepts an important role for the individual and natural law. The second concept that aided in the development of the incorporation of natural law principles is the idea that the Constitution in some way represents fundamental legal principles, which give it superiority over all ordinary legislative acts.

Finally, American governmental theory identifies the courts as the authoritative interpreters of that fundamental law that is incorporated in the Constitution. Consequently, the concept of natural rights became a judicial, rather than a political, concept, creating a natural hostility from many legislators and politicians whose authority is limited by its principles. Thus, by incorporating the principles of natural law and natural rights into constitutional theory, the Constitution gives force to the concepts of judicial review, due process, and equal protection, each of which is based on the recognition that certain fundamental rights must be protected from interference. While some legislators did indeed view such ideas as an interference with the authority of the legislature, such sentiments among early Americans were weak and unquestionably not shared by those in judicial authority.

It is clear that, after the passage of the Constitution, many Americans saw the revolutionary principles of natural law as far too unstable to act as the foundation of an emerging nation. However, it is equally clear that many justices believed that incorporating the principles of natural rights into the Constitution provided the theory of natural law not only with the ability to produce stable law but also with the authority to overrule positive law. For example, one of America's first Supreme Court justices, James Wilson, rejected the contention that any "exterior human authority can bind a free and independent man" (Wilson 1896, 1:192). Justice Wilson was also a strong advocate of natural law and principles and higher law theory (Wilson 1804, Ch. 3).

Indeed, one of the primary reasons many of the founding fathers called for the addition of a Bill of Rights to the American Constitution was their belief that it was needed to explicitly protect man's natural rights. It was exactly this argument that Mason, Henry, Jefferson, and Virginia Governor Randolph made in a 1788 bill calling for a Bill of Rights to be added to the national Constitution. The bill read, in part, that there should be "a declaration or bill of rights, asserting and securing from encroachment, the essential and unalienable rights of the people"(Congressional Record, State of Virginia, 1788).

Because of the influence of natural law theory, the Bill of Rights is one of the most important and uniquely American documents ever produced. Susan Ford Wiltshire, who has done an extensive study of the Bill of Rights and its origin, maintains that

> Statistically, the Bill of Rights is an American innovation. The ten amendments contain a total of twenty-seven separate rights. Only six of these, or about 20 percent, were first stated in the Magna Carta. Twenty-one, or about 75 percent, had already been formulated in colonial documents written before the 1689 English Bill of Rights. Only the Ninth Amendment could not be found in several of the state constitutions written between 1776 and 1787. (Wiltshire 1992, 98)

Wiltshire goes on to point out the significance of this document, particularly the Ninth Amendment, which is the only Amendment in which a right receives its first guarantee of protection in the Constitution. Although the

Ninth Amendment lay unused for almost 175 years, its uniqueness is one more example of the influence of natural law on American constitutional theory. If the founders had not been so influenced by the principles of natural law, they most likely would have enumerated a much longer list of rights and then simply left all remaining activity to the will of the legislature. However, the founders strongly embraced these ideas; as a result, the Ninth Amendment represents one part of the Bill of Rights that embodies the principles of natural law, as they were first understood by the Stoics and later developed into the principles of natural rights (Wiltshire 1992, 168-169).

As a result of this strong belief in natural rights, judicial decisions throughout American history have reflected the place of natural law within the Constitution. For example, in 1793, Federal District Court Judge Nathaniel Chipman published a book entitled *Sketches of the Principles of Government,* in which he made considerable use of the theory of natural law. In this work, Chipman maintained that each individual possessed a moral sense that, although fallible, should serve as "the final arbiter of justice." Although he admitted that many of the principles of this moral sense were vague, at best, he still maintained that certain "foundation stones" could be identified, the most important of which represented man's natural rights (Wright 1962, 52, 84-86, 112). While it is difficult to gauge the breadth of this work's influence, it is clear that American judges not only recognized the theory of natural rights but also incorporated it into their decisions, particularly when cases related to the private rights of individuals.

It was in this sense that Justice William Paterson contributed to the development of a higher law theory of the Constitution in the case of *Van Horne v. Dorrance* (1795). In *Van Horne*, Justice Paterson was faced with a legislative act attempting to confiscate property from those who had been British sympathizers during the revolutionary period. With the prospect of having to make a very unpopular decision, Justice Paterson turned to the principles of natural law, stating, "[i]t is evident that the right of acquiring and possessing property, and having it protected, is one of the natural, inherent and inalienable rights of man. . . . This legislature therefore has no authority to make an act divesting one citizen of his freehold, and vesting it in another, without just compensation" (*Van Horne v. Dorrance*). Justice Paterson argued that the government and the Constitution had been created to protect the natural rights of American citizens and that these higher law principles thereby limited the authority of the legislatures to create contradictory positive law.

This same reasoning was continued in the Virginia case of *Elliott's Executor v. Lyell* (1802), in which the court ruled that in order for a statute to be accepted as good law within the State of Virginia, it had to be consistent with the vested rights of the citizens of that state. This higher law of vested rights concept found fertile ground in the United States, and soon the idea was adopted by the Supreme Court of North Carolina in the case of *Trustees of the University of North Carolina v. Fay* (1804). This is not to say that all justices of this time accepted the principle of vested rights. In fact, the *Fay* case contains a stinging dissent, denouncing the protection of so-called vested rights. Despite strong resistance from a legislature that viewed the authority claimed by courts to protect vested or fundamental rights as an interference with their legislative authority, and in some cases as a usurpation of the legislative power all together, the principle was destined to evolve into one of the most important judicial doctrines in American jurisprudence, the doctrine of judicial review (Thayer 1893, 129-133).[1]

Inherent in the higher law principles of fundamental law or vested rights is an implied limitation on legislative authority. This limitation exists as a result of the social compact, the guarantees that flow from free representative government, but, in either instance, the courts must make use of those ideas that are found not in the letter of the Constitution, but in its spirit. The principle of judicial review would have had little impact on the political environment of early America if the principle of natural law had not been readily available to provide the basis for the doctrine's acceptance. In this sense, the Constitution is interpreted to limit the legislature by both its expressed and its implied principles.

While the legislatures did object to this principle, most objections were weak at best, thus opening the way for John Marshall to introduce, with almost no political opposition, a full theory of judicial review in the case of *Marbury v. Madison* (1803). In writing his decision, Marshall reasoned that the Constitution consisted of a set of superior obligations possessing such authority that all contrary legislative acts were void. Early proponents of this doctrine grasped onto its principles as a way of limiting legislative authority and, by doing so, tempering the harsher effects of popular rule. In addition, many saw the principle as the only way to protect the fundamental rights of the minority, principally their property rights (Haines 1914, 287). In this way, the nineteenth-century creators of the principle of judicial review found themselves in strong agreement with the political theories of John Locke, who maintained that the arbitrary use of authority by any legislature can make its enactments void. Thus, while only a few cases made specific reference to the principle of vested rights prior to 1870, Justice Marshall clearly supported the doctrine when he stated, "the government of the United States has been emphatically termed a government of laws, and not men. It will certainly cease to deserve this high appellation, if the laws furnish no remedy for the violation of a vested legal right" (*Marbury v. Madison* 1803).

Marshall's understanding of natural law theory and its role in constitutional interpretation, particularly as it relates to property rights, was also demonstrated in the case of *Ogden v. Saunders* (1827). In this case, which dealt with the right of contracts, Marshall stated that "the framers of the Constitution were intimately acquainted with the writing of those wise and learned men, whose treatises on the laws of nations had guided public opinion in the subject of obligation of contract" (Isaacs 1921, 7: 411). Along with John Marshall, Supreme Court Justice William Johnson, who served on the Court from 1804 to 1834, stated, "I do not hesitate to declare that a state does not possess the power of revoking its own grants. But I do it on the general principle, on reason and nature of things; a principle which imposes laws even on the Deity" (Haines 1965, 91).

Similarly, in the New York case of *Dash v. Van Kleech* (1811), Chancellor Kent and Justice Joseph Story were forced to deal with a legislature claiming that it could create civil statutes, the dictates of which could be made retroactive. In ruling that the legislature had no such authority, the justices stated, "It is not pertained that we have any express constitutional provision on the subject; nor have we any for numerous other rights dear alike to freedom and justice." The Court then ruled that the act of creating retroactive civil legislation was unconstitutional, citing as its authority the dicta of several preceding decisions, along with the English natural law theories of Bracton and Pufendorf. As a general rule, state constitutions contained no provision against retroactive civil legislation; however, such laws were almost universally ruled to be in violation of the "fundamental principles of Justice," "the nature of free government," "the principles of the social compact," "the principles of civil Liberty," or "natural rights" (Smith 1927, 231, 237). Both Justices Kent and Story later went on to reaffirm their acceptance of natural law theory. Kent—by continuing to cite Grotius, Pufendorf, and Bynkershoek, as well as Vattel—provided justification of his understanding of "natural equity" and "universal law." Story continually relied on the principles of natural law, "principles of natural justice," and the "fundamental laws of every free government," as laid down in "the spirit and letter of the Constitution of the United States" (Haines 1965, 94).

Although there is clear evidence of the influence of natural law theory in judicial decisions after 1810, a shifting national tide toward stronger democratic principles made the use of higher law principles in judicial decisions for the purposes of limited legislative authority infrequent, although ongoing references can still be found in the decisions of several justices, particularly Justice Story. In 1815, Justice Story invalidated state legislation attempting to limit corporate property rights, by "standing upon the principles of natural justice, upon the fundamental laws of every free government, and upon the spirit and letter of the Constitution of the United States." In addition, in 1831, Justice Green affirmed his belief in the "eternal principles of justice which no government has a right to disregard." Justice Green even went on to assert that the absence of a restriction in the Constitution did not necessitate the finding of constitutional validity for a legislative act (*Band of State v. Cooper*, 1831).

The idea that the legislature was limited by principles of fundamental law, even in the absence of a specific constitutional provision, received resounding affirmation in the federal case of *Corfield v. Coryell* (1832), in which Justice Bushrod Washington applied the higher law theory of the Constitution in the Court's attempt to enumerate the privileges and immunities guaranteed to all American citizens. He stated, "We feel no hesitation in confining these expressions to these privileges and immunities which are, in their nature, fundamental, and belong, of right, to the citizens of all free governments." The court went on to identify the right to life, liberty, property, safety, and the pursuit of happiness, among other unspecified rights, as rights to which all citizens are naturally entitled and which government is required to protect and prohibit interference.

However, these advocates of fundamental rights could not hope to stand against the rising pressures of Jacksonian democracy. As the advocates of unlimited popular rule were swept into national office, almost all references to fundamental rights were cleansed from both state and national judicial decisions. Ardent democracy is a theory that is much more compatible with the positivist philosophy of government than with the theory of natural rights. Although during this time period, state constitutions continued to contain references to natural law and natural rights, the spirit of their meaning had been washed away with the tide of democratic zeal. The one exception to this rule was in the West, where the frontier spirit of individualism provided ongoing support for both the principles of natural rights and democracy (Haines 1965, 98).

While it is true that appeals to natural law principles within the judiciary experienced a decided decline during the reign of Jacksonian democracy, during the same period there was a corresponding increase in the use of natural law principles in the political debate over the appropriateness of slavery. From 1830 to approximately 1861, the national debate over slavery extensively used the principles of natural law and natural rights.

Abolitionists adopted natural law as one of their principal authorities for opposing the moral and political justness of slavery. For example, in December of 1833, when the Declaration of Sentiments of the American Anti-Slavery Convention was framed in Philadelphia, they established their reliance on natural rights theory by asserting that liberty was an inalienable right, that "every man has a right to his own body—to the products of his own labor—to the protection of the law—and to the common advantages of society," and that, as a result, all laws providing for the enslavement of another human being are, by their very nature, null and void as "a daring infringement on the law of nature" (Wright 1962, 212).

Similarly, Gerrit Smith wrote, in an 1839 letter to Henry Clay, that he maintained the strong belief that slavery was in direct opposition to the "law of nature and my nature's God," and that the institution must be brought to an end. In addition, the Liberty Party followed this same line of thought on a much larger scale, in 1843, when it adopted the doctrine of natural equality as one of its primary planks and cited the ongoing existence of slavery as one of the most egregious violations of this natural right (Wright 1962, 213).

W. G. Brownlow made extensive use of natural law philosophers, such as Cicero and Blackstone, in making his arguments against the validity of slave legislation. He argued that it was clear from the dictates of natural law that "God inscribed upon man's forefront the law of self-ownership as clearly and distinctly as he revealed the fact that twice two makes four" and that since reason clearly revealed the moral error of slavery, such an institution must be brought to an end (Wright 1962, 215).

Finally, in 1839, when the House of Representatives refused to even consider the mounting petitions calling for the end of slavery, John Adams denounced the body for refusing to even listen to any "discussion upon the rights of man, the self-evident truths of the Declaration of Independence," and accused them of stealing from the Declaration "the principle of natural rights" that justified America's original revolution (Wright 1962, 171). Adams also proved his recognition of the rule of natural law as a judicial standard, by using it as one of the bases for his argument before the Supreme Court in the case of *Amistad*—an argument that was later published in pamphlet form in New York in 1841.

After 1840, it appears that the Supreme Court of the State of New York tried single-handedly to attempt to revitalize the higher law theory of constitutional interpretation. During the 1840s, until the advent of the Civil War, the New York state judiciary appears to have been locked into a battle with the state legislature over what it considered to be excessively liberal legislation that unduly infringed on property interests. During this period, the court invalidated more legislation than all other state courts, and even went so far as to invalidate a 75 year-old act that allowed the taking of land for the purposes of road construction without the consent of the owner. Throughout these cases, the court made extensive use of the concepts of higher law and vested rights as the foundation for its actions (Corwin 1917, 15: 281). As a result, at least in New York State, the concept of vested rights came to be synonymous with the concept of "due process of law," and when the national Constitution was amended to include the Fourteenth Amendment, in 1868, its due process clause soon took on a similar meaning.

As a result of this emerging judicial understanding concerning the meaning of the "due process of law," the principal of judicial review as based on higher law theory took on increasing importance from the 1850s to the 1890s. In addition to its judicial use, the concept of fundamental law and vested rights continued to be flown as one of the principle abolitionist banners. Pre–Civil War literature is replete with references to its principles.[2]

With the advent of the war, the attention of the nation was diverted from the judicial theories of natural rights. For many, discussing theories concerning the nature of human rights paled in comparison to the war that was being fought to make such theoretical rights real in a nation struggling for its own survival. However, with the conclusion of the Civil War and the passage of the Fourteenth Amendment came a reinvigoration of the concepts of higher law, particularly as they were incorporated into the principles of "due process of law."

Prior to 1870, the principles of due process, as found in the Fifth and the Fourteenth Amendments, were, at best, vague statements of authority that were interpreted by the courts to have only minimal protective qualities (Corwin 1911, 366-370). While the Fifth Amendment meaning of due process clearly states that "no person shall . . . be deprived of life, liberty, or property, without due process of law," the federal courts showed great reluctance in applying a restrictive interpretation to this doctrine. As a result, while American lawyers attempted to offer up the Fifth Amendment as a protective higher law doctrine, such efforts almost always failed (*Murray's Lessee v. Hoboken Land and Improvement Co.*; *Hurtado v. California*; and *Holden v. Hardy*). However, with a gradual expansion in the protective authority, the concept of due process came hand in hand with an increased use of the doctrine of judicial review, as well as an increased understanding within both the state and national judiciary of the importance of constitutional law.

No immediate revolution in judicial thought took place with the passage of the Fourteenth Amendment. Early use of the Amendment was infrequent, and when it was referred to, it played only an insignificant role in the overall argumentation of the case. As a result, the higher law interpretation of constitutional due process of law clauses would have to wait until the later part of the nineteenth century before, through successively liberal interpretations, it began once again to act as a foundation for a vested rights theory of constitutional interpretation.

Although early references to the Fourteenth Amendment were infrequent, the controversy raised by the creation of the Amendment was considerable. The original function of the Amendment, as proposed by John A. Bingham and supported by the more radical wing of the Republican party, sought substantially to place all state powers under the authority of the federal government. Despite strong sentiments in favor of added controls over the southern states, conservative Republicans, as well as the vast majority of Democrats, chose to oppose such a bold statement of federal authority. As a result, the wording of the Amendment was reworked so that it contained only vague and general terms, which both parties could interpret to satisfy their own personal desires, but which left the amendment with a less than clear meaning (Flack 1908, Ch. 1&2).

While the Fourteenth Amendment lay waiting for the more fertile judicial imaginations of the 1870s, the end of the Civil War opened the door once again for the reemergence of fundamental law principles with a slowly increasing number of cases. For example, in 1866, Justice Salmon Chase stated with confidence that "There are, undoubtedly, fundamental principles of morality and justice which no legislature is at liberty to disregard" (*License Tax Cases*), and Justice Samuel Miller made clear reference to Locke's theory of natural law when he stated that there is an "implied reservation of individual rights, without which the social compact could not exist" (*Loan Association v. Topeka*).

Further, in 1868, when T. M. Cooley published his work *Constitutional Limitations*, his belief in the theory of natural rights was clearly evidenced by his warning to jurists that, just because the Bill of Rights protects certain enumerated individual rights, it should not be understood that the Amendments themselves created these rights. He goes on to instruct his readers that the Bill of Rights is to be taken as a set of restrictions on the authority of the government and should never be interpreted to limit the rights of its citizens (Cooley 1868, 36).

Undoubtedly, the reemergence of higher law theories of constitutional interpretation opened the way for a gradual expansion of the meaning ascribed to the Fourteenth Amendment. As a result, in 1872, in the *Slaughter-House Cases*, Justice Stephen Field gave, for the time, an unusually liberal interpretation to the Fourteenth Amendment, by stating that the Fourteenth "was intended to give practical effect to the Declaration of 1776 of inalienable rights which are the gift of the Creator, which the law does not confer, but only recognizes." Two years later, in 1874, the Supreme Court used a higher law interpretation of the Fourteenth as the basis to reinvigorate the principle of judicial review, producing a stern dissent on the part of Justice Nathan Clifford, condemning the courts for a vague and "general latent spirit" to invalidate legislation that violated no specific constitutional provision (*Loan Association v. Topeka*, Dissent by Justice Clifford).

The idea that the due process clause of the Fourteenth Amendment could act as a significant limitation on legislative authority continued to find some favor in the Supreme Court throughout the early 1880s (*ex parte Wall,* 1882; *Butchers' Union v. Crescent City Co.,* 1883). For example, this idea was given great force in the case of *Barbier v. Connolly*, in which the court uses not only the due process clause of the Fourteenth Amendment but also its equal protection clause to make relevant those natural rights ideas found in the Declaration of Independence. The court asserted that "certain inherent rights lie at the foundation of all action, and upon recognition of them alone can free institutions be maintained. These inherent rights have never been more happily expressed than in the Declaration of Independence. . . . 'We hold these truths to be self-evident'"—that is, so plain that their truth is recognized upon their mere statement—"that all men are endowed"—not by edict of Emperors, or decrees of Parliament, or acts of Congress, but "by their Creator with certain inalienable rights"—that is, rights which cannot be bartered away or given away, or taken away except in punishment of crime—"and that among these, are life, liberty and the pursuit of happiness, and to secure them"—not grant them but secure them—"governments are instituted among man, deriving their just power from the consent of the governed" (*Barbier v. Connolly*, Justice Field).

This case represented the beginning of an easing reluctance on the part of the Court to interpret the equal protection clause of the Fourteenth Amendment as providing sufficient authority to overrule legislative actions. This happened when the Court found an increasing need to address issues of equality and, in doing so, returned to the principles of natural law and natural rights as found in the Declaration of Independence. In addition, this process led Justice Stanley Matthews to feel free to reject discriminatory state regulations as violative of the national Constitution, in the case of *Yick Wo v. Hopkins,* by observing, "When we consider the nature and theory of our institutions of government, the principles upon which they are supposed to rest, and review the history of their development, we are constrained to conclude that they do not mean to leave room for the play and action of purely personal and arbitrary powers" (*Yick Wo v. Hopkins*).

These cases opened the way for a reinterpretation of the due process clause of the Fourteenth Amendment during the early part of the twentieth century. By

1897, the Fourteenth Amendment served the function of incorporating the higher law principles of natural law into the Constitution and led even Justice Harlan, in the case of *Chicago Burlington & Quincy Railway Company v. Chicago,* to proclaim that the right to just compensation was to be "found in natural equity, and laid down by jurists as a principle of universal law" (*Chicago Burlington & Quincy R.R.. Co. v. Chicago*).

As the Court continued to make use of the due process clause to limit government actions, comparisons between the principles of due process of law and natural law became unnecessary because the doctrines increasingly came to represent the embodiment of higher law principles. For example, even the due process clause of the Fifth Amendment benefitted from this interpretation, leading Justice William Moody, in the case of *Twining v. New Jersey* (1908), in reference to the right against self-incrimination, to ask, "Is it a fundamental principle of liberty and justice which inheres in every idea of free government, and is it the inalienable right of a citizen of such government? If it is, and is of a nature that pertains to process of law, this court has declared it to be essential to due process of law" (*Twining v. New Jersey*).

In addition, in 1910, Justice John Harlan went so far as to state that "the courts have rarely, if ever, felt themselves so restrained by technical rules that they could not find some remedy, consistent with the law, for acts, whether done by government or by individual persons, that violated natural justice or were hostile to the fundamental principles devised for the protection of the essential rights of property" (*Monongahela Bridge Co. v. United States*). Similarly, in 1915, Justice Joseph Lamar almost offhandedly recognized the commonality of the two principles, when relying on the principles to overturn state legislation, by stating that "upon principles of natural justice, and under the due process clause of the Fourteenth Amendment," some legislative judgments are void (*Simon v. Southern Railway Co.*, 1915). So widespread was the judicial appeal to the concept of natural law that Roscoe Pound noted that "It is not an accident that something very like a resurrection of natural law is going on the world over" (Pound 1911, 162).

While the symmetry between the principles of due process and the theory of natural rights was widespread throughout the judiciary, by no means was it a universal belief. In fact, one of our most noted members of the U.S. Supreme Court, Justice Oliver Holmes, rejected the idea that there were any absolute truths and maintained that it led to a state of mind that accepted that which was familiar and commonly believed as fact (Wright 1931, 318). Justices Louis Brandeis and Benjamin Cardozo also showed their distaste for the doctrine of natural law. Brandeis condemned the concept, at least as it was used to support the economic principles of economic due process, in his dissenting opinion in the case of *Burns Banking Co. v. Bryan*, and Cardozo characterized natural law as a concept "dethroned as an exemplar" and "made to yield its place to History" (Pound 1923).

However, at the same time, the majority of the Court clearly maintained an acceptance of the concept that the Fourteenth Amendment protected fundamental rights. For example, Justice Edward Sanford asserted this belief when speaking for the majority in the case of *Gitlow v. New York.* In *Gitlow*, the majority held that freedom of speech, as protected by the First Amendment from the acts of Congress, was "among the fundamental personal rights and liberties protected by the due process clause of the Fourteenth Amendment from impairment by the States" (*Gitlow v. New York*). In addition, the court continued to hold this position in 1927, when, in the case of *American Railway Express Company v. Kentucky*, Justice James McReynolds stated that the authority of the federal government was limited in its ability to interfere with the actions of the states, unless their actions endangered the "fundamental principles which have been established in our system of jurisprudence for the protection and enforcement of private rights."

As can be seen, the application of natural law principles to legislative acts through the principles of fundamental law or natural justice has become an important part of the meaning of the due process clause. Its application is not an act of substituting judicial opinion about what is important, wise, or even best for the legislature to do, but rather it represents the Court's understanding that democratic legislatures sometimes have a tendency to use their majoritarian authority to limit or even set aside the rights of the minority. Such interpretations represent an understanding that, while the majority has the power to legislate and restrict many of the actions we take in life, these actions are restrained by the dictates of reason and, by its authority, are prevented from interfering with those rights deemed fundamentally necessary for the operation of a free government.

However, with the rise of the analytical theory of jurisprudence under the tutelage of John Austin, the references to fundamental law became increasingly infrequent. Under this school of thought, the state was seen as the center of all legal authority by virtue of its sole ability to use force as the sanction that could make law real. Thus, the analytical school maintained that no rights could be said to exist that have not been sanctioned by the state. Anything else was relegated to the status of sheer tradition or custom (Austin 1885, I:86 & 178; II: 567).[3] While this school of thought unquestionably led to a marked decline in the prevalence of explicit references to natural law, the theory never completely disappeared and we continue to find its most frequent use within the American judiciary (Haines 1965, 72).

The struggle between those who maintain a belief in the concept of fundamental law and the analytical school of jurisprudence continued for many years and, to a great extent, continues to this day. In 1937, Supreme Court Justice Hugo Black expressed a belief that the Constitution embodied everything that was necessary for a determination of cases, yet he maintained in the case of *Adamson v. California* that the

> Court is endowed by the Constitution with boundless power under natural law periodically to expand and contract constitutional standards to conform to the Court's conception of what, at a particular time, constitutes "civilized decency" and "fundamental justice." . . . . Conceding the possibility that this Court is now wise

enough to improve on the Bill of Rights, I think the possibility is entirely too speculative to agree to take that course. (*Adamson v. California*, Justice Black, Dissenting)

Justice Black's opinion represents an understanding of the American interpretation of natural law theory that sees natural law not as an independent theory that can stand against the Constitution, but as one that was incorporated into the Constitution by the collective will of the people. This conception of natural rights and constitutional theory is uniquely American and seeks to place the individual in the position of being given the ultimate authority to determine what rights are dictated by natural law.

Under this interpretation, the function of the state and the Constitution is not to make law but to protect the individuals' rights to autonomous actions, often from the dictates of majoritarianism, so that they are free to participate in the great theory of democracy. For example, the founders recognized that the majority could be oppressive of even the most basic rights of the minority. Understanding that self-interest and prejudice would always be interjected into the political process, they therefore felt it necessary to elaborate those rights that were held out as essentially guaranteed by natural law. They thus left the interpretation of these rights not to the masses, or even to their elected representatives, but to a body of politically independent individuals who, free from the pressures of majoritarianism, could give substance to those natural rights and protect them not only from the actions of the government but also against the encroachment of the majority itself. In doing so, the Court seeks to discover the collective rationality or understanding of natural law that gives authority to the Constitution. However, the people are never enslaved to the dictates of the Court. To the contrary, to the people and to the people alone is given the right, and some would say the natural right, to alter or amend this great Constitution; but to do that takes more than just a majority—it takes a collective understanding that represents not the simple will of the majority but the consensus of the nation, as a nation of individuals, as to some rights being indeed fundamental.

Not all modern jurists shared this view. For example, this interpretation of the Constitution comes into sharp contrast with that expressed by Judge Learned Hand. Hand maintained that the belief in natural law was widespread in the eighteenth century and that, in America, it represented a strain of thought that went back to the founding fathers of our nation. However, he also maintained that "the Bill of Rights neither proceeded from, nor had any warrant in, the Divine Will . . . but on the contrary that they are the altogether human expression of the will of the state conventions that ratified them. . . . This presupposes that all political power eminates from the people" (Wiltshire 1992, 97).

While many modern jurists shy away from references to such concepts as natural law and natural rights, they continue to rely on those precedents that give expansive interpretations to the equal protection and due process clauses of the Constitution. As a result, references to natural law or fundamental rights were, in this way, simply replaced by references to the sanctity of contract or the protection of private property. However, at the same time, a new venue for the theory of natural rights was emerging in what for many Constitutional scholars was an unexpected location, the Ninth Amendment.

When Madison presented his proposal for the amendment that was eventually ratified as the Ninth Amendment, he made his intentions clear by stating that:

> It has been objected to as against a bill of rights, that, by enumerating particular exceptions to the grant of power, it would disparage those rights which were not placed in the enumeration; and it might follow by implication, that those rights which were not singled out, were intended to be assigned to the hands of the General Government, and were consequently insecure. This is one of the most plausible arguments I have ever heard urged against the admission of a bill of rights into this system; but, I conceive, that it may be guarded against. I have attempted it, as gentlemen may see by turning to the last clause of the fourth resolution [which was later ratified as the Ninth Amendment]. (U.S. Congress 1789, 1:439)

The existence of the Ninth Amendment and Madison's stated recognition of a set of rights that were not created by government but nonetheless obligated and restrained the government creates great difficulties for modern positivists. Modern critics of any theory of rights find that the Ninth Amendment poses a particularly difficult obstacle to be overcome. This is particularly true of positivists who would maintain that all law is the product of positive governmental enactments, thus placing government in the position of not just not recognizing, but creating rights. The Ninth Amendment simply states, "The enumeration in the Constitution of certain rights shall not be construed to deny or disparage others retained by the people" (United States Constitution, Ninth Amendment).[4] This wording clearly implies that the creation of the Bill of Rights was an act of recognizing particular rights held by the people, rather than an act of creation. At the very least, the Amendment makes it clear that the people are believed to possess rights not created by government and that by virtue of its adoption, a vast majority of those Americans voting for its ratification seemed to agree with this premise. In addition, neither can the Ninth be argued to be simply an added protection for the theory of federalism. If it were, the Tenth Amendment, which protects those rights "reserved to the States," would become a useless redundancy (Brest 1975, 708).

Despite Madison's stated concern for these unenumerated rights, the Ninth Amendment was never used prior to 1965. It was in the case of *Griswold v. Connecticut* that the court first breathed life into an Amendment that had been characterized by constitutional scholars as a "simple technical proviso" (Wiltshire 1992, 183). In *Griswold*, the Court was faced with the issue of whether married, consenting adults could be denied access to information concerning contraceptive use. In that case, the Ninth Amendment was recognized as guaranteeing a body of rights that proceeded from no specific constitutional provision. In his concurring opinion, Justice Arthur Goldberg made the relationship between the Ninth Amendment and the theory of natural rights even more explicit, when he stated "that the Framers of the Constitution believed that there are additional fundamental rights, protected from governmental infringement, which exist alongside those fundamental rights specifically mentioned in the first eight constitutional amendments" (*Griswold v. Connecticut*).

The Ninth Amendment opened the way for the expansion of individual liberties and the acknowledgment of numerous previously unenumerated rights, among which are the "right to vote, subject only to reasonable restrictions; the right to cast a ballot equal in weight to those of other citizens; the right to associate with others; the right to marry or not to marry; the right to travel in the United States; the right to receive equal protection not only from the states but also from the federal government; the right to one's own choice about having children [and] the right to attend and report on criminal trials" (Wiltshire 1992, 172).

Bennett B. Patterson takes a much more expansive view of the Ninth Amendment. Patterson sees shadows of the Declaration of Independence in the Ninth and notes that in both documents there was an intentional effort not to create an extensive list of rights. He views both documents as an explicit rejection of the idea that rights are always created by government. Instead, he asserts that both the Ninth and the Declaration of Independence represent the idea that rights are inalienable or endowed by the Creator. In addition, both refer to an unenumerated set of rights, the Declaration by speaking of unalienable rights and stating "among these are Life, Liberty," and the Ninth by specifically referring to unenumerated rights. Under this interpretation of the Ninth it is clear that the principal function of government is not to create rights but rather to secure them (Patterson 1955, 109). While Patterson's interpretation of the Ninth Amendment opens the way for the recognition of what could be called a bottomless barrel of rights, this interpretation not only would be an uncomfortable one for most constitutional theorists, but is also unnecessary. The Ninth Amendment can be interpreted as a "presumptive" statement that seeks to protect corollary rights to those that are specifically guaranteed, while at the same time allowing for some limitations on those rights. This interpretation is in keeping with the common, though not universal, constitutional understanding that enumerated rights are not without any limits. In this sense, the guarantees contained in the Bill of Rights are subject to reasonable limitations, and so even the First Amendment protection of freedom of speech has not been interpreted to protect all speech.[5] Under this interpretation, the Ninth simply allows for the recognition of those rights that are consistent with the substantive and procedural rights already enumerated and in keeping with constitutional conceptions of due process and equal protection. In this way, the Ninth is still a reservoir of unenumerated rights, but its extent is limited by the confines of the rest of the written Constitution and its Amendments.

It was this sense of the Ninth Amendment that the Court used to resolve the case of *Richmond Newspapers v. Virginia,* in which the Court upheld the right of public access to criminal trials, which was also the last case in which the Court made active use of the Ninth Amendment. In the *Richmond Newspapers* case, the Court ruled, "Not withstanding the appropriate caution against reading into the Constitution rights not explicitly defined, the Court has acknowledged that certain unarticulated rights are implicit in enumerated guarantees" (*Richmond Newspapers v. Virginia*).

While some might like to maintain that the theory of natural law is a theory of the past, references to its principles continue to find their way into the decisions of modern cases. In 1976, Justice John Paul Stevens' dissenting opinion in *Meachum v. Fano* (1976) stated that it was "self-evident that all men were endowed by their Creator with liberty as one of the cardinal unalienable rights. It is that basic freedom which the due process clause protects, rather than the particular rights or privileges conferred by specific laws or regulations" (*Meachum v. Fano*). As little as one year later Justice William Brennan, when speaking of a family's right to privacy, made it clear that it was his belief that the right found its authority "not in state law, but in intrinsic human rights" (*Smith v. Organization of Foster Families*). Finally, as recently as 1992, the confirmation hearings for Supreme Court Justice Clarence Thomas began with a spirited debate concerning his professed belief in the authority of natural law, during which arguments were presented both opposing and supporting these theories (Arkes 1992, 13-18). When these specific references are combined with those modern cases that incorporate the fundamental law principles of the Ninth Amendment, particularly as they relate to the right to privacy, it is clear that the theory of natural rights still plays an important role in constitutional law today.

Chapter 13

The American Interpretation of Natural Law as It Pertains to the "Right to Die"

The importance of natural law theory, not only to the issue of the "right to die" but to the whole of that entity that we call the United States, is that it serves as a theoretical beacon, guiding our lumbering society through the process of history, away from the dangers of excessive authoritarianism, majoritarianism, and social conformity. Natural law serves as a guide to our efforts to determine what type of society we desire to move toward, what our political arrangements should look like, how much power should be given to the majority, and how much freedom to the individual. In attempting to answer these questions, the United States has long been influenced by the theories of natural law and natural rights.

During the colonial period, Puritan leaders ascribed to a belief in divine reason. They maintained that the dictates of natural law proceeded directly from God's reason and, by this nature, represented unchanging rules of human obligation. This religious conception of natural law later gave way to an interpretation that was more compatible with the political and legal process of the American system of republican government. This more politically compatible interpretation looked to man's relationship to the physical order of the universe and inferred from it immutable and universal laws, possessing the qualities of mathematical principles, that could be used to derive fundamental laws.

It was exactly this type of natural law theory that aided in establishing the collective authority of Rome; however, in the United States, the theory resulted in a glorification of the independent individual that the Roman state could never have conceived. In its voyage from Rome to America, the theory of natural law took many turns, providing authority for the predominance of the Catholic Church and authority for the divine right of kings, as well as helping to lay the foundation for the emergence of the modern state and, at least in part, the

Protestant Reformation. However, it must be noted that, as times changed, the essential nature of natural law need not be seen as producing contradictory results. Instead, it should be understood that, as the conditions of human existence changed, natural law was applied to differing sets of facts and, as a result, produced different answers, just as the application of a mathematical law produces different answers when applied to different sets of numbers. At the same time, we must also understand that when we speak generically about natural law, we speak not of one theory but, in reality, multiple definitions of one theory. Some variations in outcome must be expected. In this sense, when one wishes to speak specifically about natural law, it is important to specify which interpretation is used. However, when it comes to the American interpretation of natural law, as incorporated into the theory of natural rights, it is clear that the predominate interpretation of natural law theory is the version most compatible with the emergence of the independent individual.

There were, of course, versions of Greek and Roman individuality and, in some form, even Christian individualism, prior to the emergence of seventeenth- and eighteenth-century natural law theory, but it was within the American understanding of natural law and natural rights that the concept of the individual is fully incorporated into the theory of society. Through the mechanism of social contract theory, individualism was transformed into a workable political theory. The social contract achieves this task by providing a practical explanation of the individual's relationship to society and, in doing so, produces what is, for the most part, a new understanding of man as a political animal.

As such, the American theory of natural law is a revolutionary doctrine that is not so much concerned with law as it is with the idea of rights (Hobbes 1994).[1] Therefore, in America, natural law has commonly been used as a principle upon which to base revolutionary shifts in political thought pertaining to the appropriate use of state authority. As a result, when we refer to an American interpretation of natural law, we do not refer to any particular natural law, but rather to the rights that belong to each of us as a result of the foundation that natural law lays in its totality. We refer to the proposition that "to secure these rights, governments are instituted among Men, deriving their just powers from the consent of the governed" (Declaration of Independence).

The American founding fathers understood the function of government to be the preservation of the immutable and fundamental rights dictated by the principle of natural law. They recognized these rights as the minimal foundation essential for the preservation of both the individual and a free society and incorporated them into the American Constitution, thereby rendering all contrary acts of government void. By incorporating the principles of fundamental rights into the Constitution, the founders effectively left the protection of these ideas to the judicial branch of government, which, through the use of judicial review, incorporated these meanings so deeply into the fabric of American society that they are barely noticed by today's average citizen.

Even if all that has been said is true (and it is clear that the theory of natural rights has played a significant role in our nation's past), we may still wish to ask why anyone would wish to resurrect the decaying body of American natural law. For those who accept the authority of natural law, the answer lies in the binding power of the principles themselves; however, for those who may be reluctant to admit to a belief in natural law or even to those who reject it as anything other than a legal fiction, the answer may lie in the desire to achieve continuity—continuity not only with our past, but also with those political theories that make American government possible. Increasingly today, the paradox of democracy and constitutionalism found within the structure of American government has made it difficult, if not impossible, for courts and legislatures to construct a consistent legal philosophy upon which to base an acceptable American theory of rights that is consistent with both our past and our idealized visions of the future. However, by turning to the theories of natural law and natural rights, it may once again be possible to reconcile the individual with society by reconciling the individual's freedom with the democratic authority of the majority and, in doing so, to reconcile our future with our past.

Any movement to reintroduce, or even to pay homage to, the theory of natural law will, of course, not be without its detractors. One can expect that the mere suggestion of such a move would send shivers down the spines of those political scientists who have been taught to reject natural law out of hand or who possess a staunchly positivist view of legal theory. For example, many positivists today would still rally around the war cries of Professor John Burgess of Columbia University, who forcefully represented those who opposed the use of natural law during the 1890s. He maintained that "The revolutionists of the eighteenth-century who declared that nature is the source of individual liberties were entirely wrong" (Burgess 1891, 175). However, Burgess was not so quick to rule out the existence of natural law all together; rather, he maintained that the state was the only and ultimate authority and that if natural law did indeed exist, it was subject not to individual interpretation, but only to the interpretation of the state (Burgess 1891, 52). The difficulty with this argument is that when it is applied to a democratic society, it begins to break down. If only the state can interpret natural law, then what can be said of a democratic society in which the state is nothing more than a representative of the collective wills of free and independent individuals? Surely the conclusion cannot be avoided that, in order for the state to be able to interpret natural law, the individuals who make up the state must have the ability to do so as well. To conclude otherwise would be to disregard the entire conception of the social contract, which mandates that the state can have no more authority or power than the people possess and transfer to it. This argument becomes even more complicated when the idea of constitutionalism is introduced, as in America. Under such a system, individuals not only create the state but direct it to protect those rights that they, not the state, hold out as fundamental.

In the end, the greatest difficulty positivists must face is their theory's own inconsistency with the very theories that constitute American government.

Roscoe Pound once noted that despite a lack of support from the legal philosophers of his day, the average American clearly clung to an understanding of natural law and natural rights as they manifest themselves in the American concept of fundamental law. He maintained that this allegiance may well be based on a human desire to place the manipulation of law and justice beyond the bounds of human control or at least to elevate some rights to a level beyond the control of human whim (Pound 1954, 25-32).

The phenomenon to which Pound refers involves either a conscious or an unconscious recognition that law must, at least on some level, have a connection with ethics and morality and so, to some extent, must be beyond the simple manipulation of the majority. The Greeks and the Romans both maintained that jurisprudence was an inquiry into what was right or just by nature, and law and morals were seen as synonymous with this pursuit (Pound 1926). It was not until the Reformation that a clear effort was made to separate the union of jurisprudence and theology; however, this separation involved only the removal from legal considerations of an appeal to theology, not a divorce from moral ideas altogether. Thus, at the beginning of the nineteenth-century, when Immanuel Kant so clearly separated theology from law, he still maintained a belief that natural law provided an immutable ethical standard that could be used as a standard against which to measure positive law (Kant 1887, 311). Therefore, whether we are talking about Rome's interpretation of natural law as an ethical standard, the medieval interpretation that created a rational-ethical (theological) theory, or the metaphysical interpretation of Kant, each recognized the connection between natural law and ethics. This connection was continually maintained until the strong emergence of positivism and the analytical school of jurisprudence (Pound 1926).

The analytical school of jurisprudence repudiated the theory of natural law and recognized the state as the only authoritative source of law. As a result, the analytical school can maintain no relationship between law and ethics, and we are faced once again with an assertion, painfully reminiscent of the Sophists, that law is nothing more than a matter of social convention and, that thus the only reason to obey its dictates is the fear of getting caught.[2] In support of this contention, Justice Oliver Holmes maintained that, by eliminating all words of moral content, the law would "rid ourselves of an unnecessary confusion" and "gain very much in the clearness of our thought" (Holmes 1920, 179). However, this view is not shared by all schools of American jurisprudence.

While analytical jurists concentrate on the positive laws of the state, they do recognize that these laws may have been influenced by custom, religion, or even societal ethics, but they see the law itself as separate from these principles. However, for this school of legal theory, the principal task for the lawmaker is to discover the sovereign will of the majority and translate it into law. Under such conditions, any mention of fundamental rights would be tantamount to heresy.

In comparison, the historical jurist pays particular attention to tradition and custom and would maintain that all law is derived from these origins. Finally, and in stark contrast to these two schools, there is the philosophical jurist. This school sees not a symmetry but a close relationship between law and morals. This school of jurisprudence has ties with metaphysical and theological thought, producing fertile ground for natural law concepts; even when theology has been stripped from the school of thought, it has frequently found its foundation in ethics (Pound 1926, 103). Such is the case for the theories of such Continental theorists as Stammler, Kohler, Duguit, Krabbe, and Del Vecchio. Each of these philosophers prescribed an ethical standard to which all just laws must conform.

The philosophical school of jurisprudence maintains that positivists have failed to maintain, and thus to take into consideration, a full understanding of the factors that make law binding on the minds as well as the bodies of mankind. As a result, despite the natural tension between the analytical school of jurisprudence and natural law concepts, such jurists rarely escape the influence of natural law, even if its effects are well hidden. Consequently, positivists have always been bound by the ethical concepts of justice and fairness; in the United States, they have the additional burden of complying with the principles of equality, privacy, and autonomy.

Within the confines of American constitutional law, any concept of a mechanical application of law becomes even more tenuous when justices are asked to apply such doctrines as implied powers, due process, and equal protection and to construe such vague phrases without any aid from a body of common law precedents. In response to such a conception of judicial decision making, Justice Cardozo stated that it "would indeed be intolerable in its hardship and oppression if natural law, in the sense in which I have used the term, did not supply the main rule of judgment to the judge when precedent and custom fail or are displaced" (Cardozo 1922, 142-143). Under such conditions, natural law and its requirement of the application of reason become more of a restraint on judicial interpretation than do the words of the Constitution itself. Natural law limits both the legislatures and the judges from infusing personal prejudice or opinion into their decisions and provides guidelines that all legal decisions should meet.

It was in this sense that the Greeks and Romans envisioned natural law not as a list of specific dictates, but rather as a standard against which positive enactments were to be measured. This conception was slightly modified during the Middle Ages, by adding to it an eternal or religious component; however, for the most part, any theological element has been stripped from the American interpretation, leaving American natural law theory with one of two possible interpretations. The first characterizes natural law as statements of universal laws based on man's constitution and his relationship to society. The second concentrates on those principles of natural law that can be stated as rights and that are established, or at least should be established, within any political system seeking to produce justice. It is in this latter sense that natural law and natural rights theory has most frequently been used by the American judiciary.

In this sense, natural law is conceived as a criterion against which the development of law should be compared, thus giving rise to particular identifiable requirements such as legal equality, maximum personal autonomy consistent with the well-being of society, and the maintenance of a realm of personal privacy in which the state has no authority. The modern conception of this theory does not recognize one changeless standard but the identification of a set of principles or rules that produce different results as applied to differing situations. Therefore, natural law is not a rigid dictatorial standard, but a principle against which legal enactments can be tested; an idealistic version of reality, not actually to be obtained, but to serve as an indicator of appropriateness and encroachment. Thus, natural law can be viewed not as a formal part of positive law but as an influential component of its formation and as a standard against which its dictates are to be justified or criticized.

Such a theory of natural law may still antagonize those who believe that law is the product of authority and force, as embodied in the state. Although those who favor the hypothesis of force have, for the most part, predominated during the modern era, the products of such a theory have failed to find popular acceptance. In the end, if all that there is to law is positivism, then there can be no permanent standard upon which to base ongoing consensus concerning what it means to be just. As a result, concepts such as "rights" are constantly subject to change at the whims of the citizenry. Thus, our legal system has tended toward discord and strife and cannot be said to be characterized by anything even remotely similar to universal assent. In a real sense, law cannot be viewed simply as an outgrowth of custom, habit, or force. Law must properly be understood as an appeal to reason, as discovered by man through his relationship with the world and his society. In this way, natural law and natural rights theory can guide us in our effort to determine the appropriate use of positive law.

Natural law should not properly be viewed as being either liberal or conservative. The existence of an idealized legal standard does not necessitate that positive law must be overruled when the two come into conflict. Thus, in today's society, natural law could not be considered a workable tool for the lawyer outside of a narrow constitutional context. Despite this fact, it must be noted that natural rights, when incorporated into our political ideology and Constitution, are not to be construed as something given to American citizens by a benevolent legislature or even as something created by the majoritarian instincts of our citizens. Instead, they must be viewed as pre-political rights that have been recognized as guiding principles for our society. True or false, such a theory serves as a valuable ideology for protecting those rights that our society holds as essential for the enjoyment of the good life.

In such an incarnation, natural law is clearly a legalistic doctrine. While the concept is sufficient to cover most aspects of human life, it is best applied in the legal realm. The theory of natural rights thus serves as an ordering system based upon a perceived set of universal principles, derived by human reason from natural law principles and contemporary facts. In this way, natural law sets out the broader theoretical objectives toward which human law should aspire. These principles, by their nature, cannot be overly precise, but they offer guidance for the application of positive law. Along these lines, natural rights represent the implementation of those principles into political action by setting certain realms of human conduct apart from the intervention of positive; and in so doing, they may produce rules that themselves are sufficiently bound to provide for latitude of execution, varying modes of application, or even error.

Natural rights establish the boundaries of permissible action but do not determine which actions, in and of themselves, are good or bad. Under such a construction, once the parameters are set, the majority has no power to interfere with actions that take place within those defined boundaries. It is for this reason, the protection of individual rights, that the founders recognized the danger of unrestrained majoritarianism. Thus, the first rule that can be derived from a truly American interpretation of natural law is that government must be limited. For example, in his great defense of Parliament's resistance to the King of England, Jonathan Mayhew (1749) stated that Parliament's actions represented a "defense of natural and legal rights of the people, against the unnatural and illegal encroachment of absolute, arbitrary power" (Thornton 1860, 93). Similarly, Thomas Paine expressed the idea that the human person possesses rights not because of the beneficent actions of some government that can later remove what has been granted, but by virtue of his existence as a creature capable of being his own master; therefore, each human being is not merely a means to some communal end but an identifiable end in and of himself. It is in this sense that an individual is the possessor of rights, rights that are owned, not given, recognized, not given; in this sense, government is, at best, "a necessary evil" that exists only for the protection of these rights. Government actions must be restricted in scope if such rights are to continue to exist (Paine 1945).[3]

The importance of these ideas is that they identify American government as a government of limited powers, whose principal purpose is to aid in the development of the maximum expression of freedom and autonomy consistent with the common good. While this pursuit of the common good is also the foundation of authority and may be exercised directly by the people or through representatives, this is an authority over free citizens, not the authority of a master and servant. These maxims place an emphasis on a conception of liberty that cannot be justly restrained any further than is necessary for the enjoyment of this same right by all of society's members. These ideas make up the core of the American legal system and can never be accurately reduced to any stable set of positive laws. Within the American context, at least, they represent the idea of limited government for the protection of individual liberty.

Thus, in America, the Hobbesian principle that no law made by the state can be unjust is specifically rejected (Hobbes 1994, Ch. 30). The American interpretation of Locke's theory of the social contract clearly holds that the citizen never surrenders all sovereignty to the state. Man divides, and always has divided, his allegiances between all those social and political institutions that affect his life; to a great extent within modern political life, he retains this sovereignty for himself. It is from this perspective that an expectation of privacy and autonomy is formed. American citizens consent to the sovereignty of the state only within defined limits, and the Constitution, with its Bill of Rights and additional Amendments, is an effort to set down in writing the nature of those limits. Limitations of exactly this nature were, for the Greeks and Romans, to be found in the principles of natural law. It was similarly these principles that the American founding fathers believed they were incorporating into the Constitution. The positivist glorifies the democratic nature of American government, attempting to set into law the will of the majority. However, the U.S. Constitution, by its design, seeks not only to protect the majority, but also to protect the minority from the majority. In this regard, the concept of natural rights stands as the foundation for resistance to the majoritarian authority of the state (Elliot 1925).

When these principles are applied to the question of the "right to die," two things may be learned. First, while it may not be possible to list exactly what rights Americans possess, it is clear from the mere fact that we have a limited government that we possess some rights. When the powers that a government can justly exercise are limited, a realm of free action is created for the enjoyment of its citizens. Whatever rights we, as citizens, do possess must be free from the arbitrary interference of government, to the extent that government may interfere only for the benefit of other citizens and not simply to provide some paternalistic interference with a citizen's freedom of action. For this reason, it has been maintained that "the state should interfere as little as possible with the private affairs . . . the great natural rights of the people must be secure from usurpation" and freedom of thought must be recognized as absolute, and censorship as the "greatest of political evils" (Merriam 1924).

The second principle of American natural law theory that is directly relevant to the issue of the "right to die" involves the establishment of particular rights. As early as 1771, Massachusetts clergyman John Wise wrote that mankind possessed a natural liberty that was held by him by virtue of the law of nature and provided each human being liberty "as to his mind" and "to his person," giving him "free use of his own reason" to guide his personal actions (Wright 1931, 53). This interpretation of natural law is important because it places the possession of rights in the hands of the individual rather than the society. In this sense, American natural law theory is the same as the classical liberal theory of rights, in which "rights define a sphere of moral jurisdiction that persons have over certain resources in the world—including their bodies. This jurisdiction establishes the boundaries within which persons are free to do what they wish. As long as people are acting within their respective jurisdictional spheres, their acts are deemed to be 'rightful' (as distinguished from 'good'), and others may not use force to interfere" (Barnett 1989, 40).

It is under this interpretation of American natural rights theory that rights can be said to spring not only from the positive law but also from those fundamental rights incorporated into the American Constitution. As a result of these fundamental principles, Americans are said to have a right to universal suffrage, free speech and association, political equality, equality before the law, and a constitutional form of government to secure these rights. In addition, American courts have ruled that Americans enjoy a "right to privacy in matters purely private" that is derived "from natural law" (*Pavesich v. New England Life Insurance Co.*). This sentiment was echoed forty years later, when it was ruled that "the right to privacy, having its origin in natural law, is immutable and absolute and transcends the power of any authority to change or abolish it" (*McGovern v. Van Ripper*).

The significance of this characteristic of American natural law, as it pertains to the issue of the "right to die," is that it demands the recognition of fundamental personal rights as they are manifest in the concepts of freedom and autonomy. In this way, a distinction is set up between positive law and natural law in regard to the intended benefactor of its authority. Positive law is primarily based on an attempt to benefit society as a whole, while natural law and natural rights are concerned with the individual. The two coexist peacefully only when it is realized that positive law has authority over only those acts that involve the coordinated actions of several individuals (social activities), while natural law pertains to unitary (private) activities. Thus, the proper aim of positive law is not the promotion of virtue, but the maintenance of social stability. Therefore, positive law does not forbid every evil act, but only those acts that endanger society. Nor does positive law require all citizens to perform every act that is good, but only those acts that are required for the general welfare of society (Aquinas 1948, 1a 2ae, 72, 4; 96, 2 & 3).

Jacques Maritain argues that natural law demands the recognition that

> every human person has the right to make his own decisions with regard to his personal destiny, whether it be a question of choosing one's work, or marrying the man or woman of one's choice or of pursuing a religious vocation. In the case of extreme peril and for the safety of the community, the state can forcibly requisition the services of each of us and demand that each risk his life in a just war; it can deprive criminals of certain of their rights but the state becomes tyrannical if it tries to "become master of man's souls." (Maritain 1971, 79)

Such an interpretation of natural law creates a sphere of individual privacy and autonomy in that the individual must be allowed freedom of action, actions which government may not restrain so long as they do not directly and negatively affect another person. Even when governmental restrictions are allowed, they must be limited so as to protect the rights of autonomous action as much as possible.

The final element of the American interpretation of natural law can be characterized as an issue of self-ownership. The American conception of rights theory rejects the Aristotelian conception of the individual as, in some way, belonging to the collective state. In the United States, the individual is viewed as possessing complete and exclusive ownership of his or her self; by virtue of that ownership, we are said to be entitled to all those rights that enure to a free man. It was exactly these ideas that came to the forefront of American political thought when the nation was thrown into a national debate over the moral wrongness of slavery. Throughout the extended period of this debate, the theory of natural law was extensively used in support of a concept that has become an almost unquestioned part of American political philosophy today—the idea that every man has a right to his own body "and that God [or reason] has inscribed upon man's forefront the law of self-ownership" (Brownlow and Pryne 1858, 63-67).

No analysis of American natural law and of the "right to die" in America would be complete without an understanding of the personal nature of these rights. Perhaps Jefferson provided the most eloquent expression of this nature of natural rights, in his *Notes on Virginia*, when he stated that government possesses the authority to regulate all rights submitted to them by the people, but that it must always recognize that the right to conscience is not among those rights and never could be, because it is not only a fundamental right but an inalienable right, a right that can not be taken nor given, not even in return for some corresponding set of rights (Jefferson 1782, 291).

In this way, rights can be divided into the distinct categories of primary and secondary rights. Primary rights are of the highest priority and involve those matters that pertain purely to the individual; they are reflected in issues concerning a person's right to free thought, conscience, or self-ownership. Such rights are fundamental and inalienable and, as such, can never rightly be subjected to civil regulation or, for that matter, to the regulation of any authority other than the individual to whom they belong. In contrast, secondary rights represent the right to put into action our desires within the social world. This would involve the right to buy, sell, and acquire material goods for our own happiness or for the happiness of others. These rights, while important to the individual, inherently involve social activity and so open themselves to civil regulation (Wright 1931, 247).

The importance of these characteristics of American legal philosophy to the issue of the "right to die" is that they separate legal authority into distinct social and personal realms. Within the social realm of interactive activity, the state is vested with full authority to regulate through the mechanism of positive law. However, once a person is acting within the private realm, state activity can no longer be considered a simple act of lawmaking. When the state attempts to regulate the private matters of its citizens' lives (such as whom they can marry, what occupation they can follow, or what religion they may profess) beyond the extent necessary to maintain social order, then the state is no longer attempting to regulate society but private morality; within the United States, moral experience is essentially a matter for the individual. Positive law has a social or objective character, while morality has an individual or subjective character and, thus, cannot be subjected to the regulations of positive law (d'Entr'eves 1965, 85). In essence, American legal philosophy requires a setting aside of certain areas of individual activity and designates them as involving issues in which the community has no authority to interfere and with which each individual must struggle. Without theoretically setting aside a private sphere of activity from the control of government, Americans would be forced to accept the proposition that the state is an absolute sovereign and that, in the end, "might makes right," a proposition that is clearly unacceptable to many who are strong believers in the principle of rights.

The importance of the American division between the authority of the private individual over his or her own life and the authority of the state over public matters is that it recognizes the need to reach a balance between civil order and freedom. In the United States, it is the goal of the Constitution and its amendments to achieve this balance—a balance between the natural law traditions of the early Greeks and the Roman reverence for positive law. Thus, when the Constitution speaks of a right to "Life and Liberty," it speaks of rights that are not held by the community, but by the individual. It speaks of a right that allows each of us to use that life as we see fit, so long as it does not directly bring harm to others. As a corollary to this right is the unquestioned right to self-ownership within the United States; by virtue of this right, we are free to do with our bodies those things that we believe to be morally correct as long as they do not infringe on the freedoms of others.

Chapter 14

Applications

The American Constitution embodies a balance between the two competing impulses of majority rule and individual rights, a balance that recognizes that in order for both theories to exist, both must in some way be limited. Thus, the Constitution attempts to incorporate the concept of fundamental rights into the scheme of American government without giving way to the chaos of personal opinion that can result from excessive individualism. The Constitution incorporates the principles of natural rights, but recognizes that those principles must be limited by reasonable dictates necessary for both social stability and personal freedom; in so writing, the founders created a legal framework that allows both democracy and individual liberties to peacefully coexist (Pollock 1923).

A review of natural law and an application of its principles to the question of the "right to die" thus aids in a determination of whether, for Americans, such a right can be said to exist. The American interpretation of natural law is very similar to that used to rule ancient Rome, in that it recognizes natural law as an appropriate guide for the creation of civil law. However, while Roman natural law theory was concerned almost exclusively with the good of man as a common identity (community), American political theory recognizes both the individual and the community as entities deserving of protection. As a result of this need to compromise between the principles of majority rule and individual rights, the Constitution gives special status to the rights of the individual. However, even in Rome, where individuality was a mere shadow of its present existence, interference with a citizen's decision to die was seen as beyond the realm of state power. Such a decision was viewed as a private matter, not concerning the community unless the actor was under legal indictment.

Similarly, while the medieval interpretation of natural law placed great authority in the hands of the state, it recognized that the individual is the ultimate judge of what constitutes justice. In addition, as has been shown and will be discussed in further detail later on, medieval natural law offers us a flexible understanding of the theory that, even when liberally mixed with Christian ideology, allows for a limited sense of passive euthanasia, as long as it does not involve the removal or refusal of ordinary care.

Further, seventeenth- and eighteenth-century political thought brought us a new and dramatic emphasis on the theory of rights that, when merged with the theory of natural law, produced the theory of natural rights that was so influential on the American founding fathers. Several natural law theorists of the eighteenth century viewed the act of rational self-killing as an unquestionable right protected by the dictates of natural law. They developed the idea that, while each of us surrenders some of our rights to the community in return for the stability provided by government, we do not surrender all of our rights, and the government is limited in its ability to restrict these rights. It was from this fire that the American theory of fundamental rights was first forged. Within American political thought, the theory of natural law was fully transformed into a theory of natural rights and incorporated into the Constitution as fundamental law. As a theory, it does not seek to characterize particular acts as being right or wrong, but recognizes certain categories of human activity as being beyond the appropriate control of the state. Examples of such categories include, but are not necessarily limited to, the right to life, the right to privacy, self-ownership, and the right to autonomy in making decisions of conscience. Thus, when we examine the theory of American government we find that it is characterized by several dominant principles directly related to its natural law heritage.

First, American government is an institution of limited power, possessing the authority to regulate the personal affairs of its citizens only to that extent necessary for the maintenance of health, education, and welfare of its collective citizenry. As a result of these limitations, its citizens are said to possess particular civil liberties that guarantee that government will not illegally interfere with their right to personal security, ownership of property, or speech.

Second, citizens are conceived of as possessing both collective and individual rights. Collective rights represent those entitlements created by government and, as such, open to full governmental regulation. Private rights represent those rights recognized as fundamental by the nation's citizenry and are protected by the Constitution and its Bill of Rights. These rights, considered to be inalienable, are beyond the power of the government to remove or the citizenry to give away. Such private rights are said to be recognized, but not created, by government. Nevertheless, they are dependent upon governmental authority for their effective existence.

Third, government is not only restrained from interfering with the private rights of its citizens, but also affirmatively obligated to protect its citizens' rights, not only from its own actions but also from the actions of other citizens, in some instances even from actions supported by the majority. When we apply these principles to three rights that are readily recognized within our society (the rights to life, self-ownership, and privacy), we can begin to construct answers to the many questions surrounding the issue of the "right to die."

When we begin seriously to consider questions concerning an individual's right to rationally decide to terminate his or her life, we soon discover that we face not one question, but a set of increasingly complex questions that are characterized more by a sliding scale of intensity than by a binary equation. In order to draw rational conclusions, the preceding principles must be applied to a series of questions, rather than to the singular question of whether there is a "right to die."

A RIGHT TO PASSIVE EUTHANASIA?

The first, and least complex, of the questions that must be addressed is whether a person who is facing imminent death has the right to order the removal of life-sustaining procedures. Such activities generally fall under the heading of passive euthanasia and meet with the highest level of popular support.

In determining whether a person has a right to engage in passive euthanasia, we can start by examining three rights that in our society have attained near universal acceptance. First, it is clear that our society recognizes a right to life. However, having boldly asserted that right, the clarity of its meaning immediately comes into question. At its very minimum, the right to life means that once born, human beings have a right to continued existence if they so choose.[1] In its strongest sense, the right to life recognizes life as a paramount good without which no other right can be enjoyed, and so as deserving of the highest level of protection. Indeed, in accordance with the third principle of American political ideology listed earlier, government does in fact have an obligation to protect the lives of its citizens. The question then becomes to what extent the government can use its authority to do so.

It is clear that American government does seek to protect its citizens from such life-threatening events as violent crime, poorly tested drugs, and drunken drivers. However, government does not seek to protect its citizens from all dangers, particularly not those that are voluntarily entered into. In this regard, Americans are allowed freedom to participate in a wide variety of life-threatening activities such as skydiving, bungee jumping, motorcycle racing, or even cigarette smoking. Given these facts, how do we reconcile this lack of governmental intervention with the inalienable right to life and the governmental obligation to protect it? The answer to this apparent contradiction is found in an exploration of the right to self-ownership and privacy.

While it is unrefuted that there is a right to ongoing life, it is also clear that American political ideology radically differs from that of Greece and Rome, where the individual is inseparable from the community. Under the American theory of natural rights, life is something not owned by the state or the community, but owned fully and completely by the individual; as such, it is beyond the appropriate control of the state, as long as its use does not threaten the stability of the state or the rights and well-being of its other citizens. This principle becomes even clearer when we add to it even the simplest understanding of the right to privacy. The right to privacy guarantees the citizen freedom from governmental and public scrutiny in matters that are personal to the individual and do not directly affect the rights or well-being of other citizens.

If we apply these observations to the first issue of a terminally ill individual, we are forced (willingly or unwillingly) to conclude that, under American political ideology, this individual does indeed have a right to order the removal of life-sustaining procedures. First, it is clear that the decision to order the removal of life-sustaining procedures is one of the most personal decisions individuals can make. It is a decision that pertains to their bodies only and involves a decision about their personal beliefs and consciences, as well as a decision about the way they choose to live the remainder of their lives. In addition, it is clearly an issue of self-ownership. If we can truly be said to own our bodies, then, at a minimum, we must be able to control what happens to our bodies, so long as our decisions do not directly harm others. While the removal of life-sustaining medical procedures may cause others grief or moral indignation, this is not the type of harm that can justify state intervention. Finally, although government has the obligation to protect the life of its citizens, it may not intervene except to protect the rights of the individual seeking the removal of such procedures, because the government's ability to protect the life of the actor is limited by the actor's exercise of his or her right to self-ownership within the realm of private action. As a result, the individual's wishes must be upheld.

A RIGHT TO ACTIVE EUTHANASIA?

The second question that must be addressed moves us a little bit farther down the slippery slope of "right to die" issues. Does a terminally ill person have the right to take positive actions to terminate his or her life? This question presents certain complexities that were missing from our first scenario. First, rather than involving the extraction of care, which allows nature to take its normal course, this question involves the interjection of some unnatural agent whose sole purpose would be to bring about a premature death. However, all moral and religious considerations aside, the issue is still one of rights the question is whether the variations between the first and second scenarios are sufficient to set aside a person's right to self-determination, self-ownership, and privacy.

From the perspective of the individual who is choosing to die, all relevant factors seem to be the same. The individual is still engaged in a private decision that will not harm any outside party; however, the government's position has changed slightly. In the first scenario, the actors were not taking action against their lives, but were merely exercising their rights not to have their bodies subjected to ongoing medical treatment. In the second scenario, the government's obligation to protect the lives of its citizens requires it to inspect more closely such a decision. First, the government must be sure that the actor is possessed of rational decision-making capability.[2] If the government finds a lack of rational decision-making capacity, then it has an obligation to protect the life of that citizen from harm. However, if it determines that the individual is capable of making rational determinations in regard to his or her life course, then the government has no authority to intervene.

A second consideration that may change the responsibility of government involves the possibility of an outside party. In the first scenario, which involved the removal of life-sustaining procedures, the activities of the third party (more likely than not, medical personnel) were not directly related to the death of the citizen. However, in the present scenario, the act of dying will likely involve some third party who supplies the actor with the means for achieving the desired end. Involving an outside party changes the government's situation to extent that it, at least temporarily, overrides the private nature of the act.

The American conception of privacy provides conflicting results when applied to this issue. Generally, the law recognizes the existence of a realm of doctor-patient confidentiality, but this confidentiality is not absolute and can be set aside in cases of extreme danger. In addition, it is clear that a majority of American states presently do recognize such acts as sufficient bases for the intervention of the criminal law.[3] The question, however, is not what the law presently allows, but what it should allow, based on our natural law heritage. Natural law traditions, by their nature, place a great deal of emphasis on a person's ability to use his or her individual capacity to reason, to determine the course of life that should be taken. Given this tradition, modern criminal laws making suicide and the act of assisting in a suicide a crime can be seen as encompassing an overly broad category of human actions. While it is clear that the state has an interest in protecting the life of its citizens, this authority is appropriately used only in an effort to prevent those acts of morbid suicide that are not accompanied by a process of rational decision-making. In such instances, the state has the responsibility of saving the individual from his or her own irrationality and is justified in its effort to prosecute any individual who aids another in the commission of such a devastating act. It must be noted, however, that such an act is of a markedly different quality from those acts with which we are concerned when we speak of a "right to die." As was outlined in the first scenario, the state does have an affirmative responsibility to be sure that the actor is capable of making a rational decision about death. However, once rationality has been established, the state's authority to intervene is limited by our rights to self-ownership and autonomy as rational creatures.

As to third-party providers of means, any governmental effort to regulate their efforts must be limited to ensuring that such aid is provided only in those instances where the actor is capable of rational decision making. In doing so, the state is entitled to place the burden of affirmatively proving rational capacity on the provider of means or requiring that state standards for a determination of minimal rationality are met. Once such conditions have been met, the state's legitimate authority to regulate the provision of means is severely limited.

A limitation on the state's authority to regulate the provision of means can be rationally argued on another foundation as well. If we assume that rational individuals do indeed have a "right to die" and that the only issue with which we are concerned is the state's legitimate authority to regulate the provision of means, a resolution to the issue becomes much clearer. If a person has a right to a particular action, those things necessary for the commission of that act cannot be governmentally forbidden without a functional removal of the right. An analogy to a less controversial right might make this argument clearer. Under the U.S. Constitution, Americans who meet the minimal requirements of rationality have a right to vote.[4] As a result of that right, the government's legitimate authority to interfere with those things necessary for the exercise of this right is severely limited. For example, a law that made it a crime to transport voters to the polls or to travel on roads that led to the designated polling place would most assuredly be considered an unconstitutional interference with the right to vote. Similarly, if, as this work advocates, there is a "right to die," then the government may not regulate the provision of means out of existence. However, that government can regulate who may distribute the means for terminating life, under what conditions they may be distributed, or even which means can be made available. Although the government has some regulatory power, there is nothing concerning the provision of means to a rational individual that empowers the government to forbid and punish such actions.

In addition, when outside parties are in some way aiding in the process of death, it is equally clear that their involvement is, at most, tangential to the actor's decision to use the provided means. The decision to die is still a private decision, and the actual use of the means of death does not directly involve any outside party. In the end, the life at stake is still the individual's to do with as he or she sees fit. As a result, there are not, justifiable bases upon which government intervention can be maintained beyond the determination of rational decision-making capacity. Under such conditions and within the bounds of established American political ideology, there is no room for the doctrine of governmental paternalism.

A RIGHT TO ASSISTED SUICIDE?

The next difficult issue to be addressed concerns the question of whether an individual has the right to direct another person to terminate his or her life. This question raises some of the strongest issues pertaining to active euthanasia and involves the question of whether we have a right not just to die, but also to obtain "assisted suicide." This scenario differs from the previous example in that, the third party may or may not provide the means of bringing about death, but does commit the affirmative act that causes death to occur. While in today's society we would generally assume that any active assistance needed for an individual to commit suicide would come from some member of the medical profession, there is no technical reason for this presumption. Therefore, while saving issues of medical ethics for later discussion, we will assume a generic assistant.

In the first two instances, our analysis indicated that American political ideology would tend to uphold a person's "right to die." The issue of assisted suicide begins to introduce factors that must be addressed in any effort to determine a person's right. Many of the elements to be considered are the same as in the first two instances, therefore leading us to the conclusion that the individual still has a right to make personal decisions concerning self-ownership. However, in the present case, we have introduced an outsider who is much more than a passive provider of information or technology. We have a third-party participant whose sole function is to initiate the biological processes that bring about the death of another. While the right to assisted suicide may exist, such acts fall into the realm of permissible governmental regulation.

By interjecting an active third party, particularly a third party that may be paid, the veil of privacy is drawn open, and at least some level of governmental regulation is allowed in. It is for this reason, among others, that government is justified in regulating prostitution, though to a much smaller extent promiscuity between consenting unmarried adults, and the sale of particular forms of pornography, but not necessarily its personal possession within the home. However, while the introduction of an active third party allows for some governmental regulation, the question then becomes how much regulation is permissible? Generally speaking, once citizens begin to engage in public actions, particularly market activities, the government has the needed authority to regulate the activity as a whole. As stated earlier, government may regulate not only for the good of its individual citizens but also for the protection of social stability.

Several arguments have been advanced against the legalization of active euthanasia, such as the "wedge argument" and the "desensitization argument," which were outlined in the first part of this book but deserve brief reiteration here. Both arguments are essentially reducible to the proposition that, if we allow individuals to voluntarily euthanize themselves, we, as a society, will slowly become less sensitive to issues of death, and this desensitization will lead the public to allow not only voluntary but involuntary euthanasia of the old, the handicapped, or even the socially undesirable.

There are three potential responses to such a position. The first possibility is that the argument can be dismissed as an effort to impose one particular religious code onto the actions of free individuals. While such arguments are sure to be viewed in this manner by some, by and large this is an effort to avoid the argument rather than deal with it. It is true that some speakers may simply be using arguments about desensitization to encourage conformity with their preferred religious code; however, morality involves much more than religious belief. After all, the atheist can have a moral code. Morality is that common set of beliefs that holds society together and, in this sense, any action that threatens morality can be viewed as a threat to the stability of society. It is for this reason that a good many criminal laws exist that make acts illegal, not because they are physically harmful but because they diverge from those moral norms that stabilize society.

THE RIGHT TO DIE AND SYSTEMS OF REGULATION

While the proper role of morality in law has long been a subject of debate,[5] a few relevant observations allow for ready application to the present debate. The first of these observations is that, outside of any particular religious context, it is impossible for anyone to lay claim to an authoritative understanding of what acts constitute violations of society's moral code.[6] While it may be possible to make reference to generalized societal agreement on some topics, it is readily apparent that U.S. moral agreement contains more gray areas than black and white. In addition to the lack of any clear nonreligious moral standards, at least within the United States, morality is an evolutionary rather than an absolute standard. Even a brief historical retrospective will demonstrate that moral standards concerning the treatment of minorities, human sexuality, and the environment have all changed. While some may argue that moral codes have not changed but that society has simply begone to recognized that which has always existed, the fact remains that in a society which stands for religious freedom and the right to individual choice in matters of conscience, any effort to freeze morality in one place is inconsistent with our governmental theory and historical practice. As a result, while arguments about our need to preserve our moral code are important, the threat of a change in that moral code cannot be used as a justification to make active euthanasia illegal, absent some other showing of social harm.

A second response to the social desensitization argument characterizes it as worthy of examination but inherently too speculative to provide a basis for limiting individual liberty, particularly as it pertains to private decisions concerning health and self-ownership. Exactly this position was taken by the U.S. Supreme Court when it set aside state-advanced arguments in favor of limiting access to information concerning the use of contraceptives in the case of *Griswold v. Connecticut.*

In *Griswold,* the Court ruled that the Constitution and Bill of Rights protected a citizen's right to privacy, that, when state regulations result in a significant encroachment of personal liberty, the state must be engaged in more than speculation concerning the proposed danger that it seeks to avoid, and that, indeed, the state must show a necessary relation between a permissible state policy and the proposed law.[7] In the present case, while the arguments made against legalization do raise a worrisome specter of future violation of the most basic of human rights, there is no evidence to support the proposition that this danger could not be resolved in a less restrictive manner than absolute prohibition. As a result, once again, while the desensitization argument is a matter of concern, it cannot be used as a justification for absolute prohibition.

The Active Restrictive Mode

The final approach to the desensitization argument is to accept the proposition that active euthanasia is inherently incompatible with the stability of society and, therefore, the state must take what this author would call an "active restrictive" posture. Such a position would require the state to adopt a clearly defined set of laws against active euthanasia and to punish all violations of those laws in the same way it punishes violations of current homicide statutes. There are, however, several difficulties with this position. First, despite the fact that active euthanasia is a criminal act throughout almost all the United States, violators of such laws overwhelmingly go unpunished or receive only light probationary punishments because either district attorneys refuse to prosecute or juries refuse to convict.[8] While the lack of enforcement is not a justification for making such acts legal, the phenomenon demonstrates a lack of social support for the proposition that such acts constitute a crime. By and large, Americans characterize such acts as private decisions and freely define them as mercy killings, for which they are unwilling to hand down harsh penalties.

While this argument smacks of a type of democratic rule more in keeping with an argument stemming out of legal positivism than natural rights theory, it varies in several important ways. First, it demonstrates none of the problems that result when positivism is the sole ideology used for the making of society's laws. The positivist argument, that the state has the absolute authority to make all laws it sees fit for the benefit of society, may produce good law in a democratically based society as long as there is a strong public sentiment concerning the issue to be legislated. However, when public opinion is strongly divided or the public is ambivalent, legislation produces either a law that is so lightly enforced that it produces no real deterrent effect or a law that is simply not enforced (such as present-day laws against adultery). As a result of this fictitious state-sponsored forbearance, the state becomes powerless to regulate authoritatively those acts that are in theory illegal but in reality occur with shocking regularity. When such a situation results, the state's posture of active restriction deteriorates into the most undesirable of all possible situations, the "passive permissive" mode.

The Passive Permissive Model versus the Active Permissive Model

If we accept the proposition that in the United States it is not possible to successfully implement an "active restrictive" mode of regulating the "right to die" then there are only two alternative modes that can be used to address this issue. The first is the "passive permissive" mode in which an act is technically illegal but is socially tolerated. In essence, society either turns a blind eye to the ongoing violations of the law or simply refuses to convict defendants when they are charged with such criminal acts. The second alternative is the "active permissive" mode in which the state legalizes those acts which they wish to control and then strongly regulates them so as to guarantee the protection of its citizens.

The advantages of the "passive permissive" mode are largely political. It allows for an official stance against an act while, at the same time, pacifying those who dislike the law through nonenforcement or weak enforcement and minimal penalties. Such a position allows politicians to have their proverbial "cake and eat it, too." However, the danger with such a system is that it allows government to claim that it is protecting its citizens' rights, while in fact it places them in greater danger.

Within the context of euthanasia, the best example of a passive permissive system is represented by the approach of the Dutch government from 1969 to 1993. During this time period, several Dutch criminal codes made all forms of euthanasia illegal. However, such laws were seldom applied; when enforcement was undertaken, the penalty for violations constituted little more than an official slap on the wrist. The difficulty with this situation was that, while one part of the government was declaring that euthanasia was illegal, another part was not only allowing violators to act without any real sanction but was also setting up informal guidelines to be followed by future actors. In such a situation, the courts were attempting to protect the rights of Dutch citizens through a reactive mode, since the proactive (legislative) branch was content with its fictitious prohibition. As a result of these inconsistent forces, the worst of all possible situations arose. Doctors began to practice euthanasia without regulation and thus without reporting to any supervising authority. As a result, some Dutch doctors practiced not only voluntary active euthanasia, but also involuntary euthanasia (Halper 1993, 7-20, 25). So extensive was this passive permissive system that, in 1990, 454 cases of euthanasia were reported to the Dutch authorities without a single prosecution.

As the United States becomes more involved in the issue of euthanasia, the danger is great that we, too, could fall into the grasp of a passive permissive system. As public support for euthanasia increases and district attorneys become more hesitant to prosecute (and juries less likely to convict), the system becomes more dangerous, not because more people will be able to terminate their own lives, but because such acts will take place without supervision and therefore without protection. As a result, we will have gained a "right to die," only to have lost a right to live beyond the fear of involuntary termination. The only alternative that will allow for both the right to die and the protection of life is an "active permissive" mode.

The significance of this conclusion to the earlier question of the permissibility of assisted suicide is that, although the legalization of such acts may indeed raise a risk of future violations of human rights, these potential violations are best protected against not by prohibition, but by strong government regulation that seeks not only to protect an individual's "right to die" but also every individual's "right to live."

The active permissive mode of managing "right to die" cases leads us to the conclusion that, while autonomous individuals may have a right to terminate their own lives passively, actively, by individual act, or with the assistance of a third party, the government has an obligation to regulate such events for the purposes of guaranteeing that all acts of euthanasia meet minimal standards. Active permissive regulation would allow the government to regulate euthanasia for the purposes of assuring that

- all acts of euthanasia have been voluntarily requested;
- the individual requesting euthanasia is capable of rational decision making and is free from undue duress and influence;

- the request is informed, genuine, and not accompanied by a morbid desire for death that could be the result of depression or other psychological impairment;
- those assisting in the act of death are capable of making the above determinations; and
- the actual act of bringing about death is performed in a humane manner.

Such a regulatory scheme would allow the government not only to protect an individual's right to decide his or her own course in life, but also would give strong protections to every individual's right to life itself.

While the active permissive mode of managing euthanasia does allow for the simultaneous protection of individual rights and human life, it is not a panacea. Those who believe in the absolute sanctity of all human life and who reject the contention that anyone has the right to voluntarily terminate his or her life will reel at the thought of making such acts legal. However, I would argue that the ultimate danger of sliding down the slippery slope of death making to the unacceptable act of involuntary euthanasia can only be avoided by either strong, active government prohibition or active government regulation. In both instances the innocent are protected, but only in the latter is the autonomous individual's right to make decisions of conscience equally protected. In addition, today's political environment clearly suggests that active prohibition does not have a sufficient core of public support to make it politically feasible and that any effort to prohibit euthanasia will simply degenerate into a passive permissive mode, which provides no efficient protection of life. Under such conditions, the active permissive mode is for some the best of equally unsatisfactory positions.

Applying the Active Permissive Mode

At this point, it is best to raise another of the successively more difficult questions pertaining to euthanasia—the application of euthanasia and the active permissive mode to the case of the deeply unconscious adult. The "deeply unconscious adult" is an individual over the age of 18 who is in what is commonly known as a persistent vegetative state or deep coma.

In some ways, such cases can be viewed as easier than the previous cases discussed in that most individuals so situated are dependent upon the mechanical equipment for the maintenance of their existence, and, therefore, the removal of such technology allows death to occur. However, in a small number of cases, the simple removal of technology is not sufficient, and then caregivers are faced with the choice of having to remove food and/or hydration or in some other way induce a painless end. In either event, the administrator of the active permissive mode is concerned with two issues, the first being the protection of innocent life and the second being the protection of an individual's right to exercise his or her rights of privacy, conscience, and self-ownership. The principal mechanism for achieving a balance between these two rights is the concept of consent.

Although the active permissive mode of managing "right to die" decisions allows for the removal of life-support equipment, it must be made equally clear that it would allow for such a removal only under conditions of consent. By using the mechanism of consent, the active permissive system can protect the rights of those who place a high value on life and would not request euthanasia if they were competent to communicate their beliefs. At the same time, it protects the rights of those who have chosen an alternative course of action.

While at first glance the concept of consent looks to be an ideal method of legislating "right to die" cases, examination reveals that it is considerably more complex. Consent has built into it several distinct qualifiers that must be met for the act to be valid. The first element of consent that must be considered is the rationality of the individual at the time consent was given. If the act was performed at a time of questionable competence, for example, during a period of stress or while the individual was under duress, the validity of the consent is subject to challenge. Under the active permissive mode, if such a challenge is to be raised, the state must balance the right to continued life against the right to die. However, in doing so, it must be recognized that only clear statements of consent will be sufficient to override the preeminent right to life.

The second element of consent that must be considered is the durability of the consent or its ongoing and unwavering nature. The question must be asked as to whether a consensual statement once made is always binding. Must there be periodic restatements of such a consent? In this instance, the state must determine whether the consent is "fresh" or whether it was made under such conditions that its application to the presenting situation would be "stale."

In addition to these elements, the state must consider whether the consent is absolute or is conditioned upon the occurrence of a given set of facts. In the first instance the court would be correct in allowing for the removal of life support or even nutrition and hydration, while in the latter, consent would be conditioned upon the occurrence of any number of events or limited to particular types of actions, such as the removal of a ventilator but not the removal of hydration.

The final element that must be dealt with raises the issue of whether the consent was genuine and informed. For consent over such a fundamental issue as the termination of ongoing existence to be valid, it must be an act based on accurate information concerning one's condition and potential options. Without such information, the act of consent becomes speculative in nature. This is, however, not to say that a generalized consent cannot be given; however, to be valid such an act must be sufficiently broad to cover a wide variety of situations, regardless of their unique natures.

While all of these concerns complicate the concept of consent, each issue can be resolved by applying a standard of proof that is protective of life while also being respectful of a person's autonomy and self-ownership. However, the most important element in this standard of proof must be an understanding that, in the absence of sufficient proof, a preference for life must be presumed. The logical reason for this presumption is that ongoing life is the basis for all rights, in that only living individuals can be said to possess them. While it may be argued that a dead body is afforded certain protections by the law, these safeguards cannot be said to rise to the level of rights. Therefore, built into the active permissive mode is a preference for continued life, but the question that still remains is how strong that preference should be.

The Emergence of Active Permissive Standards in State Courts

Within the realm of judicial decision, few national precedent-setting cases have emerged that deal directly with the "right to die" issue. Those state court cases that have dealt with the question have been limited to determining under what conditions, if any, life-sustaining medical procedures may be discontinued. Two alternative standards have emerged. Both are concerned with the need to balance an individual's right to die with the generalized and superior right to continued life. Each standard seeks to protect both rights while recognizing the absolute nature of a person's right to continued life. While both are judicially evolved, the two standards vary broadly in the burden they place on the parties seeking to give legal effect to a right to die.

The first standard we will examine is the Missouri standard set down as part of the well-known case of *Cruzan v. Director, Missouri Dept. of Health.* The case centered around the fate of Nancy Cruzan, who, in January of 1983, was involved in a one-car accident. When Nancy was found, she was in a comatose state without respiratory or cardiopulmonary activity. She was hospitalized; and over a three-week period, her condition improved slightly so that the oral ingestion of food was possible, although she never regained consciousness. Eventually a gastrostomy feeding tube was surgically implanted to facilitate the feeding process. As time passed and it became apparent that Nancy's condition was not likely ever to improve, her parents requested termination of all life-support activities and equipment so that their daughter could die a natural death. This request was supported by statements from one of Nancy's former roommates, who testified that, at age 25, Nancy had expressed her desire not to be kept alive in the event of a serious accident or illness unless her recovery would allow her to go on living a halfway normal life.

Despite these statements, the State of Missouri refused to allow medical staff to discontinue life-sustaining treatment, stating that the roommate's statements did not meet the necessary standard of reliability to meet the state standard of proof. Speaking to this point, the Supreme Court acknowledged the right of a state to establish the burden of proof that is necessary to determine a person's wishes concerning the discontinuance of treatment. In keeping with this rule, the State of Missouri established that only "clear and convincing evidence" of a patient's wishes could be sufficient to allow the termination of life-support procedures (*Cruzan v. Director, Missouri Dept. of Health*). To date, the State of Missouri has recognized only two forms of evidence that will meet this standard of proof. The first is a formal and explicit oral communication directing the future actions of medical personnel, which, in the case of an incompetent patient, must be made in advance of the need for treatment. The second is the existence of a living will.

The State of Missouri maintained that such a restrictive standard was necessary because of the importance and finality of the decision. The logic behind this standard recognizes that courts are not omnipotent institutions of justice and, if an error were to be made, it should be an error on the side of life. The court argued that such a standard was acceptable, particularly given the fact that a decision to sustain life can always be overturned upon the presentation of further evidence, while a decision for the removal of lifesupport is rarely reversible.

The principal criticism that can be levied at the Missouri standard is that, in an effort to protect the right to continued life, it tramples on an individual's right to die. The Missouri standard gives such a strong preference to continued life that it runs the danger of forcing continued existence on those who, until the 1950s, would have died what was considered a natural death. This is particularly true in the case of an individual who has become unconscious or rendered incapable of communication and who has not executed a living will.

While some would argue that the Cruzan case serves as a warning, anyone who feels strongly about these matters will see such an argument as faulty in two ways. First, under the Missouri living-will statute involved in this case, life-sustaining treatment could be withdrawn only in cases where death was anticipated within a short period of time. In addition, the statute excludes the removal of nutrition and hydration from the authority of the living will (Missouri Revised Statute 1989, § 459.010). The State of Missouri itself recognized this difficulty and, in 1991, passed a health care proxies bill that allows for the removal of all medical technology in any case where there is no prognosis of recovery. However, the bill still requires that competent individual's have expressed their desires in writing (*New York Times*, 17 May 1991, A11). It is this requirement for a written statement of desire that is at the center of the second objection.

In deciding the *Cruzan* case, Justices Sandra Day O'Connor and William Brennan both recognized the relatively low rate at which citizens executed living wills in those states whose statutory law allowed for such documents. Justice Brennan went on to suggest that many citizens may be unwilling to consider the possibility that they may be placed in the position of needing such a document or alternatively may lack the financial or legal resources to execute such.

The importance of these observations is made even clearer when we return to the question of whether the right to die can be considered a fundamental right. If, indeed, the right to die is a fundamental right, the requirement of a self-executed written document for the enjoyment of such a right is inconsistent with its nature. This is particularly true in the case of an incompetent individual who is either unconscious or in a persistent vegetative state. To make the enjoyment of a fundamental right conditional upon the commission of some prior act is to, in effect, rob it of its fundamental nature.

Some may counter that the requirement of a living will or a conclusive oral statement is not a condition placed upon the right, but merely a standard of proof to determine an individual's true desires. While on one level this observation is correct, it fails to recognize that the state may be able to determine a person's desire for continued treatment without resorting to such a restrictive standard. The fundamental nature of the right would require a selection of a standard that is least restrictive of the right to die, while still being protective of the superior right to continued life. With this goal in mind, our examination now turns to the second common standard of proof, that known as the New Jersey standard. Over the last two decades, the New Jersey Supreme Court has engaged in the process of carefully evolving a detailed procedure for making "right to die" determinations that are respectful of both life and the right to terminate treatment. At the core of this standard is the desire to see that the wishes of the individual in question are always followed. To achieve this goal the court was forced to evolve not one test, but three.

What becomes clear immediately upon examination of the second standard is that it sacrifices the simplicity found in the Missouri standard for a heightened degree of flexibility and, hopefully, accuracy in determining an individual's wishes for treatment. One of the principal distinctions between the two methods is that the New Jersey standard divides individuals seeking to exercise their rights to refuse treatment into three distinct categories and then applies a different test to each situation. The first, most straightforward test applies solely to competent individuals who wish to refuse or withdraw treatment. In such cases, the court applies tests developed in the case of *In re Farrell.* The *Farrell* test consists of a four-step process of determination:

1. The individual's competency must be established.
2. Evidence must be submitted to demonstrate that the individual has been made aware of his or her prognosis, alternative treatments, and the risks of each.
3. The individual's consent must be voluntary.
4. The individual's request must be balanced against the state's interest in
    a. preventing suicide,
    b. preserving life,
    c. protecting innocent third parties, and
    d. protecting the integrity of the medical profession.

The thrust of this test is to determine whether the individual's request is competent, informed, and voluntary. If these three standards are met, it has been determined by previous New Jersey case law that a competent person's right to refuse medical treatment outweighs the state's interest in the four areas listed (*In re Conroy*). Therefore, barring special circumstances, all competent individuals in the State of New Jersey have the right to refuse or to discontinue all medical treatment.

It should be noted at this point that the terms of the New Jersey standard do not vary significantly from those of Missouri's. In both states a competent individual's right to refuse treatment will be respected. The true difference between the two standards comes into play only when we are faced with individuals not capable of making their wishes known when treatment is to be given. In such instances, we are faced with the process of making determinations for an individual who is either incompetent or in a vegetative state.

The New Jersey standard distinguishes between an individual who is simply incompetent and one who is in a vegetative state, and applies distinct standards to each situation. In cases where the individual for whom the discontinuation of treatment is sought is found to be incompetent, the court applies one of three alternative standards developed in the case of *In re Conroy*. The determination of which test to apply is made by examining the nature of the evidence available to demonstrate the individual's wishes.

The first criterion for removing life-sustaining treatment, called the "subjective test," is applied only in the face of clear and convincing evidence of the individual's wishes. The standard requires either a living will or some other strong prior statement sufficient to allow the court to determine what the patient would, in fact, direct if he or she were currently able to make such determination. In absence of such strong evidence, the court moves on to the "limited objective test."

The criterion for the limited objective test is "the best interest of the individual." However, this alone is insufficient to terminate treatment. The parties must also meet two additional burdens: They must demonstrate by "trustworthy evidence" (1) that the individual would have requested the removal of life-sustaining treatment and (2) that the medical burden of continued life outweighs the benefits of such an existence.

In both the subjective test and the limited objective test, six types of evidence may be considered and their relative weight determined. These varying forms of evidence include living wills; a durable power of attorney; past medical care decisions; prior oral communications as expressed to medical staff, family, or friends; testimony as to opinions expressed by the individual concerning the medical treatment of others or of herself or himself; and the religious beliefs of the individual in question.

The final part of the Conroy standard applies only to the cases of incompetent patients where no evidence of their stated desire exists. In such a case, the New Jersey standard applies what is called the "pure objective test." Under this test, no evidence of the individual's desires is necessary, but the applicant must meet two stringent standards in order for life-sustaining treatment to be discontinued. The applicant must submit sufficient medical evidence to demonstrate that the burden of ongoing treatment clearly and markedly outweighs the benefit of continued life. In addition, evidence must be submitted, demonstrating that the pain accompanying continued treatment is so severe and unavoidable that the administration of life-sustaining treatment constitutes an inhuman act.

The application of this part of the New Jersey standard produces markedly different results from the Missouri standard. While under the case law of the state of Missouri the subjective test would be allowed, it is clear that the limited objective and pure objective tests would be considered impermissible standards of proof. As a result of these limitations, an individual's ability to exercise the right to refuse medical treatment in order to allow death to take place is limited solely to those patients who have made prior provisions against such an event. By imposing such a requirement upon the exercise of that right, the majority effectively blocks many from putting their rights into action.

Given these different standards, a determination must be made as to which is best. Ultimately, the answer to this inquiry rests in the varying opinions concerning the "right to die" itself. If one takes a positivist view of law and maintains that the right to refuse medical treatment, in order to allow death, is a right created by government, then there is no inconsistency in allowing each state to fashion its own rules and limitations. Under such conditions, it would not be possible to say that the Missouri standard is better than that of New Jersey, for both are permissible options. However, if the right is determined to be "fundamental" in nature, then only one standard can prevail—a standard that not only seeks to protect an individual's right to continued life but also endeavors to protect the physical person from the intrusion of unwanted medical treatment, by upholding the individual's rights to privacy and self-ownership. Of the two standards offered, only that of New Jersey seeks to strongly protect both rights.

The New Jersey standard recognizes an individual's absolute right to continued life, and its rulings recognize the preservation of life as one of the State's principal interests (*In re Farrell*; *In re Conroy*). However, at the same time, it recognizes that the state is not the owner of this life and that the right to privacy and self-ownership allows the individual to determine when and under what conditions life-sustaining treatment should be rendered. Above all else, the New Jersey standard seeks to guarantee that the wishes of the particular individual in question are followed, and only a standard of this nature can be equally protective of the right to continued life and the refusal of medical treatment.

CONCLUSIONS

It is clear that the controversy over the existence of a "right to die" is not likely to be resolved in the near future, but we all must become aware that as we argue among ourselves about the morality and propriety of legalizing such acts, they are, in fact, occurring within our society at an alarming and increasing rate. While many states have passed legislation outlawing acts of euthanasia, their ability to enforce those same laws can be seriously questioned. The case of Dr. Zancope, a veterinarian, who openly admits injecting a 33-year-old terminally ill woman with a fatal dose of phenobarbital on 28 August, 1997, is a prime example. Despite the fact that New York had passed clear legislation making assisted suicide illegal, the criminal justice system proved to be ineffective in producing an active restrictive system for regulating euthanasia. Despite clear evidence, in July of 1999, a Manhattan grand jury refused even to indict Dr. Zancope for his act. In short, private citizens simply did not consider Dr. Zancope's acts a crime and refused to let him be tried (*New York Times*, 17 July 1999, B1). When we combine the actions of Dr. Zancope with those of Dr. Kevorkian, Dr. Quill, and a host of others, it becomes clear that the United

States simply does not have the public support necessary to regulate the right to die through an active restrictive system. To continue to insist on doing so is simply to allow our society to skip along blindly in a state of delusional righteousness where we can proudly proclaim that euthanasia is illegal, when in fact it is occurring all around us without any of the virtues of government regulation.

In the worst case scenario, the United States is destined to develop a passive permissive system for regulating euthanasia similar to that created by the Dutch between 1969 and 1993. In that system euthanasia was officially illegal but in reality, was practiced to such an extent that today it is widely accepted that citizens were euthanized without their consent. In effect, because of a lack of public support, an active restrictive system of regulating euthanasia failed and, in the end, produced the very nightmare that it sought to prevent. It allowed the lives of innocent elderly and physically ill citizens to be terminated without their consent.

At best, if the United States insists on continuing to limp along the path of using an ineffective system of active restriction, it will default into a passive permissive system of regulating euthanasia, which will allow a secret and shadowy market in death to gradually grow until we truly are desensitized and the thin edge of the wedge has been firmly planted into the side of our society. That wedge will allow our laws against euthanasia to pass into the category of dead-letter laws that includes those prohibiting adultery and fornication.

In short, the United States has little choice other than to pursue an active permissive system of regulating the "right to die"— system that will legalize such acts, regulating them in such a way that it protects and holds sacred all life and ensures that only those who meet strict legislative guidelines are allowed to practice euthanasia. Doing so may legalize some forms of death, but it would also reinvigorate our society's ability to protect innocent life. For by providing legal boundaries within which the "right to die" can operate, American citizens may once again be willing to indict those who violate our laws and American juries may be willing to convict them. In so doing, we once again will have the ability to protect the sanctity of innocent lives.

In making such a move we, as a society, must face the reality that promulgating clear guidelines in this area will be difficult. Making them will require us to refocus our attention on questions that involve not right and wrong conduct, but the ways in which we can meet the needs of the dying, relieving their pain, including them in our world, and giving their lives the meaning that they need to maintain a will to live. We must pursue a system of action that, while allowing death, provides the dying individual those attributes of care necessary to experience a meaningful personal state of comfort, peace, and love.

Appendix A: One Man's Decision to Die

If we were faced with the choice between life and death, most of us would unquestionably choose life. Despite our grumblings to the contrary, most of us consider life to be good, particularly when we are making a judgment about our own life or the life of someone close to us. Generally speaking, we approach any discussion about the "right to die" with the *a priori* assumption that existing life should be preserved as a matter of course, unless some overriding principle can be proffered that supersedes the innate value of an ongoing life. It is for this reason that most states have laws against attempting suicide or assisting someone in such an attempt. With increasing frequency, however, the American public is being asked to consider cases in which individuals maintain that they have met the criteria necessary to overcome the presumed value of ongoing life and wish to exercise their right to die. Whether we are reading about the most recent exploits of Dr. Kevorkian or being admitted into a local hospital for surgery, all of us are exhorted to come to grips with our personal opinion about how we wish to be treated should the normal course of our lives be disrupted and we be faced with a life less than what we have been conditioned to believe is complete. Under such conditions, how would we react? Would we want to live, or would we want society to allow us to die?

The pages that follow (Appendix A and Appendix B) contain excerpts from two interviews with people who have experienced events that profoundly altered their lives. In both instances the individuals were left severely handicapped and faced with the question, "Do I want to live, or do I want to die?" In both interviews the individuals involved seek to help us understand what it was like for them to undergo such dramatic changes and how they went about making their particular decisions.

THE CASE OF LARRY MCAFEE

The first interview I conducted took place on March 9, 1994.[1] Through personal connections, I had acquired an interview with Larry McAfee, a quadriplegic, who has the distinction of being the first person in the State of Georgia to be heard before the state's Supreme Court to win the right to turn off his respirator, thereby bringing about his own death.

Larry James McAfee graduated from college with a degree in electrical engineering and was, by all accounts, a talented, athletic individual who enjoyed engaging in a wide variety of sporting events, one of which was motorcycling. It was this particular passion that led to a dramatic course of events in McAfee's life. His journey began in 1985 at the age of 29 when he suffered severe injuries as a result of a motorcycle accident. His spinal cord was damaged, leaving him paralyzed from the neck down and unable to breathe on his own. Instead, he remains perpetually connected to a ventilator that controls his respiration by mechanically infusing and extracting air from his lungs. Extensive medical tests have determined that Mr. McAfee's condition is permanent and that there is no known treatment for his condition.

On the day of the scheduled interview I had to wait 45 minutes before beginning, while Mr. McAfee's lungs were being suctioned. Secretions that build up in his lungs, from hours of sedentary activity and the inability to breathe deeply on his own, have to be removed to ensure that his lungs are clear and working properly. The procedure requires two assistants to force the secretions in his lungs into his trachea by performing a procedure that is similar to CPR, compressing his lungs, or chest area. A third assistant simultaneously stands over Mr. McAfee with an Ambu bag, or hand-operated ventilator, timing his or her contractions of the bag with the chest compressions. Then the two assistants compressing the chest area apply pressure to his lungs and hold them in a compressed state while the third removes the Ambu bag. Finally, an assistant inserts a suction catheter into Mr. McAfee's tracheostomy and maneuvers the tubing down his trachea and into his lungs, so that any built-up secretions can be extracted by a small suction pump. This procedure is clearly invasive and uncomfortable for him.

When I was finally called into Mr. McAfee's room, I was introduced to a man who was over six feet, six inches tall and weighed approximately 280 pounds. Even after eight years as a quadriplegic, he still has the impressive build of a professional football player, though much of the muscle tone that he must once have possessed has gone soft after years of being trapped in a body that gives his muscles little or no exercise, except for the involuntary spasms that from time to time cause one part of his body or another to contract and contort. This hulk of a man was seated in a motorized wheelchair that, through computer technology, he can control with a drinking straw through which he puffs and sips air in particular patterns, thus regulating the speed, direction, and angle of the chair. At the foot of his hospital bed is a small crane (or Hoyer lift) that is somewhat reminiscent of an engine jack. It is used each morning to lift him from his bed and place him in his chair. Each evening it returns him safely to his bed. In all ways, Mr. McAfee seems to be a man who has grown comfortable with these added pieces of equipment in his life, though at the same time it is equally clear that he may never be comfortable with the limitations of his life itself.

As a result of his injuries, not only was Mr. McAfee's physical condition impaired, his entire way of life was thrown into upheaval. Larry McAfee was a man who believed in mathematical precision in every facet of his life. Mr. McAfee's mother commented that, upon entering his apartment after his accident, she found a scene of absolute organization. In the closet were white shirts, blue shirts, green shirts—all separated. In his dresser drawers were white socks, blue socks, and black socks—all in separate compartments. His underwear was folded, his personal items set out as if they were on display in a museum, Mr. McAfee was heretofore a man who exerted strong control over his life. Now he is almost completely dependent upon others.

As the interview began, the constant rhythmic whir of the ventilator that artificially inflates and deflates his lungs punctuated our conversation, the machine dictating, to some extent, Mr. McAfee's speech patterns, resulting in a well-metered, calm delivery. The volume of his voice rarely rises except when he is angry, and his speech usually follows the comfortable rhythm of the respirator. He expresses emotion through his eyes and in subtle changes in the inflection of his voice. Despite these limitations, there is never any doubt about how Mr. McAfee feels about any given subject. His excitement, anger, and passion are all clearly communicated to the listener, as is the earnestness with which this man approaches life.

In preparing for this interview, I had spent many hours thinking about what it must be like to be paralyzed, what it must be like not being able to move your hands, your arms, your legs, or even to feel any sensation in your body from the neck down. I have always had a secret fear of being paralyzed; the thought invokes an almost claustrophobic response that could easily rise to the level of terror. In my life I have had only one experience to which I can relate this feeling. It was when I was undergoing abdominal surgery and was placed under the control of a deep anesthetic. In the recovery room after the operation, I suddenly became aware of my surroundings, but found myself unable to move. I could hear and speak, and with great effort I could open my eyes, but I was powerless to move the rest of my body. Luckily, I managed to keep my composure until the anesthesia wore off, but to this day I remember this event as one of the most singularly unpleasant experiences of my life.

Despite of my perceptions of what paralysis was like, my conversations with Mr. McAfee made me realize that the inability to move would not be the worst aspect of being paralyzed. By far the most terrifying thing would be the inability to control your own life. I asked Mr. McAfee about his life after his accident and what control he had over what happened to him.

McAfee: Once the insurance policy that I had was exhausted, no one wanted anything to do with me, even though I was on Medicare and Medicaid and had all the privileges that it brought. The level of care was so intensive that nursing homes weren't going to get involved, and hospitals didn't want a long-term patient because it (my condition) certainly wasn't going to improve, and I was going to be like this and require a high level of care until the day I die. So there was nothing available anywhere close in the Southeast, at that time . . . that was early '87. And there was a nursing home in Ohio . . . Berea, Ohio, a suburb of Cleveland, that had a ventilator-dependent wing and had about thirty people on ventilators, mostly older people. There were . . . I think about five of us who were younger and had our mental faculties and could relate and understand what was going on. But, other than that, the rest were old and, I guess, they were there so they could die. And that was very depressing. There were no vocational opportunities whatsoever. The staff were accustomed to dealing with and caring for the older residents, and their approach to the patients was one of: "I'm here to do what's really necessary . . . just necessary, and do my job, and make eight hours, and go home, and nothing special. You don't deserve anything special, and I'm certainly not going to give it or offer it."

Whiting: So it's the loss of control that's most difficult?

McAfee: That's it! You become their property and not an individual anymore. Just a slab sitting . . . laying in a room with a room number. Not even a name and a personality.

Whiting: Did this affect your attitude?

McAfee: Yes, I'm afraid so. I was a real ass for a long time. Very demanding, very upset with the way things were done and my lack of control. I just would not fit into their mold. I was the square peg they tried to put into a round hole.

Whiting: Were they asking you to conform?

McAfee: Oh, very much so. Very much. I just could not do it. It just . . . that wasn't me.

One of the major problems with being disabled to any degree in our society is that people begin to treat you as if you are less than a human being. It is almost as though the injured party loses status as a person and becomes some lesser form of life. As a result of this perception, society often attempts to exclude the disabled from the regular activities of life and shut them away in an institution that we rationalize as being better for them anyway. The fact is, however, that this isolation is simply a form of ongoing rejection that serves only to exacerbate the original injury. Everyone's goal after a major accident is to return to a life as close to normal as possible, but Mr. McAfee came to believe that his life could never be normal again.

McAfee: It's just . . . people look at you, and the expressions on their faces are such that . . . you're almost like a circus sideshow. And if they communicate, it's always to the person with you. How is he doing, or what happened to him? Or, . . . it's like, they don't want to involve themselves with you, personally. They're afraid of you, or afraid it might rub off or affect them.

Whiting: Do you find that the people in the medical community are better or worse?

McAfee: Good question. There were a few professionals that were more in tune, and those that understood your injury. And the ones that became aware that you are able to communicate and how you communicated, and at what level you could understand or comprehend them or interact with them. And they would approach you. But until they found that out, they were a little skeptical and tended to be real careful. Some would try not to hurt your feelings, and then some would . . . I guess act in a more common way, and ask your friend or your relative questions and side-step you. That's frustrating from the people that you think should know better.

Whiting: It's hard to imagine the pain you must feel. Do you get used to it?

McAfee: You tolerate it, more . . . depending on your attitude at that time. If you're having a good day, it just rolls right off. If you're having a bad day, it really hurts. It depends on your environment, I mean, not your outlook, but hope for the future. If you're stuck in a nursing home like I was for so long and you're so depressed it's worn you down so much, that little things, little things that normally wouldn't affect you, just almost devastate you. Just go right through you. I mean, if something would have happened today, I'd just consider the source . . . say, well, they're not informed, or not caring, and just go about my business. But, if I was emotionally down already, or depressed, that just would tend to feel like adding onto it more and more. And the next thing . . . next time something like that would happen, it would be even worse, because it would be the added burden of the previous incident

In times of incredible upheaval in our lives, most of us seek solace and comfort in the love of our family, and Mr. McAfee is no exception. His decision to pursue what he conceives as his right to die does not arise out of a lack of support from his family and friends. Quite the contrary—Mr. McAfee's family has always been highly supportive of him, and that support continued to exist whether he was seeking to live a better life or whether he was trying to secure his right to die. But Larry realized that, just as the accident had, his decision to die would affect his family.

Whiting: You've always had very strong family support, haven't you?

McAfee: Very, very strong. They've done everything they could possibly ever have done. They've spent time, and energy, money, travel, talked to everybody they could. But both my parents work, and I couldn't live there, and they certainly weren't financially able to support me either. I don't know what I would have done without them. I probably would have gone over the edge, or just totally given up, and just totally ceased to communicate. I just wouldn't care what happened.

I know this guy who was paralyzed as a result of a random shooting. The bullet hit him rather high in the neck, and he was about the same level [of paralyzation] I was. And he was at Shepard Spinal Center, and his family came up to visit, and Shepard takes your family through a fairly extensive training session or program where they teach you how to do all the procedures necessary to take care of someone that's been injured, to their level. And the first day of the training his family was there. They took a break, and his family left and never came back.

Whiting: That's terrible!

McAfee: Yeah, he's in Ohio in a nursing home all by himself. I don't know how I would have reacted if it had been me.

Whiting: Was your family involved in your original decisions and discussions about your wanting to die, and how did they feel about that?

McAfee: Yes, they were involved. They were very emotional, and I tried not to involve them a lot. Just to express my opinion and get their reaction to it without going into deep philosophical discussions or go into detail with them, because it was such an emotional subject for them; and they were already devastated by the injury, and what it had done to me; and how it had affected their lives and the whole family.

The support of friends and family is the most important thing, at least to me. I don't care what other people think. It's those I'm closest to that matter the most. I don't care what the law says. I don't necessarily look up to or respect some authorities as much as I respect my family and my friends. It's your family and those that you are closest to, it's the group that you have chosen, that is important. It's a personal decision. It's not a democracy. It's a path that you've chosen to involve yourself with. So, those are the ones I care about most.

As the interview progressed, it became apparent that the largest factor in Mr. McAfee's decision to pursue the right to turn off his respirator was not his physical disability. On the contrary, it was the institutionalized lifestyle that his injuries seemed to be forcing upon him. Within the institution, the day-to-day casual social contacts and friendships that many of us take for granted rarely occur. Instead, they are replaced with paid-for relationships in which nearly all the "patient's" or "client's" daily social contacts are with individuals who are interacting with him or her chiefly because their job requires it. As a result, friendships are replaced by worker-client relationships in which the worker must service a large number of individuals and there is little time or energy for personal entanglements. In fact, within such facilities, detachment often becomes a necessity if one wishes to avoid emotional burnout.

Whiting: Why would you want to die?

McAfee: I couldn't see past the institution, being locked up with the elderly, with no hope. This was at a time, I guess—middle to late '80s—when there were a few places, as there are today, just becoming available where independent living lifestyles are offered, and people recognized the need for them; and programs have been created to supply that need. But—then, four or five years ago, I wasn't aware of that. I didn't know anything like that existed. I just thought I was destined to spend the rest of my life in one nursing home or another.

You see, in the condition I was in, there was no hope other than an institution. I hadn't been presented with any other possibility or any other type of facility other than being placed in an institution principally designed for the elderly, for people that are just there to wait . . . wait out their time. You can sense that in their eyes, and in the eyes of their families when they would come to visit. It's just a real solemn place, and I'd never experienced a place like that or wanted to; nor could I accept a life like that. Not for my age and my ability to understand, not at least for what I wanted out of the rest of my life.

Whiting: Was life in the institution really so bad you'd rather die?

McAfee: I always valued the ability to rely upon reason, and that was about the only thing I had left. That and the ability to communicate. And because I valued those highly and wasn't going to take anything for granted, I thought things out very carefully, and over longer periods of time than perhaps I should have. I gave it five years in this condition before I even considered taking steps to turn the ventilator off. I mean, I really gave it a try. I just could not adjust to life in an institution.

I thought about it long before that, even within a few months of the injury . . . after the injury, I began talking about it somewhat, and someone told me that, if I was real serious about it, I should explore all the other options, and at least give myself a chance to live in an institution, live that type of lifestyle, to see if I would adjust to it. So, I thought that was a fair and reasonable thing to ask, and, so I did. I gave myself five years.

This waiting period is an important distinction in Mr. McAfee's case. In our conversations it became clear that he had made a genuine, sustained effort to adjust to his conditions and surroundings, and that effort gave him the justification that turning off his respirator would not be suicide but, rather, the exercise of his right to die. While the distinction is subtle and, to some, undoubtedly illusory, Mr. McAfee makes a convincing argument that there is a difference. The basis of his argument is that suicide is an act of desperation, while exercising one's right to die is an act of deliberation. Thus, suicide is characterized by a high level of emotion and is influenced by such elements as trauma and depression. Conversely, the decision to exercise one's "right to die" can be characterized as a function of reason, in which one weighs all available evidence and, through deliberation, draws a conclusion.

The difficulty then arises of the determination of who should judge when a person is acting rationally and when he or she is too emotionally unstable or depressed to make such a decision. Mr. McAfee's response would undoubtedly be that this is what the extended waiting period is for—reflection, treatment, and certainty.

Whiting: Do you see a difference between committing suicide and the "right to die"?

McAfee: I think committing suicide is done more at a spur of the moment, so it's different from the right to die. I associate the right to die with terminal illness or physical conditions that have put a person in a situation where they can't improve it. They can't change it. If you have someone with the ability to change their situation, or change the reasons for them wanting to commit suicide, then I think it's their loss not to take advantage of that ability to change it and improve their life in such a way that they would think it would be worthwhile. But, in my case, I didn't have that ability. I was stuck in an institution, nobody wanted me, no one . . . well, my family wanted me, but they certainly didn't have the ability or the finances to do anything about it, and I wasn't going to ask, even if they did. And the institutions are just too damn depressing.

Whiting: Do you think it's ever too soon to start considering terminating your life?

McAfee: It depends . . . it would vary with each person because of the different phases you go through, from denial to acceptance, to regrets, to . . . there's no certain time each person takes to pass from one stage to the other, so . . . .

Whiting: Well, should there be a certain stage that everyone must reach before we allow them to consider such actions?

McAfee: That's a good point. I would try to wait until you can accept your injury . . . and your family and friends have accepted it . . . and can talk to you about what has happened, without getting emotional. And I think at that point, then you can, I guess, decide, or make decisions with a clear conscience or a clear head. You won't be influenced by emotions.

I think that there should be mandatory adjustment phases. It would help you determine whether you can accept your condition, if those around you can accept what has happened, and just whether or not you can then live with that. If you look at other alternatives, will it change, can it be cured? Will it be cured after a certain period of . . . or some period of time. Or will it go away, or will it just diminish some of your lifestyle, or part of your life, you know. I think it needs to be through phases rather than periods of time, because people just don't always go through life at the same speed.

Whiting: Should everyone have the right to terminate their life, if they want to?

McAfee: If they have the mental faculties to decide? If they have a good enough reason. If it's a decision that's been thoroughly thought out, and if it's for a reason which they can't change, then yes; if it's something that they cannot change, like terminal illness or, they're put in a situation in which they have no control or it won't end, or they can't ever foresee it ending, or that other people don't think it will ever end.

Whiting: On a more personal note, do you believe in God?

McAfee: I believe in a higher being. I don't know if I believe in a person, and what type of powers, if any, they possess, or what type of control they have over our lives and the future of our lives, or day-to-day activities, or decisions. I don't know. I think it's comforting to believe there is something else.

Whiting: Did any of those beliefs enter into your thoughts or decisions about possibly terminating your life?

McAfee: Yeah, I considered them. I weighed them, and, yes, they did play a part in many decisions that I've made.

Whiting: Do you think there's a heaven?

McAfee: I like to think there is. I would hope so.

Whiting: What do you think [that your conception of] God would think about your actions if you were to terminate your life?

McAfee: I've read, I'm referencing the Bible that it probably would not be looked upon very favorably, but, I would like to think that there is a compassionate and understanding being that would consider the same things that I've considered, and weighed the reasons as heavily as I would.

In August of 1989, Larry James McAfee made the decision to pursue his desire to terminate his life, and with the assistance of his attorney, filed a petition in Fulton County Superior Court of the State of Georgia, asking for a judicial determination concerning his right to turn off his ventilator and have it left off, thus resulting in his death. Mr. McAfee requested that he be allowed to have a switch installed in his ventilator that he could trigger by use of his wheelchair control mechanism that would allow him to deactivate his ventilator personally. In addition, he requested that medical personnel be allowed to administer sedatives to him for the purpose of alleviating pain prior to his activation of the ventilator switch. Finally, Mr. McAfee requested civil and criminal immunity for anyone who assisted him in the completion of these requests.

After he had received an affirmative determination on his petition for declaratory relief, Mr. McAfee's case was appealed by a group of individuals who identified themselves as advocates for the "right to life" and who believed that Mr. McAfee's case would set a dangerous precedent for future cases. As a result, the case eventually found its way to the Georgia Supreme Court.

Whiting: How do we decide who has the right to die and who doesn't?

McAfee: I think it should be reviewed on a case-by-case basis. The reasoning for this is that it all depends on the person's ability to understand and comprehend, and the possibility the future might offer something different. That situations might change. Everyone should at least give it a chance, if that opportunity might be in the future. However, I feel it [the decision] is up to them and I wouldn't want to just apply a stringent set of rules. Just let each person make their own decisions and their own circumstances. It's such a controversial issue that I wouldn't want to make that decision for anyone else, and I wouldn't appreciate anyone else making that decision for me.

Ultimately, it's a personal decision. If weighed heavily, if it's adequately considered, then I think it is my decision. I mean, if it's something I've thought out for a long enough period, and it's the only reasonable choice.

Whiting: Advocates for the right to life would say that your decision somehow harms all of us. That your decision to terminate your life devalues life, or encourages others to devalue people in your position.

McAfee: I think it's the opposite, because my act places more emphasis on the individual and improves their rights. It shows how valuable life is, and that decisions aren't always made and shouldn't be made lightly. Each individual case is so different that it strengthens the argument for life itself.

Whiting: Did it trouble you when they joined the appeal against your right to die?

McAfee: Yes, it really did. I thought, and still believe, that it's a personal decision, and it should be left up to each individual, and not at the control of others.

Mr. McAfee's case was decided by the Supreme Court of Georgia on 21 November, 1989. The court ruled in the case of *State of Georgia, by Michael J. Bowers, Atty. Gen. v. Larry James McAfee* that, as a competent adult, Mr. McAffee had the "right to refuse medical treatment in the absence of a conflicting state interest." The court further concluded that, of the four potential state interests: preservation of life, prevention of suicide, protection of the integrity of the medical profession, and protection of innocent third parties, only the state's generalized interest in the preservation of life was directly involved with this case.

As a result of this ruling, the Georgia Supreme Court appears to have concluded, without discussion, that any action taken by Mr. McAfee to shut off his ventilator would not constitute suicide, but would rather be characterized as an exercise of Mr. McAfee's right to refuse medical treatment, even when such a refusal would unquestionably result in his death. The court went on to rule that the state's generalized interest in the preservation of life was insufficient to overcome Mr. McAfee's right to make such a refusal.

In addition to that ruling, the court held that the "right to be free from pain at the time the ventilator is disconnected is inseparable from his right to refuse medical treatment" and that, although no living will was involved in this case, the right to construct such a document and have its wishes followed when an individual was suffering from a terminal condition rose to the level of a constitutional right in the State of Georgia.

THE DECISION NOT TO DIE

After having won his right to terminate his life, one might reasonably expect that Mr. McAfee also became the first person in the State of Georgia to exercise that right; however, he did not. To a great extent it seems that simply knowing that he had the right to control his own destiny gave Mr. McAfee the desire to see what else he could achieve. Prior to winning his "right to die," Mr. McAfee had, indeed, tried to end his life by disconnecting his ventilator. However, the extreme pain caused by oxygen deprivation forced him to abandon the act and restart the machine. But now that Mr. McAfee had the right to end his life painlessly, he began to discover other rights, such as the right to live outside the confines of an institution and to be surrounded by people of his own choosing—rights that restored his belief in the intrinsic value of living. Rights that gave him the power to control his own life, and death.

Whiting: Once you won your case, why didn't you exercise the right you had fought so hard to have recognized? In essence, I'm asking you why you are still alive to give me this interview?

McAfee: I think basically that [getting out of the institution] was the main thing that caused me to not turn it off. Having the ability, or the hope and the promise that there was something better and it would be made available, and I would have control over my life. It was something I hadn't experienced, and it was something that I wanted to try, to see if it was worthwhile, as they said it might be. And, I've tried it, and this lifestyle is worthwhile for me . . . I have control over things that most everyone takes for granted. I have those things back. The ability to say what I want to wear, what I want to eat, who I want to have working for me, how the procedures are done, and when they're done. If I want to go outside, I go outside. If I want to go work on the computer, if I want to stay in bed all day, if I want to work on physical therapy, I can do that. I can set my own schedule. And I can change that schedule every day, if I want to, as long as I don't take advantage of the people that are working for me.

Whiting: Have you rediscovered a lust for life that at one point in your life might have been gone?

McAfee: Given the ability to live outside of an institution, I've learned how to even more appreciate the freedom that I have now, the ability to make my own decisions, even in this condition I'm in. Whereas, if I was placed in an institution again, with that loss of control, I would regret that even more now, having experienced life on this side, or having experienced the control.

Whiting: So, if, as life progressed, things get worse and you are institutionalized again, would that cause you to reconsider the possibility of terminating your life?

McAfee: Very much so. And what would be even worse, or the factor, would be whether or not there was the possibility of rekindling that independent living program.[2]

Interview ends.

Appendix B: A Talk with a Formerly Comatose Patient

For years now, whenever I have formally or informally entered into conversations concerning the "right to die," the discussion invariably makes its way to the topic of the comatose patient. When this happens, the emotional level of the conversation almost always begins to peak and two or three views typically emerge.

The first view is expressed by those who are opposed to euthanasia, usually on religious grounds. These individuals consciously harden their stance, principally from the perspective that we are now talking about removing medical support from an individual who has no way to participate in the decision-making process. The second view is a countervailing assertion by those who assert a "right to die" based on human dignity. While these first two responses are readily anticipated, the third response has always been more perplexing to me. With respect to the comatose patient, individuals who have otherwise been ambivalent toward, or even mildly opposed to, euthanasia in other circumstances suddenly make emphatic statements such as, "If I were ever in a coma, I wouldn't want to be kept alive," and, "Who would want to live like some vegetable to be wheeled into the sunshine and watered every day?"

What has always struck me about these statements is that they assume that being in a coma is an unpleasant experience that no sane person could possibly prefer to death. The inference drawn is that the condition is analogous to that of a tortured soul locked inside an unwilling and unresponsive body. As I have listened to these assertions over and over, I've wondered if they are correct. Is being in a coma really such a horrifying experience, or is it simply an altered state of consciousness, much more reminiscent of a semiconscious dream state? If it is a dream state, after all, I've had some pretty good dreams, and I can think of far worse things than sleeping my life away. On the other hand, I've had some pretty bad dreams. If the comatose individual is caught somewhere between the universe of consciousness and a world of visions, sometimes trapped in isolation and other times floating in a cosmos of infinite possibility, would such a state be torment or simply a different condition of existence that is more cerebral than physical?

In order for reasonable individuals to make an informed decision as to whether they would rather die than be in a comatose state, they must first reach some rational determination of what it is to be in a coma. The best place to go for that information is to the comatose patient.

This interview is not intended to draw any absolute conclusions about what a coma is like. Clearly, even if it were my desire to make such conclusions, the information garnered from the interview is far too limited and, at times, even sketchy to draw any scientific conclusions. This does not mean, however, that the interview is without merit. Quite the contrary. Despite her handicaps, the woman I interviewed was able to open several doors just wide enough to give us a peek inside the world of one formerly comatose patient.

THE INTERVIEW

The interview began on a warm summer day in 1994, with a long drive out into the countryside of Georgia's Central Savannah River Area. We were driving out to talk to Jan Grover, who was a woman I had known casually for some time. I had once heard her mention to a friend that she remembered what it was like to be in a coma. When I asked her if she would talk to me about her experience, she was delighted.

When I, accompanied by a friend (Linda Day), arrived for the interview, Jan was sitting outside enjoying a cigarette. Jan lives in a nice house with several other physically impaired individuals. The house itself is owned and run by a family who live on the premises and provide assistance as needed. Jan is a thirty-four-year-old woman whose smile is virtually continuous. She shows an amazingly positive attitude for an individual whose life was so violently uprooted.

At the age of nineteen, Jan was a bright and talented woman who could play the clarinet, alto clarinet, bass clarinet, oboe, bassoon, and saxophone. She actively enjoyed such diverse activities as being a flag bearer for her high school marching band, rock climbing, and rappelling. She served as a volunteer in her community and was engaged to her high school sweetheart. When she went to college, she was selected as a residential assistant for her dorm. After her first year of college, Jan's life was radically changed when a drunk driver struck her Volkswagen Beetle head-on while she sat in the parking lot of a neighborhood grocery store.

The Accident

Whiting: How did your accident happen?

Grover: Oh, I . . . I got hit by a drunken driver. It was a head-on collision, and after he hit me, I . . . I was in a coma for six months. And after . . . , I couldn't walk, I couldn't talk, I couldn't even do anything. But he also hit three other cars besides me, and, of course, they were in Kroger's, you know, and I was just leaving Kroger's when that happened.

Whiting: What kind of injuries did you sustain?

Grover: Oh, brother (laughing). I can't . . . I really can't get my arm or my leg right [to move right] anymore, you know. Especially my arm, you know, but then again, my leg . . . uhm, now, I walk with a limp, and I didn't use to. And I still don't know my right . . . I never did know even before I had the accident (laughing) . . . you know, I'd . . . you see, what I did was, Marilyn . . . anyway . . . she was a flag director, she'd . . . ok, go right, so I . . . automatically, I'd go left and left and I'd go right (laughing), so, she said, ok, let's see, go this way or that way. Ok, now I can understand (laughing).

Although at this point in her life Jan is more concerned with the injuries to her right arm and leg, the collision caused Jan to suffer considerable head trauma. As Jan's car was struck, the force of the collision caused Jan's head to strike either the steering wheel or the windshield. As a result of the blow, Jan suffered a severe brain contusion on the left side of her head, which, along with cerebral edema (swelling), caused permanent damage to the part of her brain that controls her speech and auditory skills. Jan additionally suffered a severe contusion to her brain stem, that resulted in a state of unconsciousness, or coma, that lasted six months, a state of existence which Jan reports to distinctly remember.

Life in a Coma

Whiting: Do you have any memories of being in the coma?

Grover: Yeah! I remember that, uh, there was God, and . . . and God was with me, you know, and . . . all the time. . . .

Whiting: What was it like when you were in the coma?

Grover: Well, God was with me, you know, and also Jesus, Buddha and Mohammed. Even the nonbelievers, you know?

Whiting: Could you see?

Grover: I wasn't really seeing . . . I saw . . . I saw a face, but I just knew that God was with me.

Day: Do you remember hearing anything, any sensory smells or touches or feelings?

Grover: Well, you know, it was sharp until after, when I woke up . . . I had . . . I had the coma, and I said, wait a minute, I can't smell anymore. You know. . . .

Whiting: When you were in the coma, could you hear someone standing by your bed talking to you?

Grover: Yeah, I did, but I couldn't get it . . . I couldn't get it back . . . I couldn't . . . I couldn't, respond. You know, I just didn't say anything, and I wonder why, but . . . can't help it, you know.

Whiting: How did you emotionally feel while you were in the coma?

Grover: I just can't believe it. I'm really in this place. I don't understand why. I . . . I. And also . . . well, then, Don and I were engaged to be married, and . . . and I was worrying about him, and I was thinking, well, listen, there is life, over and over and over, you know, and it kinda renews it, you know.

Whiting: Were you worried that you were going to die?

Grover: Yeah. I mean, six months . . . wouldn't you be?

Whiting: But, did you know that it was six months you were in the coma?

Grover: No, I didn't, but I . . . I knew it was an awful long time.

Day: Did it feel like it was one long day, or were there any kind of divisions to it?

Grover: No, it was just . . . constantly. I could just feel it, you know.

Whiting: When you were in the coma, did you know where you were?

Grover: No. I . . . all I knew is there was . . . there was a God, you know, and . . . and I did know that . . . that Mom and Daddy . . . anyway they were really disappointed of me [*sic*], you know, and Mom, you know, she just stayed with me, and she spoke to me, you know, and . . . and Daddy. . . .

Whiting: How do you know that she was there?

Grover: Because I could . . . I could see her, you know, I couldn't respond, but I could see her.

Whiting: So, you could actually see?

Grover: Uhm hum (affirmative).

Day: Could you hear them?

Grover: Yeah, but I couldn't . . . I couldn't respond.

Whiting: Was it frustrating?

Grover: Are you kidding (laughing)? What's so bad is that, in my coma, I could talk and walk and everything just fine, you know, and all of a sudden, (I woke up and) gee whiz, what happened to me? Why am I in a wreck, and why am I talking so funny? I don't understand it.

Whiting: So, it was only after you came out of the coma, that you realized you couldn't walk or talk.

Grover: Yeah.

Whiting: Was your coma state like a dream?

Grover: Uhm hum (affirmative).

Whiting: Were you doing things in . . . in that state?

Grover: Uhm hum (affirmative).

Day: What kinda stuff were you doing?

Grover: Uh, I could walk and talk just normally, and not with a limp, like I do now, you know.

One of the points repeatedly made during the interview was that, for Jan, the experience of the coma itself was less of an ordeal than was her life after she awoke. She reports that in her comatose state she apparently floated somewhere between consciousness and sleep so that she could observe the world around her, but could not directly or actively participate in it. However, it is important to note that despite how unpleasant this must sound to some, for Jan it was not an agonizing experience. Quite to the contrary, she reports that in her comatose state she experienced a sense of peace—a sense of being with God—and perceived herself as being fully well, able to walk and talk. Perhaps most important, Jan goes on to tell us that within this coma state she had a continual desire to live.

The Awakening

Whiting: What was your life like after the coma?

Grover: Oh, it was awful. I couldn't walk, I couldn't talk, I couldn't even think, practically. I mean, I could think, but I couldn't express it out loud, and it was very frustrating. Uh, in my coma, I was walking, you know, and then . . . and then, I couldn't . . . I couldn't even go to the bathroom.

Day: So, you'd gone from being this really independent, active person before the accident to someone who is very dependent and very constrained. At any point during that, did you think about just saying, to hell with it, I quit, I want to end it all?

Grover: Uh, a little bit, only . . . not really, but I was just thinking, why me, why now? I'm . . . I'm alive, you know, and I'm . . . I'm fine.

Day: Was it a thought that . . . that you really contemplated, though?

Grover: A little bit. You see, I was I think that . . . I don't understand it. In my coma, I was alive, and now I'm not, and I don't understand it. And . . . and its terrible. Why am I in this condition? And . . . and I know that . . . that . . . I think, one time, I would just like to end it all, but, of course, I didn't have the resource, you know. That was . . . oh, goodness, that was one year after I was in the coma.

Whiting: When you were in your coma, did you think about living or dying, or ending it or anything?

Grover: Yeah, in fact, I died three times while I was in . . . in my coma. And I . . . I . . . I would revive, you know, because they caught it in time, thank goodness.

Whiting: So, you didn't want to die?

Grover: No. I mean, not now. Later, yeah, but . . . (laughing). No, I mean, then I thought that I could be married, you know, and just be normal again . . . in my . . . in my coma.

Whiting: Because everything was fine.

Grover: Yeah, and . . . and now, I don't know if I'll ever get married because who would have me (laughing), you know.

Whiting: Just one last question. Do you believe that people do have the right to die, if they want to?

Grover: Well, if . . . I think that if . . . if someone wants to die, I would say, well, you can, but it's just terrible. Now . . . now . . . now I . . . I wasn't that concerned, 'cause I knew that there was a God, and also Jesus, Buddha and Mohammed.

Day: Is that a choice that you could ever make for yourself?

Grover: Uhm, well, I don't know, but, I think that . . . if I'm, well, I mean, if I'm well, and all of a sudden, I die, you know, that's different, but if I'm suffering, I would cheerfully say, listen, extinguish it. . . . Because I believe that . . . that . . . that you should have that right, you know.

Whiting: Are you happy now?

Grover: Yeah, now I am.

Whiting: Do you enjoy your life?

Grover: Yes, I do. Of course, the bad thing is, they're all women here (laughing).

Despite the fact that this is only a single account of what a coma is like, perhaps not typical, it is clear that, at least for Jan, being in such a state was not a hellish experience. Rather, it seems simply to have been an altered state of consciousness in which she existed in a world within the world. She was very much alive, experiencing a state of existence that enabled her to observe our world while we were unable even to perceive hers. Perhaps it is our inability to understand the world of the comatose patient, combined with our instinctive fear of the unknown—that leads so many of us to adamantly reject the prospect of living in such an altogether mysterious state. For many of us, this rejection is so profound that we automatically express a preference for death over a comatose or vegetative state. Is this an irrational fear, or simply a personal preference? It is difficult to say.

A WORD OF ADVICE

Whiting: Do you have any advice for the families that might have sons or daughters in a coma?

Grover: Just be there, and . . . because they will come out of the coma one day, you know, and they might be . . . let's see . . . a week or a month or a year, or whatever and . . . and God is in there. And don't . . . don't take their word for it [the doctors] because, uhm, I almost died, you know, and . . . and they said, well, listen, Mr. and Mrs. Grover, your daughter is never going to get out of the coma, or if she does, she'll only watch, uh, let's see . . . Ryan's Hope, and she doesn't . . . she doesn't read at all, she doesn't do anything, and I'm sorry, but she's . . . and she's gonna be . . . be in a wheelchair all of her life, and (laughing), of course, I don't anymore. But, Mom and Daddy said, well, listen, uh, I don't think it's so, you know, and we're not going to take her in the nursing home, like we were saying, instead we're going to work . . . going to work her, and we're going to make her remember, you know. Because then . . . they thought that I could go back to school again, you know, but . . . and now, there's just one chance in a hundred that I'll go back and . . . but I kinda doubt it. But, that's ok.

Whiting: Can you read?

Grover: Oh! In fact, I was just reading . . . right now.[1]

Interview ends.

Appendix C: Universal Declaration of Human Rights

(obtained from United Nations Web Page at http://www.un.org/Overview/rights.html)

On December 10, 1948 the General Assembly of the United Nations adopted and proclaimed the Universal Declaration of Human Rights the full text of which appears in the following pages. Following this historic act the Assembly called upon all Member countries to publicize the text of the Declaration and "to cause it to be disseminated, displayed, read and expounded principally in schools and other educational institutions, without distinction based on the political status of countries or territories."

PREAMBLE

Whereas recognition of the inherent dignity and of the equal and inalienable rights of all members of the human family is the foundation of freedom, justice and peace in the world,

Whereas disregard and contempt for human rights have resulted in barbarous acts which have outraged the conscience of mankind, and the advent of a world in which human beings shall enjoy freedom of speech and belief and freedom from fear and want has been proclaimed as the highest aspiration of the common people,

Whereas it is essential, if man is not to be compelled to have recourse, as a last resort, to rebellion against tyranny and oppression, that human rights should be protected by the rule of law,

Whereas it is essential to promote the development of friendly relations between nations,

Whereas the peoples of the United Nations have in the Charter reaffirmed their faith in fundamental human rights, in the dignity and worth of the human person and in the equal rights of men and women and have determined to promote social progress and better standards of life in larger freedom,

Whereas Member States have pledged themselves to achieve, in co-operation with the United Nations, the promotion of universal respect for and observance of human rights and fundamental freedoms,

Whereas a common understanding of these rights and freedoms is of the greatest importance for the full realization of this pledge,

Now, Therefore THE GENERAL ASSEMBLY proclaims THIS UNIVERSAL DECLARATION OF HUMAN RIGHTS as a common standard of achievement for all peoples and all nations, to the end that every individual and every organ of society, keeping this Declaration constantly in mind, shall strive by teaching and education to promote respect for these rights and freedoms and by progressive measures, national and international, to secure their universal and effective recognition and observance, both among the peoples of Member States themselves and among the peoples of territories under their jurisdiction.

Article 1.

All human beings are born free and equal in dignity and rights. They are endowed with reason and conscience and should act towards one another in a spirit of brotherhood.

Article 2.

Everyone is entitled to all the rights and freedoms set forth in this Declaration, without distinction of any kind, such as race, colour, sex, language, religion, political or other opinion, national or social origin, property, birth or other status. Furthermore, no distinction shall be made on the basis of the political, jurisdictional or international status of the country or territory to which a person belongs, whether it be independent, trust, non-self-governing or under any other limitation of sovereignty.

Article 3.

Everyone has the right to life, liberty and security of person.

Article 4.

No one shall be held in slavery or servitude; slavery and the slave trade shall be prohibited in all their forms.

Article 5.

No one shall be subjected to torture or to cruel, inhuman or degrading treatment or punishment.

Article 6.

Everyone has the right to recognition everywhere as a person before the law.

Article 7.

All are equal before the law and are entitled without any discrimination to equal protection of the law. All are entitled to equal protection against any discrimination in violation of this Declaration and against any incitement to such discrimination.

Article 8.

Everyone has the right to an effective remedy by the competent national tribunals for acts violating the fundamental rights granted him by the constitution or by law.

Article 9.

No one shall be subjected to arbitrary arrest, detention or exile.

Article 10.

Everyone is entitled in full equality to a fair and public hearing by an independent and impartial tribunal, in the determination of his rights and obligations and of any criminal charge against him.

Article 11.

(1) Everyone charged with a penal offence has the right to be presumed innocent until proved guilty according to law in a public trial at which he has had all the guarantees necessary for his defence.

(2) No one shall be held guilty of any penal offence on account of any act or omission which did not constitute a penal offence, under national or international law, at the time when it was committed. Nor shall a heavier penalty be imposed than the one that was applicable at the time the penal offence was committed.

Article 12.

No one shall be subjected to arbitrary interference with his privacy, family, home or correspondence, nor to attacks upon his honour and reputation. Everyone has the right to the protection of the law against such interference or attacks.

Article 13.

(1) Everyone has the right to freedom of movement and residence within the borders of each state.

(2) Everyone has the right to leave any country, including his own, and to return to his country.

Article 14.

(1) Everyone has the right to seek and to enjoy in other countries asylum from persecution.

(2) This right may not be invoked in the case of prosecutions genuinely arising from non-political crimes or from acts contrary to the purposes and principles of the United Nations.

Article 15.

(1) Everyone has the right to a nationality.

(2) No one shall be arbitrarily deprived of his nationality nor denied the right to change his nationality.

Article 16.

(1) Men and women of full age, without any limitation due to race, nationality or religion, have the right to marry and to found a family. They are entitled to equal rights as to marriage, during marriage and at its dissolution.

(2) Marriage shall be entered into only with the free and full consent of the intending spouses.

(3) The family is the natural and fundamental group unit of society and is entitled to protection by society and the State.

Article 17.

(1) Everyone has the right to own property alone as well as in association with others.

(2) No one shall be arbitrarily deprived of his property.

Article 18.

Everyone has the right to freedom of thought, conscience and religion; this right includes freedom to change his religion or belief, and freedom, either alone or in community with others and in public or private, to manifest his religion or belief in teaching, practice, worship and observance.

Article 19.

Everyone has the right to freedom of opinion and expression; this right includes freedom to hold opinions without interference and to seek, receive and impart information and ideas through any media and regardless of frontiers.

Article 20.

(1) Everyone has the right to freedom of peaceful assembly and association.

(2) No one may be compelled to belong to an association.

Article 21.

(1) Everyone has the right to take part in the government of his country, directly or through freely chosen representatives.

(2) Everyone has the right of equal access to public service in his country.

(3) The will of the people shall be the basis of the authority of government; this will shall be expressed in periodic and genuine elections which shall be by universal and equal suffrage and shall be held by secret vote or by equivalent free voting procedures.

Article 22.

Everyone, as a member of society, has the right to social security and is entitled to realization, through national effort and international co-operation and in accordance with the organization and resources of each State, of the economic, social and cultural rights indispensable for his dignity and the free development of his personality.

Article 23.

(1) Everyone has the right to work, to free choice of employment, to just and favourable conditions of work and to protection against unemployment.

(2) Everyone, without any discrimination, has the right to equal pay for equal work.

(3) Everyone who works has the right to just and favourable remuneration ensuring for himself and his family an existence worthy of human dignity, and supplemented, if necessary, by other means of social protection.

(4) Everyone has the right to form and to join trade unions for the protection of his interests.

Article 24.

Everyone has the right to rest and leisure, including reasonable limitation of working hours and periodic holidays with pay.

Article 25.

(1) Everyone has the right to a standard of living adequate for the health and well-being of himself and of his family, including food, clothing, housing and medical care and necessary social services, and the right to security in the event of unemployment, sickness, disability, widowhood, old age or other lack of livelihood in circumstances beyond his control.

(2) Motherhood and childhood are entitled to special care and assistance. All children, whether born in or out of wedlock, shall enjoy the same social protection.

Article 26.

(1) Everyone has the right to education. Education shall be free, at least in the elementary and fundamental stages. Elementary education shall be compulsory. Technical and professional education shall be made generally available and higher education shall be equally accessible to all on the basis of merit.

(2) Education shall be directed to the full development of the human personality and to the strengthening of respect for human rights and fundamental freedoms. It shall promote understanding, tolerance and friendship among all nations, racial or religious groups, and shall further the activities of the United Nations for the maintenance of peace.

(3) Parents have a prior right to choose the kind of education that shall be given to their children.

Article 27.

(1) Everyone has the right freely to participate in the cultural life of the community, to enjoy the arts and to share in scientific advancement and its benefits.

(2) Everyone has the right to the protection of the moral and material interests resulting from any scientific, literary or artistic production of which he is the author.

Article 28.

Everyone is entitled to a social and international order in which the rights and freedoms set forth in this Declaration can be fully realized.

Article 29.

(1) Everyone has duties to the community in which alone the free and full development of his personality is possible.

(2) In the exercise of his rights and freedoms, everyone shall be subject only to such limitations as are determined by law solely for the purpose of securing due recognition and respect for the rights and freedoms of others and of meeting the just requirements of morality, public order and the general welfare in a democratic society.

(3) These rights and freedoms may in no case be exercised contrary to the purposes and principles of the United Nations.

Article 30.

Nothing in this Declaration may be interpreted as implying for any State, group or person any right to engage in any activity or to perform any act aimed at the destruction of any of the rights and freedoms set forth herein.

Notes

CHAPTER 1: CONTEMPORARY ATTITUDES ABOUT DEATH

1. For an exploration of the cost of medical care during the last days of life, see M. W. Riley, "Aging, Social Change and the Power of Ideas," *Daedalus* 107: 39-52.

CHAPTER 2: A BRIEF MODERN HISTORY AND DEFINITION OF TERMS

1. The establishments of Concern for Dying and the Society for the Right to Die have now combined and are called the Euthanasia Society of America.
2. In essence, this New York rule simply made legally permissible what was a common practice behind drawn hospital curtains in the past.
3. See *Tate v. Canonica,* 5 Cal Reptr. 28 (District Court App. 1960), quoting Blackstone (1778: 189): "Self-Murder is not the pretended heroism, but the real cowardice, of the Stoic philosophers, who destroyed themselves to avoid those ills which they had not the fortitude to endure and was punished by the Athenian law with cutting off the hand. And also the law of England wisely and religiously considers that no man hath a power to destroy life . . . and, as the suicide is guilty of a double offense—one spiritual . . . the other temporal, against the king who hath an interest in the preservation of all his subjects; the law has, therefore, ranked this among the highest crimes" at 31-32. See also *McMahan v. State*, 53 So. 89, 90-91 (Ala. 1910), footnotes 9 and 10; Donald Beschle, "Autonomous Decision Making and Social Choice: Examining the 'Right to Die.'" *Kentucky Law Journal* 77 (1989): 323.
4. James Carpentier lectured at Columbia University and at the Association of the Bar of the City of New York. An expanded version of these lectures was later turned into a book, G. Williams, 1972, *The Sanctity of Life and the Criminal Law* (New York, Knopf, 1972). In this work Williams openly advocated the decriminalization of contraception, and the availability of voluntary sterilization and abortion, and he even went so far as to argue in favor of infanticide.
5. Several revisions of the Roman Catholic Church's position on euthanasia have been made, the last being approved by Pope John Paul II, "The Sacred Congregation for the Doctrine of the Faith 'Declaration on Euthanasia,'" issued on 5 May, 1980.

6. In the last decade, the last states with statutes making attempted suicide a crime have repealed those statutes.

7. For state legislation distinguishing between suicide and the withholding or withdrawal of life-sustaining procedures see the following state legislative acts: VA. CODE. ANN. sect. 54.1-2991 (1950); N.M. STAT. ANN. Sect. 24-7-8 (1953); UTAH CODE ANN. Sect. 75-2-1116 (1953); ME. REV. STAT. Ann. tit. 22, Sect. 2929 (1964); DEL. CODE ANN. Tit. 16, Sect 2507 (1974); ALA. CODE Sect. 22-8A-9 (1975); TENN. CODE ANN. 32-11-110 (1984); GA. CODE ANN. Sect. 31-32-9 (1985); HAW. REV. STAT. Sect. 327D-14 (1985); WASH. REV. CODE ANN. Sect. 70.122.070 (1975); W. VA. CODE Sect. 16-30-8 (1985); ALASKA STAT. Sect. 18.12.080 (1986); ARIZ. REV. STAT. ANN. Sect. 36-3208 (1986); FLA. STAT. ANN. Sect. 765.11 (West 1986); NEV. REV. STAT. ANN. Sect. 449.650 (Mich 1986); COLO. REV. STAT. Sect. 15-18-111 (1987); VT. STAT. ANN. tit. 18, sect. 5260 (1987); ARK. STAT. ANN. Sect. 20-17-210 (Sup. 1989); IOWA CODE ANN. Sect. 144 A.11 (West 1989); WIS. STAT. ANN. Sect. 154.11 (West 1989); CAL. HEALTH & SAFETY CODE Sect. 7192 (West Sup. 1990); IND. CODE ANN. Sect. 16-8-11-18 (Burns 1990); LA. REV. STAT. ANN. Sect. 40:1299.58.10 (West Sup. 1990); MD. HEALTH-GEN. CODE ANN. Sect. 5-613 (1990); N.C. GEN. STAT. Sect. 90-321 (1990); TEX. HEALTH & SAFETY CODE ANN. Sect. 672.017 (Vernon 1991).

8. Upon the removal of the respirator, Karen Ann Quinlan began to breathe spontaneously and continued to live for another ten years.

9. See *People v. Campbell*, 124 Michigan App. 337-338; 335 N. W. 2d at 29-30.

10. Similar decisions were reached in the cases of *In re Gardner*, 534 A.2d 947 [Maine 1987], and *Corbett v. D'alessandro*, 487 So.2d 368 [Florida 1986]. Both cases allowed for the removal of artificial feeding tubes and hydration, despite the existence of state statutes that required the ongoing provision of following "comfort care," which was broadly understood to include both of these measures.

CHAPTER 4: ANATOMY OF A RIGHT

1. "Neither your own persons nor the estate are your own; both belong to your whole line, past and future, and still more absolutely do both lineage and estate belong to the community." Plato, *Laws* 923a, translated by Taylor. "We must not regard a citizen as belonging just to himself: we must rather regard every citizen as belonging to the state." Aristotle, *Politics* 1337aa 8-29 (8.I.4), translated by Barker.

CHAPTER 5: OPPOSITION TO THE "RIGHT TO DIE"

1. The court also noted that this right must be balanced against the recognized state interest in protecting life.

2. For general information on the position of various religious groups see Gerald A. Larue, "Euthanasia and Religion: *A Survey of the Attitudes of World Religions to the Right-to-Die* (Los Angeles, California: The Hemlock Society, 1985).

CHAPTER 6: ROMAN NATURAL LAW THEORY

1. Voeglin stated this situation best when he wrote that negative views about natural law were at one time so prevalent that "to be found guilty of adherence to natural law theories is a kind of social disgrace." H. Voeglin, "Kelsen's Pure Theory of Law," *Political Science Quarterly* 42 (1997): 268-276, 269.

2. I witnessed a good example of such avoidance at the 1993 Midwest Political Science Association in Chicago, where a young scholar was delivering a paper on the subject of "Fundamental Law." After listening to his presentation, I inquired of him as to why he had not made mention of the natural law theories that were so important to his topic. He responded to my query by assuring me that he had discussed natural law in his paper, but then added, somewhat sheepishly, that his lead professor had made him remove all references to natural law and place them in the

endnotes of his work.

3. "Neither your own persons nor the estate are your own; both belong to your whole line, past and future, and still more absolutely do both lineage and estate belong to the community." Plato, *Laws*, 923a, translated by Taylor. "We must not regard a citizen as belonging just to himself: we must rather regard every citizen as belonging to the state." Aristotle, *Politics*, 1337aa 8-29 (8.I.4), translated by Barker.

4. In this work, the author posits the idea that the American and French revolutions would never have taken place and that no ideas of freedom or equality under the law would have developed without the influence of natural law.

5. It should be noted that customary law can be maintained as a third category, however. This category cannot be cited as a source of private law, given the lack of sufficient social stability and the length of uninterrupted social practice necessary to establish customary actions sufficient to take on the force of law.

6. In her book *Greece, Rome, and the Bill of Rights*, Susan Ford Wiltshire cites Lionel Cassion as saying, "Imagine, if you will, a time without lawyers at all; civilization flourished in Egypt and ancient Greece with little help from lawyers, but then came Rome and our troubles began." *Smithsonian* 18 (October 1987): 122. To be fair, however, Wiltshire also points to the work of Robert J. Bonner, who concluded that litigation was so common in ancient Athens that rather than conclude that there were no lawyers, it is more accurate to see them as a "nation of lawyers." *Lawyers and Litigants in Ancient Athens* (Chicago: University of Chicago Press, 1927).

CHAPTER 7: NATURAL LAW THEORY THROUGH THE MIDDLE AGES

1. This collection of church laws was completed in approximately 1140 and was part of a larger collection of Church documents known as the Corpus Iuris Canonici, so named by the Council of Basle in 1441. This collection is an essential reading for anyone interested in the specifics of the Medieval church's understanding of natural law.

CHAPTER 8: THE DEVELOPMENT OF NATURAL RIGHTS THEORY

1. Although Hobbes is often cited in defense of positivism, it is clear that he held a view of natural law that, although radical, still maintained that its principles restricted human action and were eternal and immutable. See Hobbes' *Leviathan*, chap. 15.

2. Locke states that "The state of nature has a law to govern it, which obliges everyone: and reason, which is the law, teaches all mankind, who will but consult it, that being all equal and independent, no one ought to harm another in his life, health, liberty, or possessions."

3. The influence of Aristotle over Locke is profound, and this influence is reflected throughout Locke's works on government and natural law. It is, however, difficult to determine whether this influence is directly taken from Aristotle's work or has been translated through the works of St. Thomas Aquinas. Thus, in Locke's work, *Essays on the Law of Nature* (ed. W. von Leyden, Oxford: Clarendon Press, 1970), Locke argues that the principal function of man is to contemplate God's works, to preserve life in society with other men, and to maintain society by the gift of speech and language (p. 158). This statement is extremely reminiscent of Aristotle's understanding of the nature of man and that which separates man from other animals (language), as well as being reminiscent of Aquinas's statement that all men are called to "preserve oneself, to know the truth about God, and to live in society" (*Summa Theologica*, Ia, 2ae, 94, Art. 2).

4. A similar view of Locke's theory has been expressed by Christian Wolff and is

cited in the work of Susan Ford Wiltshire, *Greece, Rome, and the Bill of Rights* (University of Oklahoma Press: Norman and London, 1992).

CHAPTER 9: THE EVOLUTION OF NATURAL LAW THEORY AND THE "RIGHT TO DIE"

1. Van Hooff citing Seneca, *Epistulae*, 91, 21; 58, 34; 54, 1-2; 77, 9, recounting Seneca's deliberations concerning his own death.
2. Otto Gierke observes that many medieval thinkers had theories concerning the existence of individual rights. See Otto Gierke, *Political Theories of the Middle Ages*, translated by F. W. Maitland. (Cambridge, England: 1922).

CHAPTER 12: NATURAL LAW AND THE CONSTITUTION: THEN AND NOW

1. James B. Thayer maintained that an understanding and acceptance of the principles of natural law undoubtably helped lead to the American practice of judicial review.
2. See American Anti-Slave Society, *Declaration of Sentiments of the American Anti-Slavery Society in Philadelphia* (New York: American Anti-Slave Society 1835) 31; *Works of William H. Seward* (Boston: Houghton, Mifflin and Company, 1884) I: 66, 74; William Hoser, *The Higher Law in Its Relation to Civil Government with Particular Reference to the Fugitive Slave Law*, 1852; Justice Chase in *Jones v. Van Zandt,* in C. E. Merriam, ed., *A History of American Political Theories* (New York: Macmillan Co., 1906), 212.
3. For additional support on this aspect of the analytical school see George Lawrence Scherger, *The Evaluation of Liberty* (New York: Longmans, Green, and Co., 1904), 11.
4. The principal function of the Ninth Amendment was to specifically defeat the rule of legal interpretation, still operative today, which holds that any item or requirement not enumerated is to be interpreted as intentionally excluded.
5. For counter opinions one can see the opinions of Justice Hugo Black, who believed in the absolute nature of the First Amendment. See *Smith v. California*, 361 U.S. 147 at 157 (1959); *Konigsberg v. State Board of California*, 366 U.S. 36 at 61 (1961).

CHAPTER 13: THE AMERICAN INTERPRETATION OF NATURAL LAW AS IT PERTAINS TO THE "RIGHT TO DIE"

1. Hobbes distinguished between Law and Rights by noting that "Rights" consist of the liberty to do or not do some act, whereas "Law" represents a determination of what one must and must not do. *Leviathan*, Chap. 14.
2. Perhaps it should be noted that it was exactly the repugnant nature of this assertion that led Greek philosophers to try to identify foundational principles upon which man's obligation to the legal order and society could be founded.
3. A similar view was expressed by Jacques Maritain, *The Rights of Man and Natural Law* (New York: Gordian Press, 1944).

CHAPTER 14: APPLICATIONS

1. While many would argue that the "right to life" also protects the unborn, such questions involve considerations that are beyond the scope of this book.
2. It should be noted that evaluating rational ability is markedly different from determining whether or not an action is rational. This exercise would be similar to a determination of whether a testator, or the maker of a will, possesses a sufficiently rational state of mind to execute a legal document. During such a determination, the court does not seek to examine the rationality of the individual bequests that may be

contained in the will, but only to examine the testator's state of mind at the time of its making. Similarly, in the case of a "right to die" decision, the government should not be involved in characterizing the rationality of the decision but, rather, the rationality of the decision maker.

3. It is exactly this type of situation that has given rise to the controversy surrounding the actions of Dr. Jack Kevorkian, who has aided numerous individuals in their efforts to terminate their lives, by providing various "suicide machines" or means by which the individuals could painlessly terminate their lives. In addition, the reader may wish to take note of the present debate among criminal law theorists concerning the plausibility of a "compassion defense" to charges of assisted suicide. Jeremy Horder, "Assisting in Suicide: Keeping the Debate Alive," *Journal of Criminal Law* 54 (May 1990): 253-256.

4. It is also true that an individual can forfeit her or his right to vote by committing crimes against society.

5. One of the most famous was the debate between Patrick Devlin, who advocated the strong use of the criminal law to protect society, and H.L.A. Hart, who advocated that the criminal law was an improper moral instrument.

6. It is clear that within the religious context of the Roman Catholic Church strong guidelines have been established that attempt to delineate exactly what actions its members may take to alleviate suffering and which actions would be considered to be morally wrong or sinful.

7. In *Griswold v. Connecticut* (1965), Justice Goldberg's concurring joined Warren and Brennan. Also see "Griswold, The Right to Be Let Alone," *Northwestern University Law Rev.* 55 (1960): 216.

8. Perhaps the most striking example of this phenomenon is the case of Dr. Jack Kevorkian, who, at the time of this writing, had assisted in the deaths of 18 people and who was only reluctantly charged by a Michigan prosecutor, who himself believed that euthanasia should be legalized and who stated that he would not seek a prison sentence for Dr. Kevorkian, even if he were convicted.

APPENDIX A: ONE MAN'S DECISION TO DIE

1. Additional information about Mr. McAfee was obtained with Mr. McAfee's permission through an interview with Robin P. Whiting, who worked as a private care attendant for Mr. McAfee from 1992 to 1993.

2. In November of 1993, Larry McAfee experienced a severe staph infection that required prolonged hospitalization. During this time, Mr. McAfee continued to live with the hope that he would recover from this setback and would once again be able to return to living outside an institution. However, Larry McAfee's wish never came true, and he died at University Hospital, Augusta, Georgia.

APPENDIX B: A TALK WITH A FORMERLY COMATOSE PATIENT

1. Jan Grover began making plans to reenter college in Augusta, Georgia, in November of 1996.

Selected Bibliography

Adams, John. *The Works of John Adams, Second President of the United States.* Edited by Charles F. Adams. Boston: Little, Brown, 1865.

Adams, Randolph G. *Political Ideas of the American Revolution.* Dunham: Trinity College Press, 1922.

Almgren, Gunnar. "Bedside Decisions Pertaining to Artificial Nutrition and Hydration: Influences of Public Versus Nursing Home Industry Structure." In Henry R. Glick, *The Right to Die: Policy Innovation and Its Consequences.* New York: Columbia University Press, 1992.

Aries, Philippe. *Western Attitudes Toward Death: From the Middle Ages to the Present.* Translated by Patricia M. Ranum. Baltimore: Johns Hopkins University Press, 1974.

_____. *The Hour of Our Death.* Translated by Helen Weaver. Hammondsworth: Penguin, 1981.

Aristotle. *Art of Rhetoric.* 1373b4 and 1375a27. Translated by J. H. Freese. Cambridge, Massachusetts: Harvard University Press, 1926.

_____. *Nicomachean Ethics.* Bk. I, 1098 a7-8, and bk. V, 1134 b18. Translated by Martin Oswald. Indianapolis: Bobbs-Merrill Educational Publishing, 1962.

_____. *Politics.* 1294 a7-9. Translated by Carnes Lord. Chicago: University of Chicago Press, 1984.

Arkes, Hadley. "Natural Law: Its Reappearance and Why It Continues to Matter." *Constitution: A Journal for the Foundation of the U.S. Constitution* 4, no. 1(1992): 13-18.

Aquinas, St. Thomas. *Summa Theologica.* Translated by Fathers of the English Dominican Province. New York: Benziger, Bruce and Glencoe, 1948.

Austin, John. *Lectures on Jurisprudence and the Philosophy of Positive Law*, 5th ed., Vol. 1. Edited by Robert Campbell. London: John Murray, 1885.

Barker, Sir Ernest. *Greek Political Theory: Plato and his Predecessors.* London: Methuen and Co. Ltd., 1918.

_____. *Traditions of Civility: Eight Essays.* Cambridge, England: University Press, 1948.

_____. *Essays on Government.* Oxford: Clarendon Press, 1951.

Barnett, Randy E. *James Madison's Ninth Amendment: The History and Meaning of the 9th Amendment.* Fairfax, Virginia: George Mason University Press, 1989.

Bass, David M. "The Hospice Ideology and Success of Hospice Care." *Research on Aging* 7, no. 1 (1985): 319-367.

Becker, Carl L. *The Declaration of Independence.* New York: Knopf, 1966.

Bentham, Jeremy. *Anarchical Fallacies,* in "*Works.*" Edited by John Burton. Edinburgh: W. Tait, 1843.

Beschle, Donald L. "Autonomous Decision Making and Social Choice: Examining the 'Right to Die.'" *Kentucky Law Journal* 77 (1988-89): 320.

Borchard, Edwin M. "Government Responsibility in Tort." *Yale Law Journal* 36 (1927): 794.

Brest, Paul. *Processes of Constitutional Decisionmaking: Cases and Materials.* Boston: Little, Brown, 1975.

Brownlow, W. G., and Abram Pryne. *Ought American Slavery to Be Perpetuated?: A Debate Between Rev. W. G. Brownlow and Rev. A. Pryne.* Philadelphia: J. B. Lippincott & Co., 1858.

Burgess, John W. *Political Science and Comparative Constitutional Law.* Boston: Ginn and Co., 1891.

Burns, Alfred. "Athenian Literacy in the Fifth Century B.C." *Journal of the History of Ideas* 42 (1981): 371.

Burns, Edward McNall, Robert E. Lerner, and Standish Meacham. *Western Civilizations: Their History and Their Culture.* New York: Norton, 1984.

Calhoun, George M. "Greek Law and Modern Jurisprudence." *California Law Review* 11, 1923.

Callahan, Daniel. *Setting Limits: Medical Goals in an Aging Society.* New York: Simon and Schuster, 1987.

Candiotii, Susan, Correspondent. Paralyzed Woman Dies After Winning Legal Fight: Prosecutors Collect Evidence Against Her Mother. 19 May 1999. Available [Online]: <http.//www.cnn.com/US/9905/19/daughter.shot.02/index.html> [28 May 2000].

Cardozo, Benjamin N. *The Nature of Judicial Process.* New Haven: Yale University Press, 1922.

Carlyle, A. J. "The Political Theories of St. Thomas Aquinas." *Scottish Review* 27, no. 126 (1869): 141.

Carlyle, A.J., and R. W. Carlyle. *A History of Medieval Political Theory in the West,* Vol. 1. New York: Barnes and Noble, 1903.

Cassirer, Ernest. "The Individual and the Cosmos in Renaissance Philosophy." Translated by Mario Domandi. In Susan Ford Wiltshire, *Greece, Rome, and the Bill of Rights.* Norman: University of Oklahoma Press, 1992.

Channel 6000. AMA to Fight Oregon's Assisted Suicide Law: Medical Org. Delegates Debate Ethical, Legal Issues. No Date. Available [Online]: <http://www.channel6000.com/health/storieshealth-19991209-025111.html> [28 May 2000].

Choice in Dying. Recent Legislation. 11 February 2000. Available [Online]: <http://www.choices.org/legal.htm#Legislation> [28 May 2000].

Cicero, Marcus Tullius. "De Republica, De Legibus." In A. P. d'Entr'eves, *Natural Law: An Historical Survey.* New York: Harper and Row, 1965.

_____. *De Republica, De Legibus.* I, x, 29; xii, 33. Translated by C. W. Keyes. Cambridge, Massachusetts: Harvard University Press, 1966.

Claiborne, William, and Thomas B. Edsall. "Affirmation of Oregon Suicide Law." *Washington Post*, November 6, 2000, A:19. Available [Online]: <http://www.washingtonpost.com/wpsrv/politics/97/stories/initiative1106.html> (28 May 2000).

Cole, J. J. "Moral Dilemma: To Kill or Allow to Die?" *Death Studies* 13, no. 4 (1989): 393-406.

Coleman, Phillipson. *Great Jurists of the World*. Edited by Sir John MacDonell and Edward Manson. Boston: Little, Brown, 1914.

Congressional Record. State of Virginia. Excerpt from the Journal, authored by John Beckly, Secretary to the convention. Richmond: Aug. Davis, printer to the honorable convention (1788).

Continental Congress. 1774-89. *Journals of the Continental Congress, 1774-1789*. Edited by Worthington C. Ford et al. 34 Vols. Washington, D.C., 1904-37.

Cooley, T. M., and Thomas McIntyre. *A Treatise on the Constitutional Limitations which rest upon the Legislative Power of the States of the American Union*, 2d ed., Boston: Little, Brown, and Co., 1868. Microfilm.

Corwin, Edward S. "The Doctrine of Due Process of Law Before the Civil War." *Harvard Law Review* 24 (1911): 366-370.

_____. "The Extension of Judicial Review in New York." *Michigan Law Review* 15 (1917): 281.

DeathNet. Assisted Suicide Bill Delayed in Senate. 29 May 2000. Available [Online]: <http://www.rights.org/deathnet/Usnews_9911.html> [29 May 2000].

_____. Senate Judiciary Committee Approves Anti-Suicide Bill. 28 May 2000. Available [Online]: http://www.rights.org/deathnet/Usnews_0004.html> [29 May 2000].

_____. Four in Five Vote for the Right to Die. 30 May 2000. Available [Online]: <http://www.rights.org/deathnet/Wnews_0004.html> [30 May 2000].

_____. Kevorkian Denounces Assisted Suicide Proposal. 28 May 2000. Available [Online]: <http://www.rights.org/deathnet/Usnews_9810.html> [30 May 2000].

_____. World's Most Liberal Euthanasia Law Set to Pass in June 2000? 30 May 2000. Available [Online]: <http://www.rights.org/deathnet/Wnews_9912 html> [30 May 2000].

_____. Cape Town, South Africa: Parliament Opens Debate on Euthanasia. No date. Available [Online]: <http://www.rights.org/deathnet/Wnews_9909.html> [16 June 2000].

Dedek, John F. *Human Life: Some Moral Issues*. New York: Sheed & Ward, 1972.

d'Entr'eves, A. P. *Natural Law: An Historical Survey*. New York: Harper & Row, 1965.

_____. *Natural Law: An Introduction to Legal Philosophy*, 2d ed. London: Hutchinson, 1970.

Dickinson, E.D. *The Equality of States in International Law*. Cambridge: Harvard University Press, 1920.

Dickinson, George. "The American Way of Dying and Death." In *Dying, Death and Bereavement*. Dickinson, George, Michael R. Leming and Alan C. Mermann, eds. Guilford, Connecticut: Dushkin Publishing Group, 1993.

_____. "Euthanasia: What Is a 'Good Death'?" In *Dying, Death and Bereavement*. Guilford, Connecticut: Dushkin Publishing Group, 1996.

Docker, Chris. Timeline. No date. Available [Online]: <http://www.euthanasia.org/history.html> [28 May 2000].

Donne, John. *Biathanatos*. London: Published by Authority, for Humphrey Moseley, 1648.

Dunning, William A. *Political Theories from Luther to Montesquieu*. New York: Macmillan, 1905.

Egerton, H. E. *The Causes and Character of the American Revolution*. Oxford:

Clarendon Press, 1931.
Elliot, W. Y. "Sovereign State or Sovereign Group." *American Political Science Review* 29, no. 3 (1925): 475-499.
"Euthanasia: Controversy Around the World." *Britain: The Sunday Times* [electronic version], 12 May 1999. Section unknown. Available [Online]: <http://www.sundaytimes.co.uk/news/pages/tim/99/05/12/timnwsnws 03028.html> [28 May 2000].
Fagles, Robert. *Sophocles: The Three Theban Plays.* New York: Penguin Books, 1984. Original work published in Sophocles, *Three Theban Plays* (441 B.C.).
Feifel, Herman. "Philosophy Reconsidered." *Psychological Reports* 15 (1964): 415-420.
_____. "Psychology and Death: Meaningful Rediscovery." *American Psychologist* 45, no. 4 (1990): 537-539.
_____, ed. *New Meanings of Death.* New York: McGraw-Hill, 1977.
Finnis, John. *Natural Law and Natural Rights.* Oxford: Clarendon Press, 1980.
Flack, Horace E. Chap. 1 and Chap. 2 in *The Adoption of the Fourteenth Amendment.* Baltimore: Johns Hopkins Press, 1908.
Friedberg, Emil Albert. *Decretum Gratiani.* Leipzig: A. Edelmann, 1876.
Gentile, Marian, and Maryanne Fello. "Hospice Care for the 1990's: A Concept Coming of Age." In George E. Dickinson, Michael R. Leming, and Alan C. Mermann, eds., *Dying, Death, and Bereavement.* Guilford, Connecticut: Dushkin Publishing Group, 1994.
George, Robert P., ed. *Natural Law Theory: Contemporary Essays.* Oxford: Oxford University Press, 1992.
Gevers, Sjef. "Legal Developments Concerning Active Euthanasia on Request in the Netherlands." *Bioethics* 1 (1987): 160.
Gierke, Otto F. von. *Political Theories of the Middle Ages.* Translated by F. W. Maitland. England: Cambridge University Press, 1922.
_____. *Natural Law and the Theory of Society 1500-1800.* Boston: Beacon Press, 1934.
Glick, Henry R. *The Right to Die: Policy Innovation and Its Consequences.* New York: Columbia University Press, 1992.
Godley, Elizabeth. "'Patients' Right to Die Becoming Major Issue for MDs and MPs." *Canadian Medical Association Journal* 146, no. 4 (1992): 608-610.
Goodell, D. "An Athenian Parallel to the Function of Our Supreme Court." *Yale Review* 2, 1893.
Gray, John C. *The Nature and Source of the Law.* New York: Columbia University Press, 1909.
Grotius, Hugo. *Laws of War and Peace.* Indianapolis: Bobbs-Merrill, 1925.
Gunnison, Robert. "Assembly Panel OKs Assisted-Suicide Bill: Field Poll Says Most in State Support Practice." *San Francisco Gate News*, 21 April 1999, No Section. Available [Online]:<http://www.sfgate.com/cgi-bin/article.cgi?file+/chronicle/archive/1999/04/2/MN104227.DTL> [29 May 2000].
Haines, Charles Grove. *The American Doctrine of Judicial Supremacy.* New York: Macmillan, 1914.
_____. *The Revival of Natural Law Concepts: A Study of the Establishment and of the Interpretation of Limits on Legislatures with Special Reference to the Development of Certain Phases of American Constitutional Law.* New York: Russell and Russell, 1965.
Haley, Martine. "Euthanasia Clinics Win Public Support." *Hobart Mercury* (1 May 2000). Available [Online]: <http://www.ozemail.Comau/~dcar1946/deliverance /news/ default. Html> [30 May 2000].
Halper, Thomas. "Accommodating Death: Euthanasia in the Netherlands." Paper

presented at the Midwest Political Science Association Meeting, Chicago, Illinois, 1993.

Hamilton, Alexander. *The Farmer Refuted.* New York: James Rivington, 1775.

Harner, S. "Confusion in the Right to Die Ideology: Impact of Ethical Decision Making for Treatment of an Incompetent Client." *Georgetown Journal of Legal Ethics* 4 (1991).

Harris, William V. *Ancient Literacy*. Cambridge, Massachusetts, and London: Harvard University Press, 1989.

Havelock, Eric A. *The Greek Concept of Justice: From Its Shadows in Homer to Its Substance in Plato*. Cambridge, Massachusetts: Harvard University Press, 1978.

Helme, Tim. "Euthanasia Around the World." *British Medical Journal* 304 (1992): 7.

Hemlock Society. "Unbalanced Campaign" Defeats Proposal B. No Date. Available [Online]: <http://www.hemlock.org/press-w.html> [28 May 2000].

Hemlock Society. The New Dutch Bill. January 2001. Available [online]:<http://www.hemlock.org/hot_topics.htm#Dutch> [27 August 2001].

Hentoff, N. "The Death Doctors." *Village Voice* (8 September 1987).

Hinchman, Lewis P. "The Origins of Human Rights: A Hegelian Perspective." *Western Political Quarterly* 37, no. 1 (1984): 7.

Hirsch, Dana E. "Euthanasia: Is It Murder or Mercy Killing? A Comparison of the Criminal Laws in the United States, the Netherlands and Switzerland." *Loyola L.A. Int'l & Comp. Law Journal* 12 (1990): 799.

Hobbes, Thomas. *Leviathan.* Edited by Edwin Curley. Indianapolis: Hackett Publishing Co., 1994.

Holdsworth, William Searle. *History of English Law.* Vol. 5. Boston: Little, Brown, 1922.

Holmes, Oliver Wendell. *Collected Legal Papers.* New York: Harcourt, Brace and Co., 1920.

Hooff, Anton J. L. van. *From Autothanasia to Suicide: Self-Killing in Classical Antiquity*. New York: Routledge, 1990.

Horan, Dennis. "Euthanasia, the Right to Life and Termination of Medical Treatment: Legal Issues." In Donald G. McCarthy and Alvert S. Moraczewski, *Moral Responsibility in Prolonging Life Decisions.* St. Louis: Pope John Center, 1981.

Hume, David. *Two Essays*. London: Printed for Michael Smith, 1783.

Humphry, Derek. A Twentieth Century Chronology of Voluntary Euthanasia and Physician-assisted Suicide. April 1999. Available [Online]: <http://www.finalexit.org/more-chronology.html> (28 May 2000).

Humphry, Derek, and Ann Wickett. *The Right to Die: Understanding Euthanasia.* New York: Harper & Row, 1986.

Hunt, Gaillard, ed. *The Writings of James Madison*, Vol. 5. New York: G. P. Putnam's Sons, 1904.

Ingersoll, Robert G. *Is Suicide a Sin?* New York: Holland Publishing, 1895.

Isaacs, Nathan. "Marshall on Contracts." *Virginia Law Review* 7 (1921): 411.

Jacoby, R. "Narcissism and the Crisis of Capitalism." *Tolos* (1980): 33-64.

Jefferson, Thomas. *Notes on the State of Virginia*. Philadelphia: Princhard and Hall, 1782.

_____. "Declaration of Independence." In Francis Newton Thorpe, *The Federal and State Constitutions, Colonial Charters, and Other Organic Laws of the States, Territories and Colonies now or Heretofore Forming the United States of America*. Washington: U.S. Government Printing Office, 1909.

Kamisar, Yale. "Some Non-Religious Views Against Proposed 'Mercy-Killing'

Legislation." *Minnesota Law Review* 42 (1958): 969-971 & 1019-1024.

Kant, Immanuel. *The Philosophy of Law: An Exposition of Fundamental Principles of Jurisprudence as the Science of Right.* Translated by W. Hastie. Edinburgh: T. & T. Clark, 1887.

Kotch, Martin L. "Beyond Kevorkian." *Detroit Monthly Magazine* 17, 1994.

Kubler-Ross, E. *On Death and Dying.* New York: Macmillan, 1969.

Lacampagne, Suzanne. "Euthanasia: A Comparison of the Criminal Laws of Germany, Switzerland and the United States," *Boston College International and Comparative Law Review* 4 (1983): 533, 538-539, 547.

"Lambeth Conference: Euthanasia Wrong, Says Anglican Church." *Sydney Morning Herald* [Electronic Version], 6 August 1998, Section Unknown. Available [Online]: <http://www.smh.com.au/news/9808/06/world/world6.html> [30 May 2000].

Langer, Gary. Kevorkian Verdict Unpopular: Poll Mirrors Attitudes on Doctor-Assisted Suicide. 27 March 1999. Available [Online]: <http://www.abcnews.go.com/sections/us/DailyNews/Kevorkian_poll990327.html> [28 May 2000].

Lecky, W. E. H. *History of European Morals from Augustus to Charlemagne,* 2nd ed. London: Longmans, Green, 1869

_____. "History of European Morals." In H. R. Fedden, *Suicide, A Social and Historical Study.* London: P. Davies Limited, 1938.

Locke, John. *Essays on the Law of Nature.* Edited by W. von Leyden. Oxford: Clarendon Press, 1970.

_____. *Second Treatise of Civil Government.* Edited by Crawford B. Macpherson. Indianapolis: Hackett Publishing Co., 1980.

Long, A. A. *Hellenistic Philosophy: Stoics, Epicureans, Sceptics.* London: Gerald Duckworth, 1974.

Longwood College Library. Doctor-Assisted Suicide — A Guide to WEB Cites and the Literature. 29 May 2000. Available [Online]: <http://www.web.lwc.edu/administrative/library/suic.htm> [29 May 2000].

MacIntyre, Alasdair. "The Right to Die Garrulously." In Ernan McMullin, ed., *Death and Decision.* Presented at the AAAS Selected Symposium 18. Boulder, Colorado: Westview Press, 1978.

Maine Legislature. What the Maine Death with Dignity Act Is All About. No date. Available [Online]: <http://www.Janus.state.us/legis/bills/billtexts/id234801-1.asp> [29 May 2000].

Mair, A. W. "Suicide." In J. Hastings, ed., *Encyclopedia of Religion and Ethics* 12: 26-27. Edinburgh and New York, 1921.

Maritain, Jacques. *The Rights of Man and Natural Law.* New York: Gordian Press, 1943.

_____. *The Rights of Man and Natural Law.* New York: Gordian Press, 1971.

Masaryk, Thomas G. *Suicide and the Meaning of Civilization.* Translated by William B. Weist and Robert G. Batson. Chicago: University of Chicago Press, 1970.

Mayhew, Jonathan. *A Discourse Concerning Unlimited Submission.* Northridge, California: Santa Susana Press, 1976.

McCarthy, Donald G. "Care of Persons in Final State of Terminal Illness or Irreversibly Comatose." In Donald G. McCarthy and Alvert S. Moraczewski, *Moral Responsibility in Prolonging Life Decisions.* St. Louis: Pope John Center, 1981.

McDonald, Forrest. *Novus Ordo Seclorum: The Intellectual Origins of the Constitution.* Lawrence, Kansas: University Press of Kansas, 1985.

McIlwain, Charles Howard. *The High Court of Parliament and Its Supremacy.* New

Haven: Yale University Press, 1910.
_____. *The American Revolution: A Constitutional Interpretation.* New York: Macmillan, 1923.
_____. *The Growth of Political Thought in the West.* New York: Macmillan, 1964.
McKay, Shona. "Life, Death and the Law." *Maclean's Magazine*, 18, July 1983.
McLaughlin, Andrew Cunningham. *Foundations of American Constitutionalism.* New York: New York University Press, 1932.
McMullin, Ernan, ed. *Death and Decision.* Presented at the AAAS Selected Symposium 18. Boulder, Colorado: Westview Press, 1978.
Merriam, C. E. *American Political Theories.* New York: Macmillan, 1924.
Meucci, Sandra. "Death-Making in the Human Services." *Social Policy* 18, no. 3 (1988): 17-20.
Mojica, Stacy L., and Dan S. Murrell. "The Right to Choose: When Should Death Be in the Individual's Hands?" *Whittier Law Review* 12 (1991): note 16 on p. 473.
Mullins, M. "The Need for Guidance in Decision Making for Terminally Ill Incompetents." *Ohio Northern University Law Review* 17 (1991): 827-859.
Myres, John L. *The Political Ideas of the Greeks.* New York: Abingdon Press, 1927.
Nelson, Brian R. *Western Political Thought: From Socrates to the Age of Ideology.* Englewood Cliffs, New Jersey: Prentice-Hall, 1982.
Newman, S. A. "Saying No to Medical Treatment." *New York Magazine* 16 (1983): 74-85.
Nicholas, Barry. *An Introduction to Roman Law.* Oxford: Clarendon Press, 1962.
Nolan, Joseph R., and Jacquelin M. Nolan-Haley et al. *Black's Law Dictionary*, 6th ed. Edited by Henry Campbell Black. St. Paul, Minnesota: West Publishing Co., 1990.
O'dea, J. J. *Suicide: Studies on Its Philosophy, Causes and Prevention.* New York: G.P. Putnam's Sons, 1882.
Ogg, E. "The Right to Die with Dignity." *Public Affairs Pamphlet No. 57.* Public Affairs Committee, 1980.
Oregon Health Division. Oregon's Death with Dignity Act: The Second Year's Experience. No Date. Available [Online]: <http://www.ohd.hr.state.or.us/chs/pas/ar_smmry.htm> [28 May 2000].
Orentlicher, David, and Arthur Caplan. "The Pain Relief Promotion Act of 1999: A Serious Threat to Palliative Care." *Journal of the American Medical Association* 283, no. 2 (2000): 255-258.
Ostwald, Martin. *From Popular Sovereignty to the Sovereignty of Law: Law, Society and Politics in Fifth-Century Athens.* Berkeley: University of California Press, 1986.
Otis, James. *The Rights of the British Colonies Asserted and Proved.* Boston: Edes and Gill, 1764.
Paine, Thomas. "Common Sense." In Howard Fast, ed., *The Selected Work of Thomas Paine, Set in the Framework of His Life.* New York: Duell, Sloan and Pearce, 1945.
Parrington, Vernon L. *The Colonial Mind, 1620-1800.* New York: Harcourt, Brace and World, 1954.
Parshall, Gerald. "Snapshot: High Explosives." *U.S. News & World Report* (23 January 1995): 12.
Patterson, Bennett B. *The Forgotten Ninth Amendment.* Indianapolis: Bobbs-Merrill, 1955.
Plato. *The Dialogues of Plato.* Edited by William Chase Greene, translated by Benjamin Jowett. New York: Horace Liveright, 1927.

_____. *Plato's Apology: The Trial and Death of Socrates.* Translated by G. M. A. Grube. Indianapolis: Hackett Publishing Co., 1975.

Plucknett, Theodore F. T. *Statutes and Their Interpretation in the First Half of the Fourteenth Century.* Cambridge, England: Cambridge University Press, 1922.

Pollock, Frederick, Sir. "The History of the Law of Nature." *Columbia Law Review* 1 (1901): 11.

_____. "Review of Professor Brown's *International Society: Its Nature and Interests.*" *Law Quarterly Review* 39, 1923.

Pound, Roscoe. "Scope and Purpose of Sociological Jurisprudence." *Harvard Law Review* 25 (1911): 162.

_____. *An Introduction to the Philosophy of Law.* New Haven: Yale University Press, 1922.

_____. "Interpretations of Legal History." *Harvard Law Review* 37 (December 1923): 280.

_____. "The Theory of Judicial Decisions." *Harvard Law Review* 36 (1923): 802.

_____. *Law and Morals,* 2d ed. Chapel Hill: University of North Carolina Press, 1926.

_____. *An Introduction to the Philosophy of Law.* New Haven: Yale University Press, 1954.

Radin, Max. "Roman Concepts of Equality." *Political Science Quarterly* 38 (1923): 288.

Reeves, Richard. "The Permissive Dutch." *N.Y. Times Magazine,* 20 October 1985.

Riley, J. W., Jr. "What People Think About Death." In O. G. Brim, Jr., et al., *The Dying Patient.* New York: Russell Sage Foundation, 1970.

Robinson, B. A. Euthanasia and Physician Assisted Suicide Outside the U.S. 8 December 1999. Available [Online]: <http://www.religioustolerance.org/euth_wld.html> [30 May 2000].

Russell, O. *Freedom to Die: Moral and Legal Aspects of Euthanasia.* New York: Human Sciences Press, 1977.

Schaer, Meinrad. The Practice of Assisted Suicide in Switzerland. No date. Available [Online]: <http://www.finalexit.org/swiss.html> [30 May 2000].

Sena, Rev. Patrick J. "Biblical Teaching on Life and Death." In Donald G. McCarthy and Alvert S. Moraczewski, *Moral Responsibility in Prolonging Life Decisions.* St. Louis: Pope John Center, 1981.

Shevell, Michael. "Racial Hygiene, Active Euthanasia, and Julius Hallervorden." *Neurology* 42 (1992): 2214-2219.

Silving, Helen. "Euthanasia: A Study in Comparative Criminal Law." *University of Pennsylvania Law Review* 103 (1954): 350, 384.

Smith, Bryant. "Retroactive Laws and Vested Rights." *Texas Law Review* 95 (April, 1927): 231, 237.

Sofres, Taylor. Two Thirds of GPs Are in Favour of Euthanasia. No date. Available [Online]: <http://www.tnsofres.com/news/newsarticle.asp> [30 May 2000].

Spencer, A. W. "The Revival of Natural Law." *Central Law Journal* 80 (1915): 347.

St. John-Stevas, Norman. *The Right to Life.* New York: Holt, Rinehart and Winston, 1964.

Sullivan, Amy, Katrina Hedberg, and David W. Fleming. "Legalized Physician-Assisted Suicide in Oregon—The Second Year." *New England Journal of Medicine* 342 No. 8 (2000): 598-604.

Thayer, James B. "The Origin and Scope of the American Doctrine of Constitutional Law." *Harvard Law Review* 7 (1893): 129-133.

Thornton, J. *The Pulpit of the American Revolution: The Political Sermons of the Period of 1776.* Boston: Gould and Lincoln, 1860.

Toynbee, A., A. K. Mant, N. Smart, J. Hinton, S. Yudkin, E. Rhode, R. Heywood, and H. H. Price. *Man's Concern with Death.* St. Louis: McGraw-Hill, 1968.

Tyler, Moses C. *The Literary History of the American Revolution 1763-1783.* New York: Frederick Ungar Publishing Co., 1963.

Ubell, Tyler Earl. "Should Death Be a Patient's Choice?" *Parade Magazine,* 9 February 1992, p. 24.

Ullmann, Walter. *The Individual and Society in the Middle Ages: An Introduction to the Sources of Medieval Political Ideas.* Ithaca: Cornell University Press, 1975.

U.S. Congress. *Annals of Congress* 1 (1789): 439.

Vatican Congregation for the Doctrine of the Faith. *Declaration on Euthanasia,* Sect. 4. Vatican: 1980.

Vattel, Emmerich. "The Law of Nations III." In James Brown Scott, ed., *Classics of International Law.* Washington: Division of International Law, Carnegie Endowment for International Peace, 1916.

Vervoorn. "Voluntary Euthanasia in the Netherlands: Recent Developments." *Bioethics News* 6 (1987): 19-20.

Vinogradoff, Sir Paul. *Outlines of Jurisprudence.* Vol. 2, *The Jurisprudence of the Greek City.* New York: Oxford University Press, 1922.

Voeglin, H. "Kelsen's Pure Theory of Law." *Political Science Quarterly* 42 (1997): 268-276.

Vollmar, Valerie. International Developments. October 1999. Available [Online]: <http://www.Willamette.edu/wod/pas/pasopadateoctober 99.html> [30 May 2000].

Watson, Gerard. "The Natural Law and Stoicism." In A. A. Long, ed., *Problems of Stoicism.* London: Athlone Press, 1971.

Wells, William V. *The Life and Public Services of Samuel Adams.* Boston: Little, Brown, 1865.

Westcott, W. W. *Suicide, Its History, Literature, Jurisprudence, Causation and Prevention.* London: H. K. Lewis, 1885.

White, Mary Modenback. "The Right to Die—A Current Look." *Loyola Law Review* 30 (1994): 141.

Wilkin, Robert N. *Eternal Lawyer: A Legal Biography of Cicero.* New York: Macmillan, 1947.

Wilson, James. "Consideration on the Nature and Extent of the Legislative Authority of the British Parliament." In *Works.* Edited by Bird Wilson. Philadelphia: Lorenzo Press, 1804.

_____. *Works.* Edited by Andrew's. Chicago: Callaghan and Company, 1896.

Wiltshire, Susan Ford. *Greece, Rome, and the Bill of Rights.* Norman: University of Oklahoma Press, 1992.

Winthrop, Robert C. *Life and Letters of John Winthrop.* Boston: Ticknor and Fields, 1864-1867.

Wright, Benjamin Flecher, Jr. *American Interpretation of Natural Law: A Study in the History of Political Thought.* Cambridge, Massachusetts: Harvard University Press, 1931.

_____. *American Interpretation of Natural Law: A Study in the History of Political Thought.* New York: Russell and Russell, 1962.

CASES

Adamson v. California, 332 U.S. 46, 69, 89, 90 (1947). Justice Black, Dissenting.

American Railway Express Company v. Kentucky, 27 U.S. (1927).

Anderson v. St. Frances–St. George Hospital, 77 Ohio St. 3d 82; 671 N.E.2d 225, 269. (1996).
Aven v. State, 1925. 102 Tex Crim. 478; 277 S.W. 1080-83 (1925).
Band of State v. Cooper, 2 Yerg. 599, 603 (1831).
Barber v. Superior Court, 195 Cal. Rptr. 484 (1983).
Barbier v. Connolly, 113 U.S. 27, 31 (1885).
Burns Banking Co. v. Bryan, 264 U.S. 505, 520 (1927).
Butchers' Union v. Crescent City Co., 111 U.S. 746, 759 (1883).
Chicago Burlington & Quincy R.R. Co.v. Chicago, 166 U.S. 226, 134 (1897).
Corfield v. Coryell, 4 Wash. C.C. 371, 380-382; Fed. Case No. 3230 (1832).
Cruzan v. Harmon, 760 S.W.2d 408 (1988).
Cruzan v. Director, Missouri Department of Health, 110 S.Ct. 2841 (1990).
Dash v. Van Kleech, 7 Johns (N.Y.) 477, 505 (1811).
Elliott's Executor v. Lyell, 7 Va. 268 (1802).
Ex parte Wall, 107 U.S. 265, 303 (1882).
First HealthCare Corporation v. Rettinger, 342 N.C. 886 (1996).
Gitlow v. New York, 268 U.S. 652 , 666 (1925).
Grace v. State, 44 Tex. Crim. 193; 69 S.W. 529-530 (1902).
Griswold v. Connecticut, 381 U.S. 479 (1965).
Holden v. Hardy, 169 U.S. 366, 390 (1898).
Hurtado v. California, 110 U.S. 516, 528 (1883).
In re Conroy, 98 N.J. 321; 486 A. 2d. 1209 at 1226, 1229-1232 (1958).
In re Farrell, 108 N.J. 335, 529 A. 2d. 404, 413 (1987).
In re Fiori, 543 Pa. 592, 602; 673 A. 2d 905, 910 (1996).
In re Martin, 450 Mich. 204; 538 N.W.2d 399 (1995).
In re Quinlan, 355 A.2d 647; cert. denied, 429 U.S. 922 (1976).
Kansas v. Naramore, 25 Kan. App. 2d 302; 965 P.2d 211 (1998).
Lee v. Oregon, 869 F. Supp. 1491, 1503 (D.Or. 1994).
License Tax Cases, 5 Wall. 462, 469 (1866).
Loan Association v. Topeka, 20 Wall. 655, 663, 669, 670 (1875).
Marbury v. Madison, 5 U.S. 1 Cranch 87; 137 2L.Ed. 60 (1803).
McGovern v. Van Ripper, 137 N.J. Eq. 24, 33, 43 A.2d 514, 519 (1945).
Meachum v. Fanno, 429 U.S. 873 (1976).
Monongahela Bridge Co. v. United States, 216 U.S. 177, 195 (1910).
Murray's Lessee v. Hoboken Land and Improvement Co., 18 How. 272 (1855).
Ogden v. Saunders, 12 Wheat. 213 (1827).
Osgood v. Genessee Regional Medical Center, 94-26731-NH (1997).
Pavesich v. New England Life Ins. Co., 122 Ga. 190, 195; 50 S.E. 68 (1905).
People v. Campbell, 124 Mich. App. 333; 335 N.W.2d. (1983).
Richmond Newspapers v. Virginia, 448 U.S. 555, 579 (1980).
Row v. Wade, 410 U.S. 113 (1973).
Sherbert v. Verner, 374 U.S. 398 (1963).
Simon v. Southern Railway Co., 236 U.S. 115, 122 (1915).
Skinner v. Oklahoma, 316 US. 535 62s.d. 1110 (1942).
Slaughter-House Cases, 16 Wall. 36 (1873).
Smith v. Organization of Foster Families for Equality and Reform, 431 U.S. 816 (1977).
Southern Pacific Ry. v. Jensen, 244 U.S. 205, 222 (1916).
State of Georgia, by Michael J. Bowers, Atty. Gen. v. Larry James McAfee, 385 S.E. 2d, 259 Ga. 579 (1989).
Superintendent of Belchertown State School and another v. Joseph Saikewicz, 373 Mass. 728 (1977).
Trustees of the University of North Carolina v. Fay, 2 Hay N.C. 310, 312 (1804).

Twining v. New Jersey, 211 U.S. 78, 106 (1908).
Union Pacific v. Botsford, 141 U.S. 250, 251 (1891).
Vacco v. Quill, 521 U.S. 793; 117 S. Ct. 2293 (1997).
Van Horne v. Dorrance, 2 Dall. 304, 310 (1795).
Washington v. Glucksberg, 521 U.S. 702 (1997).
Wisconsin v. Yoder, 406 U.S. 205 (1972).
Yick Wo v. Hopkins, 118 U.S. 356, 369, 370 (1886).

Index

About the Author

RAYMOND WHITING is Professor of Political Science at Augusta State University. He has received both the University's Outstanding Faculty Member Award and a Governor's Teaching Fellowship Award.

www.ingramcontent.com/pod-product-compliance
Ingram Content Group UK Ltd.
Pitfield, Milton Keynes, MK11 3LW, UK
UKHW012043150926
475560UK00001B/159

9 780313 314742